Managing Radical Change

Managing Radical Change

Beyond Survival in the New Business Age

Jerome H. Want

omneo

AN IMPRINT OF OLIVER WIGHT PUBLICATIONS, INC.
85 Allen Martin Drive
Essex Junction, VT 05452

Oliver Wight Publications books may be purchased for educational,
business, or sales promotional use. For information, please call or write:
Special Sales Department, Oliver Wight Publications, Inc.,
85 Allen Martin Drive, Essex Junction, VT 05452.
Telephone: (800) 343-0625 or (802) 878-8161;
FAX: (802) 878-3384.

Library of Congress Catalog Card Number: 94-76394.

ISBN 0-939246-72-4

Text design by Irving Perkins Associates

Printed on acid-free paper.

Manufactured in the United States of America.

1   3   5   7   9   10   8   6   4   2

This book is dedicated to all of us who have worked within corporations, consulting firms, and service organizations with the commitment and desire to make a difference.

I also dedicate *Managing Radical Change* to businesses everywhere that are struggling to make change a quality of the organization—not just an obstacle to be overcome.

CONTENTS

Part I

Radical Change and the Business Change Cycle   1

Part II

Change in Seven Critical American Industries   119

Part III

LIST OF FIGURES AND TABLES

FIGURES

TABLES

PREFACE

Not since the industrialization of America has this country's business sector undergone so much turbulence and dislocation. Almost every industry has been rocked by the forces of business change, which have included divestiture, deregulation, industry consolidation, market globalization, increased regulation, and new technology breakthroughs. As a result, entire industries are being reshaped within months—not years. An overnight demand has arisen for exotic new skills that were once on the fringe of the labor pool, while the need for long-relied-upon capabilities seems to disappear just as quickly. The nature of managerial work is radically changing, especially at the CEO level, where dismissals are becoming more common if not yet routine. Once admired and seemingly impregnable companies disappear in the course of a late-night meeting, while seven new *Fortune* 50 companies are created with the stroke of a judge's pen. Sage business analysts and legions of industry professionals wonder when it will all stop and what is behind it. No one knows the answer to the first question: the turbulence and dislocation may *never* stop. To the second question, the answer clearly is *radical change*.

My purpose in writing this book is twofold. My first goal is to lend some clarity and insight into the forces of radical change that are impacting virtually every business and industry in America today. To accomplish this, I have provided readers with a rational framework for tracking, anticipating, and managing business change as it affects the competitiveness of companies. My second goal is to provide an inside look at change as it's actually shaping American businesses and industries today. See Figure 1.

Part I introduces real-world change forces and how they are affecting various American industries. The *Business Change Cycle* is introduced in Part 1 as an overarching framework or process for understanding how change impacts the competitiveness and internal functioning of specific companies. The *Business Change Cycle* presents strategies for managing change and accomplishing "turnaround" in mature companies, as well as strategies for planning and building new business organizations that may be more adaptable to marketplace change. Part I also compares and contrasts traditional fix-its and fads with more far-reaching change strategies. The critical issue of corporate culture also is discussed in detail—how to appraise and manage corporate culture and how it affects business performance during periods of change.

Part II offers the reader a unique glimpse into seven critical American industries as they are buffeted by change. Each chapter is authored by an authority from that industry—an industry insider such as a corporate officer or consultant. I know of no other book on the subject of business change that provides this level of contribution. Each chapter author understands the *Business Change Cycle* and applies it to the major companies discussed in these chapters. Short of employing a formal company or industrywide appraisal, this is an informed way of applying the *Business Change Cycle* to recent developments in those industries and to help readers understand how companies are functioning in a radically changed business climate. It should be noted that the constant changes that are roiling various industries made this section of the book all the more fascinating and challenging to complete. Even as the book was being prepared for printing, revisions were being made to the manuscript to reflect major changes in the marketplace, although we could not include every new development.

Park III contains my concluding thoughts on this vital issue of radical change as it impacts the business world.

Figure 1
Radical Change and the Business Change Cycle

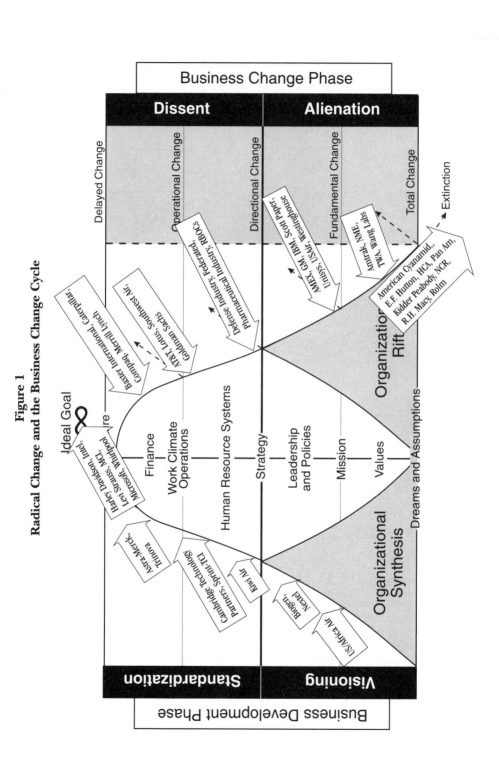

ACKNOWLEDGMENTS

The term *acknowledgments* does not adequately express the feelings of indebtedness and gratitude that most authors feel for the contributions and support of others. My book would not have come to fruition without the support, risk taking, and contributions of many other people.

For their belief in the book, despite the risks it posed, I thank my publisher, Jim Childs of Oliver Wight, who is now with John Wiley & Sons, Inc., esteemed consultant and author Marvin Weisbord, and Steve Piersanti of Berrett-Kohler, who initially recognized the book's value.

For their patience and responsiveness to the demands of publishing a collective effort, as well as for their magnificent contributions, I thank my coauthors, Lawrence J. Bolick, Rouja Brzozowski, John E. Daniels, Sarah E. Henry, Roger A. Jones, J. Jennings Partin, James G. Purvis, Nicholas J. Radell, Alan E. Schnur, and Robert N. Wilson.

For their generosity of time, thought, and shared experiences, I thank Russell Ackoff, professor emeritus of the Wharton School and chairman of INTERACT, Lawrence Brown of Centocor, Dwight Coffin of Continental Grain, Michael Farabelli of Ernst & Young LLP, Donald Kehoe of Medical Data North, Frank Kittredge of the National Foreign Trade Council, John Kubish of Becton-Dickinson, Steven Lesser of HRPlan, Alan Lutz of the Kassandra Group, Emmit McHenry of Network Solutions, Christine Oster of Intel, Stanley Schrager of Chase Manhattan Bank,

Robert Spencer of the Institute for Human Development, Joseph Stewart of Johnson & Johnson, Reyer Swaak of the National Foreign Trade Council, Susan Thompson of Levi Strauss, Richard Urevig of Towers Perrin, Bent Werbel of META Health Technologies, and John Zimmerman of MCI.

For their expert and unselfish contributions to the production of the book, I thank my editor, Miller Hudson, my graphic artist, Allison Moore, and my word processors, Brigitte Carucci and Paul Hester.

I also wish to thank my colleagues from OSI who have been so supportive of this endeavor over the past four years.

Finally, special thanks are offered to some very special people who have served as my *personal change mentors* at various periods in the course of my own growth and change cycle: Miriam and Louis, Carolyn and Buddy, Fran and Bill, and June and Jim.

PART I

Radical Change and the Business Change Cycle

1

Failure to Manage Change— and the Consequences

You can't go home again because home ceases to exist except in the mothballs of one's own memories.
—THOMAS WOLF

Despite the tendency of companies to resist new and unfamiliar conditions, change in the business world waits for no one, and failure to respond can be linked directly to the failure of countless companies—large and small—as well as entire industries. No industry has been spared the effects of change, which have included deregulation, consolidation, divestiture, increased regulation, and increasing foreign competition. Unending new technology breakthroughs challenge as much as help companies in their efforts to be competitive (see Table 1.1).

When leaders decide to do something about changing business conditions, too often they merely reach for the latest fad or fix-it: excellence, total quality management (TQM), benchmarking, just-in-time inventory management, zero-based budgeting, decentralization, rightsizing, or reengineering. The list is endless—but these fads never really change the way corporations manage themselves while trying to be more competitive.

In the 1980s, many companies went on buying binges and entered business sectors in which they had little experience. Quaker

3

Table 1.1
Impact of Radical Change on Business

First-Order Change Forces	Second-Order Change Forces	Industries Impacted
Social / Political	Deregulation	Banking, airlines, trucking, local telephone
	Increased regulation	Investment banking, insurance, health care, timber, food processing, cable TV
Scientific and technological	Divestiture	Telecommunications, consumer products, manufacturing
	Consolidation	Defense, investment banking, retail consumer products, pharmaceuticals, biotechnology, advertising, entertainment and media, banking, publishing
	New technology breakthroughs	Wireless communications, computers, biotechnology, pharmaceuticals, semiconductors, software, telecommunications, steel, agribusiness
	Foreign competition and market globalization	Textile manufacturing, steel, autos, chemicals, shipping, aerospace, telecommunications, pharmaceuticals, computers, semiconductors

Oats bought retail stores, Sears and Xerox bought financial-service companies, American Express moved onto Wall Street (and has now fled it), and Southwestern Bell went into publishing—all to compensate for the loss of market share in each of their core business sectors. They all thought they could emulate the success of GE, which has been unique in its ability to diversify beyond its core electronics business to become a truly successful, globe-spanning conglomerate (a recently retired GE executive identifies GE's ability to unload a company as being as important to its success as its ability to buy or start one).

Many companies, and most of those mentioned above, have since divested their original holdings (usually at a loss) and have learned that if they are to survive, they have to return to the basics of better managing their core businesses within a radically changed and unforgiving business environment. To reinvigorate its core business, Kodak (under its new CEO, George Fisher) divested itself of its pharmaceutical and chemical businesses. Mead Paper made similar moves to spin off its computer software business, while Sears has spun off Allstate, Dean Witter, and Sears Payment Systems. This trend will reverse the poorly conceived diversification mergers of the 1980s.

Entire industries, from banking to bomb making, have misjudged the pace and scope of change. Recent history is full of examples of companies—steel, automotive, computers, airlines, consumer products, telecommunications, health care, banking, and defense—that misjudged and underestimated change and almost always with disastrous consequences.

For years, leaders in the U.S. automotive industry thought that downsizing, coupled with government protection, would allow them to ignore their Japanese competitors. But the American auto buyer ignored the inferior products and services that Detroit's Big Three were offering. Only recently have Chrysler and Ford begun to satisfy the changing consumer demand for quality at a fair cost. Even Toyota now recognizes that there are limits to what the American consumer will pay as the quality gap narrows. Although they have downsized and driven still greater efficiencies into their businesses, Chrysler and Ford have turned the corner by making customer-driven quality an integral component of their corporate cultures. This is being accomplished principally by overhauling their decision-making processes—driving responsibility and autonomy down to supervisors, managers, and production teams in the plants—and by rethinking the larger relationship between management and labor. Just as important, they have begun to bring into their companies people from other industries with fresh new ideas. Paramount among the changes has been the emerging change in values in executives of these companies. Fat bonuses for executives are no longer automatic (as they were even during times of heavy financial losses) and are now tied more directly to performance. Detroit has finally embraced change.

Clear parallels exist between the auto industry and the computer industry, as evidenced by the problems at Digital Equipment Corporation (DEC), Wang, and IBM. IBM's attempts at decentralization could not overcome decades of unchanged culture and questionable leadership practices. Their leaders falsely believed that their mainframe technology would continue to dominate the industry at a time when alternative technologies were bypassing the mainframe. Great ideas and strategies from the past were now hurting them. The founders at Wang and DEC were too slow to recognize the technological changes that made their main product lines obsolete almost overnight. By the time John Akers (IBM), An Wang (Wang), and Kenneth Olson (DEC) finally relinquished control, the damage was done. The result was a drastic loss of market share at IBM and DEC and the near collapse of Wang (which is still predicted by many within the industry). On a larger scale, computer manufacturing has become a commodities industry driven by the software and semiconductor sectors. This poses an even greater challenge to the industry.

FAILED RESPONSES TO CHANGE

Reasons for Failure

The reasons that leaders of companies fail so persistently in their efforts to manage change effectively are as varied as their companies but most seem to fall into five major categories:

- *Micro versus macro thinking*   Senior managers devote too much of their time to operational and financial problems and not enough to issues of change and strategy. It is far too easy for them to become involved with the latest breakdown within the company when they should be constantly searching beyond the company (and even its competition) for eventual threats or opportunities for the business and the industry. Executives and managers must go beyond managing procedures or functions to manage change. A classic example may be seen in the contrasts between AT&T and MCI before the breakup of AT&T. While AT&T dug in and kept doing what it always had done, MCI's Bill McGowan had a new vision—not just for his company but for the entire industry. And it was that vision that eventually reshaped the industry.

- *Short- versus long-term goals setting* With increasing pressure from their boards and shareholders to deliver profits every quarter, CEOs have been forced to measure success in terms of months rather than years. This behavior is pushed down the line so that the entire organization reacts to immediate pressures and manufactured, short-term goals. We may be critical of the Japanese keiretsu, but it ensures current stability and resources for long-term competitive advantage. German corporate boards give labor a near-equal say with management, which reduces conflicts (strikes), while fostering a long-term partnership between labor and management. We will also look at some underutilized American advantages later in this section of the book.

- *Fixing versus reinventing the business* As a result of their short-term and narrow focus, corporate leaders tend to reach for tactical remedies for business problems that are strategic and global. Many an innovative business plan has been written but never comes close to being implemented because the culture of the organization was not capable of supporting it. Too often, operational remedies are employed and new organization charts are written when poor management practices and faulty decision making have been the real roadblocks to improved performance. For most businesses, fixing is not enough: many must be reinvented.

- *Failing to understand and manage the culture* Most CEOs and senior officers will claim to have a feel for their company's culture. Nevertheless, they continue to act as if the culture was something that sat outside the CEO's door just waiting to respond to his latest memo. A company's culture is neither an appendage of the executive suite door nor a touchy-feely thing that defies definition or management. Too often, the subject of culture is one that comes up only at senior management retreats. In reality, corporate culture can be a major asset to the business, as seen in such good companies as Johnson & Johnson, Motorola, Merck, JP Morgan, Levi Strauss, Nike, Harley Davidson, 3M, ALCOA-Tennessee, Intel, Rubbermaid, Analog Devices, and Microsoft. In these companies, culture is constantly emphasized and nurtured over structure. Conversely, the impact of a failed corporate culture can also be seen in such companies as E. F. Hutton, its successor Shearson Lehman, Drexel Burnham Lambert, and Kidder Peabody (where the failure of their cultures directly caused their collapse), as well as in other companies like Sears, TWA, GM, IBM, USAir, KMart, United Airlines, and Avis, where their failing cultures have stymied growth and performance.

• *Losing track of the customer*   When faced with failure, too many companies blame the Japanese, the last recession, labor conditions, foreign trade restrictions, or government regulations—instead of themselves. Admittedly, business organizations are extremely complex, but their goal is simple—to satisfy customer needs. The best companies strive to exceed customer demands and work closely with their customers as partners. Poorly performing companies see their customers as a necessary evil or, at best, as the cash cow to be milked. Most of those companies that I have identified in the previous paragraph for their excellent cultures are also companies that emphasize the customer.

The Magic Wand of Restructuring

In their highly regarded book, *Beyond Human Scale* (Basic Books, 1985), George Vojta and Eli Ginzberg make a strong case for the notion that the large corporation is at risk. Their premise is that the internal structure of nearly every sizable corporation works in a manner that is counterproductive to its competitive capacity.

Although their premise has much merit, a company's structure is not the primary impediment to business success, and improving structure is not a remedy for the larger problems that plague most complex organizations. If business structure was the principal problem facing American companies today, then all the restructuring and reorganizing that we have witnessed over the past decade would have put America's businesses back on solid ground. *Clearly, the real challenge facing most businesses is not the issue of structure. Structure has become the symptom of more fundamental failings of strategy, leadership, and corporate culture.* Instead of addressing these issues (which takes time and rarely yields immediate, measurable results), executives prefer to rely on the club of restructuring or downsizing, which usually does produce certain measurable results, albeit the wrong ones.

Many companies have had a legitimate need to reduce their overhead, especially since their growth levels during the go-go 1980s may not have been sustained over the long term. Nevertheless, the rush to restructure and downsize has deprived too many companies of some of their most innovative talent and at the same time contributed to the destruction of their corporate cultures. Moreover, restructuring and downsizing do little to improve decision making or overall competitiveness, as seen by the restructuring experiences at GM, NYNEX, RJR Nabisco, Sears, DuPont, KMart, Exxon, and Westinghouse. At UNYSIS, it has been more than four years since the company first initiated the downsizing and restructuring process—and its struggles and restructuring continue.

In 1992, Amoco downsized its organization by 10 percent,

immediately showed a profit, and was at it again in 1994 in pursuit of a better bottom line. In the oil patch, it used to be said, "You need only wait for the prices to rise." Now they say, "Lay off staff if you can't wait that long." In the 1980s, Xerox engaged in a massive layoff that was widely proclaimed a success. So why is it doing it again today with its stock price at an all-time high? Increasingly, the burden for producing profits and dealing with the unpleasant aspects of change is falling on the workforce when it is the primary responsibility of mahogany row. Eventually, the downsizing well will run dry.

Restructuring and downsizing will not

- Compensate for a failed corporate culture,

- Substitute for effective organization design,

- Promote improved employee performance or commitment,

- Enhance faulty decision making, or

- Correct a flawed business strategy or failed leadership.

In reality, downsizing does little more than reduce the size or cost of the organization, cut back a bureaucracy that resists change, and, at times, resolve serious political conflicts—usually through the elimination of key contenders on different sides of an issue. In fact, we are now seeing the broad economic effects of the last decade of downsizing as production companies are unable to increase capacity to meet a rising demand for goods. This hinders growth and fuels inflation. In a major consumer products company, serious interpersonal and decision-making problems existed among the seven top officers. The CEO's solution was a multimillion dollar project to restructure divisions and small business units to reduce the conflicts and "improve performance." Secession planning and leadership coaching may have been more effective and certainly less costly for the company and its shareholders—especially since the CEO and most of that officer group were replaced less than a year later. Restructuring

and downsizing almost always hurt a company's culture by reducing previous levels of commitment between the company and
its employees. We also know that the most frequent outcome of
restructuring and downsizing is more of the same. The American
Management Association notes that 65 percent of the companies
that downsize do so again the following year, with manufacturing
and consumer products leading the way in each of the last three
years.

Too often, business leaders ask the wrong questions while preparing to restructure:

CONVENTIONAL QUESTIONS

- How big should our company or division be (headcount)?

- How many management layers should we have?

- How do we get lean and mean?

- What spans of control should we have?

- Should we centralize or decentralize?

BETTER QUESTIONS

- How do we make our workforce more innovative and productive?

- How can our organization be more responsive to unexpected
  shifts in the marketplace?

- What is our real mission, and how can we project it into the
  marketplace?

- What is the best process for redesigning our business?

- How can we better serve our customers—internal as well as
  external?

- How can we get the organization to support our strategy?

- How do we increase synergy and reduce fragmentation?

In his most recent book on downsizing (*Rethinking the Corporation,* AMA, 1993), Robert Tomasko noted some startling statistics from a survey of 1,000 companies that undertook the downsizing process:

- Ninety percent wanted to reduce expenses: fewer than half succeeded;

- Seventy-five percent sought productivity improvements: only 22 percent reached their goal; and

- More than half expected to reduce bureaucracy: only 15 percent could claim success.

Companies like Hewlett-Packard and Intel rely on downsizing only when other measures have failed. At Intel they have the 90 and 120 percent solutions. The former requires those earning over $50,000 take a 10 percent pay cut, and the latter calls for those high-salaried employees to produce 20 percent more work at the same pay. Hewlett-Packard has also become famous for these innovative cost-savings strategies.

Merck is one company that continually reorganizes itself but not around new organization charts or solely for the purpose of downsizing. Instead, it continually rethinks its divisions and business units around changing missions and customer needs, new marketplace threats and opportunities, and altered distribution requirements for new products. Recent upheavals in the pharmaceutical industry have forced some downsizing across the entire industry (far less than in most others), and when public policy and pricing practices have been resolved, we will see a new focus and new directions across all companies. Nevertheless, downsizing is but one of the many incremental tools used for managing change.

The False God of Business Planning

Formal business planning was born in the late 1960s and early 1970s, when business leaders recognized that the U.S. supply of natural resources was becoming increasingly limited and expensive. This new constraint on business performance was exemplified by the 1974 oil crisis and led companies to search for a business-planning model that would allow them to plan and conserve their resources around hazards of scarcity. Subsequently, the business-planning process was enlarged to account for the entire business. With the advent of increasingly complex technologies, especially in the defense sector, the business-planning process was forced to create a future-looking scenario for people, technology, and competitor behavior, as well as for resource planning. Business planning was being asked to do things that it was never intended to do and could not do. Nevertheless, it remains a fixture in most corporations and is a primary source of revenue for a number of consulting firms.

An example of its misuse can be seen at a five-year-old software technology company where the CEO thought that it was time for the company to have a strategic business plan. Its client roster included major federal agencies and several large corporations, had doubled its revenue in each of the past two years, and had more than 500 employees. Through all of its growth, the CEO and his managers never formally thought about the organization design process and instead allowed the company to mushroom around client demand. As is typical with most fast-growing companies, support or staff positions increased faster than direct service or line roles. This almost always results in painful downsizing during subsequent business downturns. This benign neglect also was applied to the corporate culture, while human resource planning was restricted to perpetual personnel hiring for short-staffed project teams. When asked what he wanted to accomplish through the business-planning process, the CEO noted three needs: (1) to identify large companies that would have an interest in purchasing his company, (2) to identify funding sources for new technology development, and (3) to project how large his company "should" be. He wanted no organizationwide involvement in the business plan and chose to exclude from the process an assessment of critical internal issues such as leadership effectiveness, operations, culture, organization design, human resources, and customer service.

This rubbing of Aladdin's lamp typifies how business planning is approached by both large and small businesses, regardless of whether it is conducted by external consultants or internal planners. Unfortunately, the genie seldom materializes. Too many corporate leaders continue to believe that business planning can see into the future and predict a company's probable success. Unfortunately, strategic planners often try to accommodate this misguided perception and usually with disastrous results. Just look at the results of Frank Lorenzo's business planning for Eastern and Continental Airlines or the ill-fated plans of the Bell companies to expand into nonregulated business sectors after divestiture. International Harvester's revolving strategies in the 1980s may have accelerated its decline, and GM's new manufacturing strategy of the 1980s, which emphasized common design and production processes, cost it customers (customers didn't like driving Cadillacs with Oldsmobile engines). At RJR Nabisco, the business-planning process never allowed the company to dig out from its huge debt after the merger (at that time, the largest in history). TWA's 1993 business plan failed to take into account the limitations of the culture and the permanent loss of customers and markets.

Traditional business planning has largely failed for four essential reasons:

1. It usually is too quantitative and dependent on an ever-expanding economy and pool of capital: conditions that do not always exist;

2. It has persistently ignored "ground zero" operating conditions that are more familiar to operations and account managers than to planners;

3. It fails to take into account the ability of the organization's corporate culture to support new business strategy initiatives; and

4. It assumes that the business and the larger competitive environment are rational and predictable, which they are not

because they fail to take into account *change* (J. Want, and W. DuSualt, *The President*, AMA, 1990).

Business conditions change so quickly and radically that they make business plans obsolete before they can be implemented. Johnson & Johnson takes pride in the fact that it does not undertake centralized business planning. It has long understood that the discovery of new diseases and the ensuing R&D process defy traditional planning practices, especially in a complex industry.

Too often, business planning does not include operations managers who can see at first hand the potential impact of the plan on business operations. Neither does it consider whether the culture of the organization can mobilize itself to support the new business plan. In an environment driven increasingly by changing technology, the organization needs to know whether it has the right technology to compete and the right people to manage the change as well as the technology. Most important, business planning needs to be process oriented rather than product oriented so that it can make adjustments as new change issues arise and move the entire organization along the planning process.

The Latest Panacea: Process Reengineering

Early in my career, I discovered that corporate executives fled from the word *processes*. They frequently said, "Don't talk to us about improving processes around here. We don't need that process stuff—just outcomes." My consulting brethren quickly reinvented their terminology so that they would not offend prospects and clients and replaced the *p* word with *methods, steps, action plans, technologies*, and any other synonym that could be found in Roget's *Thesaurus*.

Today process reengineering is the buzz term. Each of the Big Six accounting/consulting firms is offering it as the change tool for the next century, while the Index Company claims to have pioneered it as a consulting intervention. One firm has created an entire "strategy practice" around its reengineering process, while another's is implemented by a massive corps of information systems consultants. In the 1970s and early 1980s, downsizing and operations improvement consulting kept tens of thousands of consultants employed across the world. Somewhere between 1987 and 1990, those same consultants were miraculously transformed and retrained to reengineer the processes of the same companies that they had previously downsized and restructured. Suspiciously, the end product still resembles the results of the downsizing craze.

The real problem is perception, people, and promise. The *perception* in the corporate world is that reengineering will truly transform companies and cultures while reducing to manageable proportions the problems of change that they are facing. The consulting world really believes that this is what it is accomplishing and too often *promises* results that frequently are not achieved. The reasons for the failure is that people within the organization are ignored.

Reengineering *can* improve operational processes within an organization. Compaq and AT&T's PBX business are successful examples, but separate culture-development interventions were required within each company. GTE also has claimed real gains but is in its third year of reengineering. Where restructuring in the past has failed, reengineering can help an organization to streamline—to make its operations more efficient and reduce overhead. In fact, cost reduction has become the principal objective and outcome of reengineering. But even as a cost-control intervention, reengineering seems to have limitations. In a study by Gene Hall, Jim Rosenthal, and Judy Wade, only 30 percent of the companies studied achieved any cost reduction, and many others found that profits declined and business-unit costs actually increased after reengineering (*Harvard Business Review*, November–December 1993, pp. 119–131). Reengineering was originally conceived by its originators (Davenport, Hammer, and Champe) to have broad implications and benefits for the organization. The problem may be with its implementors and surely with the expectations of the corporate world. Nonetheless, Champy and Hammer now recognize the limitations and failures of reengineering, and are now proposing the need to "reengineer" management and later the culture (*The Wall Street Journal*, June 17, 1995).

Other problems arise from process reengineering, particularly within the *people* realm. Too frequently, the workforce is ill prepared to assume the new processes that are put in place via reengineering. Mass layoffs then ensue, which are followed by new hiring and training—a very expensive cycle that offsets previous cost savings. Michael Farabelli, a former Ernst & Young reengineering partner, has frequently stated that he would rather have good people and bad processes than good processes and bad people. Too often, reengineering makes the people obsolete (Interview, May 10, 1994).

Reengineering rarely supports or improves the culture of an organization. Instead, it imposes great stress on the culture and many times destroys it. In one manufacturing and distribution business, the goal was to reduce unnecessary steps and bureaucratic interference while allowing floor managers more freedom to intervene for problem solving and product modification to satisfy customer needs. Just the opposite occurred, however, as managers complained that after the reengineering they had been further shut out of the production process and "quality engineers" became just another level of bureaucracy protecting the newly installed processes from "interfering" managers. In a highly bureaucratic, paternalistic, and authoritarian distribution company, the executive committee retained a consulting firm to improve processes and reduce costs by $1 to $1.5 billion through reengineering, while avoiding a significant reduction in the workforce. Needless to say, they failed, and the culture was sent into chaos. Senior management had to reestablish many of the old procedures, and its goal of not wanting to spin off better performing divisions had to be scrapped. Clearly, the issue was one of culture and leadership, which reengineering rarely touches.

Reengineering is a tool and a useful one—but not a panacea for change. To benefit from it, leaders must examine closely their own perceptions of what it does, how people will be affected, and the promises it holds for the business.

CREATING A PERFORMANCE-DRIVEN
CORPORATE CULTURE

Few terms have been so frequently defined, yet so widely misunderstood, as *corporate culture*. Corporate culture is the *collective beliefs that people within the organization have about their ability to compete in the marketplace—and how they act on those belief systems*. A company's culture is revealed through the attitudes, dreams, values, and behaviors of employees and management. For that reason, corporate culture is not easily manipulated or quickly redirected by memos or mission statements, but, over time, it can be developed and guided in the directions required to ensure a company's success (see Figure 1.1).

For decades, most U.S. executives have failed to understand the

Figure 1.1
Vehicles for Culture Change

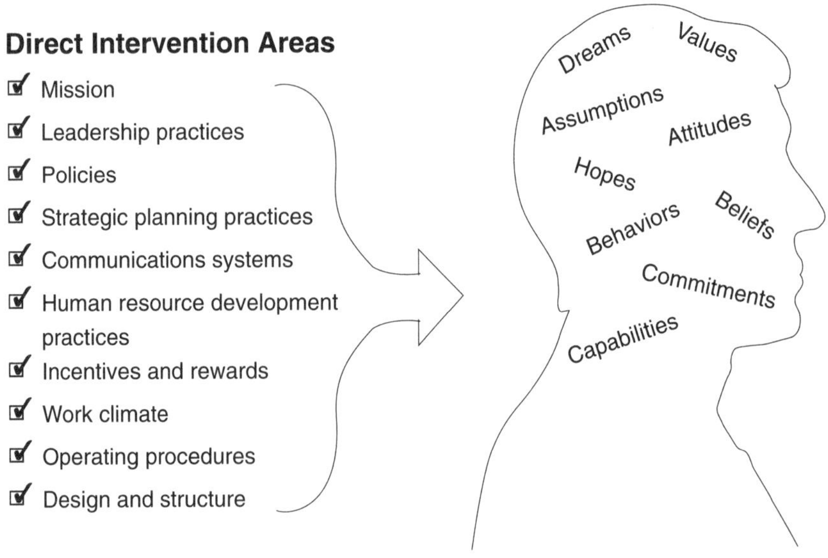

Direct Intervention Areas

- ☑ Mission
- ☑ Leadership practices
- ☑ Policies
- ☑ Strategic planning practices
- ☑ Communications systems
- ☑ Human resource development practices
- ☑ Incentives and rewards
- ☑ Work climate
- ☑ Operating procedures
- ☑ Design and structure

Dreams Values Assumptions Attitudes Hopes Behaviors Beliefs Commitments Capabilities critical link between corporate culture and the long-term success of the business. In many other countries, corporate culture is typified by a long-term commitment between the company and its employees that creates a shared investment in the success of the business. A companywide commitment to the customer flows from this internal culture of commitment and is seen at work in the marketplace.

While many overseas companies attempt to build and nurture cohesive, performance-driven cultures, thinking more typical of the Taylor school of management (mechanistic, segmented and reductionist) seems to dominate too many American companies. Labor and management see themselves as separate, and conflicts can tear apart a company—as during the conflicts in the steel industry in the 1970s and in today's labor-management conflicts in the airline industry. Within management itself, excessive political conflict exists to the detriment of the business. Ties to the marketplace are temporary and too often defined by immediate cost savings rather than by long-term mutual growth and benefit. This notion of investing in the marketplace is unfamiliar to most American companies. Nevertheless, it served Japanese auto makers quite well in the 1960s and 1970s as they learned from American consumers what they wanted in a car. This long-term investment in the American marketplace was eventually rewarded with a fairly constant 30 percent share of the U.S. auto market. When American businesses attempt to create footholds in foreign markets, they are too often seen as wanting short-term gains (though this is beginning to change). The drastic reduction in research and development by American companies over the past fifteen years is indicative of this desire for only short-term gains. American industry once led all other industrialized nations in its investment in R&D, but now it lags behind most other industrial nations, except the Netherlands. The loss of more than 12 million white-collar jobs over the same period makes it hard to refute the criticism.

Many foreign companies find it easier than U.S. companies to develop and maintain cohesive and unified corporate cultures since they often are extensions of largely homogeneous societies where national security, cultural, and business goals are inextricably linked as one and are embodied in the company. This has been especially apparent in such countries as Korea, Taiwan, Japan, Switzerland, the Netherlands, Singapore, and the former West Germany. This affords companies from these societies certain advantages, especially as they compete on a global scale:

- Management can more often be assured of the support of its workforce;

- The company can more easily engage in long-term planning for entering foreign markets; and

- The company is less often in conflict with its own national government and generally enjoys more widespread national support.

Nevertheless, U.S. companies also have certain advantages, which can be used to their benefit. They include the following:

- Access to a large and diversified labor force,

- A reputation for innovation (especially in product development) that is rarely matched by companies of other societies, and

- Being the home team for the largest single marketplace in the world.

A BLUEPRINT FOR MANAGING RADICAL CHANGE

If U.S. companies are to better manage change—and keep ahead of their competitors—they need to focus on five strategies:

Keep Innovative People and Ideas at Home

Too often companies create new ideas and innovative products and services, only to sell them to others or to let the originator of the new product or idea leave through the back door. A unique quality of our society is its ability to nurture creativity and initiative, which directly contributes to the business climate. Long-term strategies for creating, developing, and maintaining innovation must become the cornerstone for the larger business strategy. This includes incentives for keeping innovative people and their ideas within the company—not just through financial incentives but through incentives that build mutual commitment and opportunities for individual growth and creative development. This can be especially useful as mobility up the corporate ladder is less available or may not even be desired.

Close the Gap Between Business Planning and Organization Planning

Companies invest heavily in strategic business plans that rarely fulfill their promise, frequently because many underlying functions of the business are not in place to support the new strategy. For the strategy to be successful, it must first be grounded in the visioning process of the business—in its corporate values, identity, purpose, mission, and leadership. If employees do not have faith in their leaders and are unable to identify with the mission, they have no point of reference and lack the commitment to act effectively on behalf of the company.

More obvious are the consequences for failed values within the organization. When employees believe that the organization lacks the appropriate values and direction for competing in the marketplace, they will not support the strategy—or worse, they even may undermine it. Of course, none of this can remain invisible to the marketplace for long, and customers will desert the company. Again, the most obvious example can be seen on Wall Street and with many failed savings and loan institutions, as well as with the former International Harvester and Eastern Airlines.

Design, structure, operations, and human resource systems must be ready to function in support of the new strategy. Montgomery Ward has answered this challenge by creating one multidisciplinary function that integrates human resource and organization strategy with marketing, customer service, and strategy. Inefficient or failed operational capabilities will sink the strategy simply by the company's inability to deliver products and services. If the human resource department fails to provide the right people who are properly trained, it too will impede the strategy. An effective organization design is critical to the success of any business strategy. It should facilitate communication and responsiveness between the company and the marketplace.

Create a Corporate Culture That Embraces Change

After a new business strategy was established by one of the regional Bell companies, the vice chairman commented that all they now needed to do was to change the 60,000 person culture that had been retained since the divestiture. He really was saying that the culture was not ready to support the new and riskier direction that had been charted for the business and which required innovative leaders and managers—qualities not known to exist in bureaucratic, hierarchical organizations such as telephone companies. Few would challenge the notion that companies with committed, empowered cultures will outperform other companies. When we talk about a corporate culture's readiness for change, we are dealing with two broad qualitative categories:

- *Alienated cultures* have qualities that may be characterized as being rigid, arrogant, controlling, punitive, hierarchical, closed, bureaucratic, predatory, or risk averse. It is not unusual to see several of these characteristics working in tandem within the same nonadaptive business culture.

- *Change-ready cultures*—or what I call *new age cultures*—may be characterized as being flexible, searching, open, supportive, democratic, loosely or nonhierarchically structured, risk taking, and innovative. Most important, people in the company are focused on change as much as on any production process or task. A change-ready culture will usually have several, if not most, of these qualities. Organizations that exhibit these qualities will be in a better position to implement new strategies and will clearly be able to respond to change more effectively than companies with nonadaptive corporate cultures. We explore, in detail, different types of business cultures, including the new age business culture, in Chapter 5.

Identify Alternative Critical Success Factors for Managers

Increasingly, traditional styles of leadership are being questioned and openly challenged in companies, and CEOs are being removed by small and large companies alike. As competitive conditions are more frequently subjected to radically changing business conditions, a new type of leadership is required that will be typified by in-depth, thoughtful decision makers versus command-control decision makers. The CEO and other senior executives will have to

- Become students of the company's culture and learn how to manage and develop it on a long-term basis;

- Incorporate change-management planning into long-term strategies for sustained success and not just strategies for short-term financial returns;

- Find ways to disperse decision making and authority through the use of empowerment; and

- Look beyond the usual field of threats and opportunities to assess the long-term impact of regulatory, technological, cultural, and competitive changes on the business. Obstacles and opportunities for the company will be too diverse and will arise too rapidly from too many different directions to be seen by just one person or a few people at the top.

Learn to Manage Change

Managers must learn to respond to changing business conditions with differentiated change strategies that are appropriate for the challenge. Essential to managing change is to stay close to the customer: the marketplace is usually the chief indicator for change, if not the source. At the same time, corporate leadership has to maintain a strong vision that will drive company performance. Too often leaders look at what the company next door is using to decide what their companies should do. Today, many (if not most) companies are reengineering with little regard for what it can and cannot do while ignoring its track record for end results with other companies.

To compete effectively in a changing marketplace, a thoughtful, ongoing organization-wide exploration must be made, both of internal capabilities as well as of external change forces. Too often limited tactical solutions are applied when large-scale, long-term strategies need to be embraced. By employing the Business Change Cycle or similar long-term change strategies, companies will be better able to anticipate and respond to change with unique strategies that are appropriate to the marketplace and beneficial to their businesses. Those who fail to manage change will always be acted on by change. Successful managers and leaders will see change as an opportunity for developing the business and adding value to its products, as well as for growing the business. Businesses that are able to implement these types of strategies (and generate new ones) will emerge as long-term industry leaders in the struggle to manage radical change.

CHAPTER

2

The Impact of Change on American Business and the Workforce

The least democratic institutions in the world are Communism and the American corporation.

—WILLIAM OUCHI

Communism has collapsed and been consigned to the "trash heap of history" for its inflexibility and inability to respond to change. Some speculate that Ouchi's other "least democratic institution"—the American corporation—may not be far behind. In his most recent book, *The Democratic Corporation* (Oxford University Press, 1994), Russell Ackoff laments "the deterioration of the American economy and its business enterprises . . . as a complex system of interrelated problems—a mess." In his best-selling book, *The Mind of the Strategist* (McGraw-Hill, 1982) Kenichi Olmae notes that the "large American corporation is run like the [former] Soviet economy. In order to survive, it must plan ahead, comprehensively controlling a vast array of functions and every detail." The problem seems to be that the typical American corporation eventually loses its flexibility and ability to adapt to change.

RADICAL CHANGE BEYOND THE WORLD OF BUSINESS: FIRST-ORDER CHANGE

Three major change forces are now shaping our world: social, political, and scientific-technological. We went through a similar period of change in the second half of the nineteenth century with the advent of the industrial age. With it came the rise of the modern nation state, colonialism, xenophobic nationalism, and modern warfare. In addition, people became resources, interchangeable components for the new industrial machines. Despite the conflicts and pain that we see around us today, the struggles of our current change revolution hold the promise of yielding positive results. Nevertheless, radical change that we are now experiencing *is* responsible for the dislocation that is rippling through the business world in the form of changed competitive practices and industry transformation. For many, this is an exciting and profitable time to be in the business world as changing market conditions create new opportunities. For others, these changes may be a challenge.

The current wave of radical change in business began after World War II as the world moved toward a consumer-driven economy—the first in history. The emergence of the consumer society has been a powerful force for both social and business change. In the 1950s and 1960s, it was a challenge and an opportunity for American businesses to deliver goods and services to a newly affluent and growing population. That burgeoning consumerism also fueled explosive business growth as smaller companies became large corporations and large companies grew into giant conglomerates with previously unimagined revenues and profits. The billion-dollar company that we take for granted today did not come into its own until well after the war (today, a billion-dollar company barely qualifies for the *Fortune* 500).

Consumerism has recently spread to other countries, principally in Asia, where it now fuels an explosion of affluence and corporate growth on that continent. The consequences of social and political change, however, are not limited to emerging economies. Social and political changes continue to affect the U.S. business environment as companies, large and small, deal with an aging workforce, increasing numbers of inadequately trained and poorly educated young workers, and increasing employee demands for more comprehensive and cost-effective health care as well as for improved quality of life both within and outside the work environment. These social-change forces represent the beginnings of a cascading order of change starting with what I call first-order change forces (see Figure 2.1). Their impact is global in that they are first reflected at the broad macroeconomic market level through societal, political, and economic changes before they directly affect the performance of business organizations.

Figure 2.1
Hierarchical Order of Change

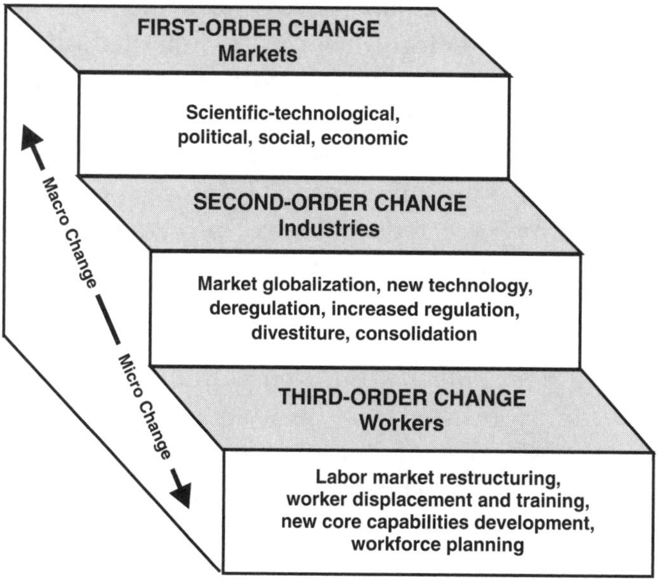

FIRST-ORDER CHANGE
Markets

Scientific-technological,
political, social, economic

SECOND-ORDER CHANGE
Industries

Market globalization, new technology,
deregulation, increased regulation,
divestiture, consolidation

THIRD-ORDER CHANGE
Workers

Labor market restructuring,
worker displacement and training,
new core capabilities development,
workforce planning

Macro Change

Micro Change

The newest form of macro change—the scientific and technologi-cal advancements that are altering the way we live and work—is unique to our period in history.

The information-technology age was born in the 1950s and 1960s when an unpredictable change force was unleashed. Sci-ence and new technology have benefited and enriched us more than any other source of change and at the same time have over-taken us before we have learned to adapt to them. New technology breakthroughs have radically changed lifestyles, revolutionized production processes, created exotic new products, and spawned whole new industries. Twenty years ago, there was no Microsoft or Lotus Development much less an entire software industry employ-ing millions. Today's health-care industry is built on new scientific and technological breakthroughs—in new medical instrumenta-tion, breakthrough wonder drugs, and biotechnology discoveries. Previously unknown companies like Amgen and Genentech allow us to treat diseases before they can be inherited, like multiple sclerosis, certain forms of cancer, and cystic fibrosis. This all con-tributes to business change.

New manufacturing processes no longer resemble the indus-trial age assembly line (the principal by-product of the industrial revolution), which created millions of production jobs. Today's social dilemma is how to deal with the massive job losses created by the new technology. Industrial robots can do the work of twelve assembly-line workers, and computers allow a handful of workers to operate a steel mill that once employed hundreds. The new manufacturing processes have been equally devastating on the white-collar workforce: millions of managerial jobs have been lost in the last fifteen years. These employment disruptions are all the product of a migration or transformation of the work world, and time is required to determine whether the transition will be suc-cessful. Clearly, there is a reciprocal—even a symbiotic—link be-tween the impact of technological and social change, and nowhere is that interaction more evident than in business.

Quite possibly the most dramatic changes in this period of radical change have come in the political arena with the astounding collapse of Communism—a rigid political and economic system. Similar changes have occurred in Latin and South America as military governments have given way to free-market, democratic economies. Politics, however, was not the sole reason for Communism's collapse in Europe and Russia. The overwhelming desire of people to lead their own lives in freedom and prosperity was a major social force that interacted with the politics of the time to ignite a counterrevolution. Today, those societies are coping with the unfamiliar social change issues associated with capitalism and democracy. East Europeans are adapting more easily than others since they have a tradition of capitalism. The liberated Russian, Ukrainian, and Asian peoples, with no experience of capitalism, are enduring a more difficult transition.

SECOND-ORDER CHANGE: CHANGE IN THE CORPORATE WORLD

The business-change forces of the globalization of markets, new technology breakthroughs, deregulation, increased regulation, divestiture, and business consolidation dominate the headlines of the *Wall Street Journal, Business Week,* and *Fortune.* Nevertheless, we tend to overlook the fact that these business-change forces are products of the larger social, political, and scientific change forces that are rocking the entire planet. During periods of radical change, enterprises that are most successful in managing the Business Change Cycle understand this critical linkage or continuum between change in the larger world—first-order change—and change in the business world—second-order change.

Globalization of markets has become a major factor in the competitive equation for many American companies. Neither the United States nor its blue-chip corporations can continue to dominate world markets as they once did. International trade agreements like NAFTA and the European Community (formerly the European Common Market) are required to level the playing field and reduce trade barriers. Additional free trade agreements probably will be seen between states in the former Soviet Union, in Asia, and in Latin and South America, as no one will want to be left out. According to Frank Kittredge, president of the National Foreign Trade Council (Interview, February 22, 1993), a strong worldwide GATT trade agreement will truly open markets and level playing fields around the world. Nevertheless, American companies still need to learn more about their target markets and continued support by the U.S. government will be required at times to level the playing field as it is doing in Asia today.

This trend will be both a blessing and a dilemma for companies that are accustomed to conducting business only within their own national borders. The opening of previously closed markets will be enticing but also problematic. Companies will have to learn to compete in strange cultures. Note how difficult it has been for Western companies to gain a foothold in Eastern Europe and Russia. In addition, the relatively unstable value of currencies has made it difficult for companies to properly price their products for overseas markets. A principal reason that the sophisticated Japanese car makers are actually losing market share—not just money—to American producers is the unstable relationship between the yen and dollar, as well as the improving quality of American autos. German auto manufacturers BMW and Volkswagen have opened plants in the United States to keep their autos competitively priced with the American and Japanese autos that are already being produced here.

For decades, American businesses have complained about the unfair competition from companies based overseas, and in many cases, their complaints were justified. In the 1980s, steel dumping by Japan, Korea, and Germany was a common practice, and more Yamaha motorcycles than Harleys were seen on TV and on the road. Many of those inequities have been corrected. In fact, you rarely see a Yamaha or Suzuki motorcycle on U.S. roads anymore. The United States' open-market practices should have prepared U.S. companies to compete effectively in selected overseas markets. American companies are already the suppliers of choice in Mexico and China, two of the largest and fastest-growing markets in the world. Companies like Caterpillar, Motorola, Ford, Bechtel, Coca-Cola, Continental Grain, and General Electric could be labeled as our first generation of truly successful international companies, given their long-term success in overseas markets. Many of our new computer software developers, semiconductor companies, and once stodgy telecommunications companies are leading the next generation of successful U.S. competitors in the expanding global marketplace.

Technology breakthroughs are enhancing virtually every industry and at times are creating headaches. A major problem is that technology-laden products seem to have an increasingly shorter half-life. This built-in obsolescence makes it difficult for businesses to keep up with the competition and with the product-evolution cycle. It is a good strategy for Intel and Microsoft to make obsolete their own products before the competition does, but what are the consequences of this planned obsolescence for customers? Corporate information technology (IT) departments (customers) barely adapt to a new system or software package before it becomes obsolete and requires updating or replacement. The IT professionals and their skills also can become obsolete as we will see in Chapter 8. Digital technology will soon make cellular communications technology seem as outdated as wired communications systems. Too many PC software and disk technologies just don't adapt to each other, and with the emergence of CD-ROM technology, system compatibility is a growing challenge. With each new technology breakthrough comes change for the consumer.

The pharmaceutical industry is experiencing significant change as the public demands additional new cures for frightening new diseases. Recent breakthroughs in medical and biogenetic labs have raised researchers' hopes, which have yet to keep pace with the public's expectations. Along with the demand for more magic bullets is the public's call for cost-effective drugs and universal health-care protection. Those on the firing line—hospitals and pharmaceutical companies—are being squeezed from all directions.

Deregulation and *increased regulation* are usually the products of governments acting on behalf of consumers. The airlines were *deregulated* with the goals of increasing efficiency and lowering prices for the flyer through increased competition. Some argue that deregulation didn't work and that the industry has actually become more chaotic—not more efficient. We examine airline industry developments in greater detail in Chapter 7.

Banking was deregulated to allow for increased competition across state lines and to promote more services for bank customers. The result has been a dwindling number of banks around the country as larger banks buy-up smaller banks. In addition, the large banks have been merging and buying each other: Bank America has purchased Continental Illinois of Chicago, and Chemical Bank merged with Manufacturer's Hanover in New York. While banks are now offering more diversified services to compete with brokerage houses, mutual funds, and insurance companies, consumers still complain about the quality and cost of conventional banking services.

Increased regulation is being seen on Wall Street and in the insurance and health-care industries. The questionable practices and outright fraud in the securities industry have led state governments, the Securities and Exchange Commission, and the National Association of Stock Dealers to tighten enforcement standards and penalties. In health care, proposed reform is intended to widen the safety net of coverage so that more Americans can be protected, to place hospitals and physicians under increasing scrutiny to justify and control costs, and to find the means to pay for the expanded coverage. Despite the involvement of Congress and the President in health-care reform, we must keep in mind that this resurgent regulatory climate was born out of the public's demand for better and more cost-effective coverage. It remains to be seen whether the proposed new legislation and laws will truly reflect the people's will.

Divestiture reflects a number of disparate business conditions. The principal reason for divestiture is to unload a poorly performing business unit, especially if the sale will generate cash for the parent company to reinvest in its core business or return to shareholders. In the past year, Kodak developed a new strategy for returning to the basics of its core imaging business, prompted by the sluggish performance of both its core business and its subsidiary chemical and pharmaceutical businesses. The revenues from those spun-off businesses will bolster Kodak for increased competition from its hard-charging Japanese competitor, Fuji Corporation. Other companies, like Cooper Industries and Quaker Oats, have sold off failed or underperforming acquisitions from the 1980s, and Ford Motor Company sold the perpetually underperforming First Nationwide Bank. One of the biggest shoppers for companies outside of its own core business—Sears—sold off its financial services, catalogue, and car rental units when it realized that its core business was hemorrhaging: it chose socks over stocks. Despite the continuing trend toward company and industry consolidation, many underperforming mergers of the 1980s have become the source of divestitures in the 1990s as corporate leaders recognize the importance of sticking to their knitting.

The mother of all divestitures was the breakup of AT&T. Mandated by the courts and the government to create more competition in the long-distance telephone market, we may never see another corporate breakup of such magnitude and with so much direct impact on the general public. The consequences of AT&T's breakup will be explored in Chapter 9.

Consolidation has been a major business trend for the last fifteen years, for reasons as diverse as there are industries. In the 1980s many large companies purchased other companies that were in no way related to their core business: tobacco companies bought food companies that, in turn, bought clothing companies; steel companies bought petroleum companies; industrial manufacturers bought banks, investment banks, and media companies; retail chains bought financial service companies; and auto manufacturers purchased computer software companies. These sales all grew out of an increasingly laissez-faire climate that some attributed to President Reagan's economic policies. Today, there is considerable doubt about the benefits—the value added or prosperity—of the merger mania of the 1980s. RJR Nabisco continues to stagger under the debt created by their merger, and Kodak is wisely unloading those unprofitable companies it bought. American Express learned that Wall Street was no place for a credit card company, and General Electric may soon follow AMEX's example. The 1986 overleveraged buyers of Macy's have collapsed under a mountain of debt that hindered the company's ability to compete. The buyer of Macy's, Federated, is now saddled with huge debts from its own past buying sprees. The 1980s also witnessed many takeovers within industries, primarily to take over a rival for its assets, and nowhere were takeovers more predatory than on Wall Street and in the commercial banking sector. The net effect has been a major restructuring of industries, the elimination of both weak and competitive companies, and a significant downsizing of the professional and technical workforce.

Business consolidation remains strong in the 1990s but largely for *different* reasons. As change affects entire industries, key players within each industry are consolidating to protect themselves in the wake of an oversupply of services and products. Banking is a conspicuous example in a country with more banks per capita than any other nation in the world. Increased automation requires fewer employees, while the lowering of barriers to interstate competition has driven out many small and midsize banks. The result is a smaller industry with fewer workers but larger institutions.

Despite the creation of seven new telephone companies out of AT&T's breakup, the telecommunications industry is actually shrinking as smaller long-distance companies like WilTel and LDDS consolidate (to form the fourth-largest U.S. long-distance carrier) to better compete for a shrinking pie. Unnoticed by many was the quiet merger in 1993 between the nation's most profitable local service phone company—Contel—and GTE to form the largest local phone service company in the country. Late last year, AT&T purchased McCaw Cellular in the largest merger in the industry.

Change is also forcing consolidation in the pharmaceutical

sector as health alliances are driving down the cost of drugs. That, along with impending regulatory change in the health-care and insurance sectors, is forcing the once gentlemanly pharmaceutical companies to feed on each other by purchasing related or competitor businesses. American Home Products leaped from obscurity to become the fourth-largest U.S. pharmaceutical company, all through acquisitions. Merck's acquisition of MEDCO Containment, a low-cost prescription drug distributor, allowed it to move into a competitor distribution sector. The intricacies of this trend will be mapped out in Chapters 10 and 11. Nevertheless, business consolidation today is occurring for different, smarter, and more rational reasons than it did in the 1980s. The net effect is that as entire industries—not just companies—consolidate and downsize, they are affecting the conventional work world.

THE WORKFORCE OF THE FUTURE HAS ARRIVED: THIRD-ORDER CHANGE

Third-order change affects the nature of work as well as workers. Just as new technologies have created new industries and jobs while eliminating others, first- and second-order change forces are transforming the landscape of the white-collar and labor markets. The nature of work itself is changing. What were once called piecework jobs have largely disappeared from the United States. These task- and output-oriented jobs with compensation based on the final piece or product could be measured by quantifying their output. For example, the textile industry and certain parts of the agricultural and food-processing industries continue to be tied to piecework labor. They are an outdated vestige of the industrial revolution's labor force.

The Irrelevant and Soon-to-Be Extinct Job

Skilled and managerial jobs have long been structured along the lines of piecework jobs as output, status, or responsibility have been measured and assigned a value. The entire industry of

compensation and benefits consulting grew up around the practices of quantifying managerial work processes, qualifications,
and output. These jobs and professions are becoming extinct.
Until now, industrial and corporate jobs were created through the
formation of large production units in factories, mines, and offices. As production units became larger and more complex, the
jobs became more specialized and stratified. The bureaucracy was
invented. Each company, like an ant colony, was a maze of jobs.
Companies had to manage their bureaucracies—the complexity—rather than business conditions. That stratification gave rise
to restructuring, downsizing, TQM, just-in-time, reengineering,
and so on. The effective work team—where one person doing
ABC and another assigned to JKL must work in harmony and
coordination with a worker doing XYZ—is a great concept that
has been long overdue and will be discussed in Chapters 5 and 6.
Nevertheless, what happens to team workers when the team has
been eliminated through reengineering, downsizing, the introduction of new technology, or outsourcing to a smaller firm that
can do the team's work for one-third the cost? This is where radical
change becomes an issue for everyone and not just for those
gathered around the board room conference table.

Jobs and tasks are becoming irrelevant. As a result, "learning
has become more important than training" (M. Weisbord, *Productive Work Places*, Jossey-Bass, 1988) just as more companies and
industries are becoming irrelevant. In 1990, a midsize financial
services company eliminated most of its human resource function
and outsourced those tasks and activities to a newly created outside firm lead by the former chief human resource officer and
staffed by former company employees. In 1991, Motorola sold off a
Texas-based production unit to its workers and helped them with
the financing: the workers would not relocate, and the company
did not want to maintain the overhead of the unit. Motorola now
outsources to the company at a lower cost, and the new company
has been able to take on other clients. These are the exceptions
and not the rule. More typically, fortunate white-collar workers
who lose their jobs or are forced into early retirement are given an

opportunity to consult back to the employer for extended periods, doing essentially what they did before while the company has less overhead and none of the long-term commitment to the employee. According to consultant Bill Bridges, "The reality we face is much more troubling, for what is disappearing is not just a certain number of jobs in certain industries or in some part of the country or even jobs in America as a whole. What is disappearing is the very thing itself: the job. That much sought after, much maligned social entity, a job, is vanishing like a species that has outlived its evolutionary time" (*Fortune,* September 19, 1994).

Developing Innovative Behaviors in a Changing Labor Market

One reason for this creeping extinction of jobs is that jobs themselves have become either so complex as to defy definition or so fragmented as to lose meaning. Products and measurable outcomes are out while such terms as *value-added* and *processes* are in (not long ago, no business executive wanted to hear the word *process* because of its association with academia). It has become increasingly difficult for companies (especially service companies and intellectual-capital enterprises) to set expectations and to measure results. This makes it harder to value workers and their contribution or output based on revenues generated.

In addition, as companies increasingly focus on the bottom line, they adopt innovative personnel-reduction practices, while some of us wish that their innovation would be turned in other directions. Professionals will have to be just as innovative in protecting their careers. Increasingly, employers are hiring temporary professionals—not just secretaries, but managers and technical professionals. Jobs are being shared by several people, and technology is always being employed. As contingent or virtual workforces grow, professionals can no longer be certain of their role and where they will be employed. The notion that most people will have a specific job that is linked to one employer may soon be obsolete, especially with the emergence of the virtual company. Some companies, especially in the service sector, rely on the widespread and long-term use of temporary employees, but without the commitment, performance, and loyalty of permanent employees. The cost of accelerated turnover, recruitment, and ongoing training of temporary employees outweighs any cost savings. There is also the increased threat of losing proprietary technology and trade secrets through an uncommitted or contingent workforce. Very few companies have yet learned how to appraise, value, and retain intellectual capital, much less apply it to make money—value added. A few companies—like Dow Chemical, Motorola, Canadian Imperial Bank of Commerce, Intel, and Hughes Aircraft—are attempting to better measure and apply their intellectual capital. But here again, the focus is on specific patent opportunities or technology breakthroughs by talented individuals. Determining what can be captured from the collective endeavors of the workforce remains a mystery for most companies.

The trend, however, is for companies to look at their workforces as overhead. If they wish to remain "employed," individuals will need to develop new attitudes and innovative skills:

- *Become the keeper of your own trade.*   You do not have to start your own company to develop a proprietary nature about your skills and capabilities. Take ownership of them—especially your own intellectual capital—as well as responsibility for enhancing your skills and capabilities. Market them proactively within the organization or industry with which you are affiliated. This requires adaptability and continual learning.

- *Adapt to changing employer needs.*   Employees become fixated on their jobs, while professionals ready themselves for new assignments and projects within the company. They adapt and market their capabilities and commitment to fit new requirements of the employer or of customers. This is value-added thinking as opposed to commodity thinking. The Intel Corporation has very little turnover because it is committed to shifting workers to new projects where their skills and thinking can be adapted to new needs and requirements. According to Christine Oster, senior business consultant for Intel, the company rarely hires people for a specific job but rather looks at their ability to fit into and contribute to the culture—to thrive on new opportunities and challenges and not the sameness or security of one job (Interview, August 30, 1994).

- *Become part of the team.* Affiliate yourself with a team that reflects your own values, career savvy, and range of capabilities (not necessarily the same skills). Inside a company, a project team may move as a unit to fulfill a new challenge within the company, or a group of loosely affiliated professionals may share similar goals and aspirations for both the company and their careers. The team can sell itself far more effectively within the company and gain more recognition for its accomplishments than can an individual. The team also becomes a powerful magnet for others in the organization. Consultants have been doing this for years. If you are outside the company and are essentially a solo vendor or consultant, the need to affiliate becomes even more important for securing information about changes in the marketplace and for linking capabilities to serve a business. A group of allied professionals also can scan the change landscape far more effectively than any individual.

- *Embrace change and risk.* Static markets and organizations provide few opportunities for change-minded professionals. Seek out dynamic, changing conditions in the marketplace or within your company that provide opportunities that can be exploited. Identifying these opportunities before others can identify them requires you to take some risks and encounter some resistance, but the rewards are commensurate with the risk. In addition, don't be afraid to alert others to changing conditions in the marketplace where you can be a change manager or coordinator of their contributions. Even better, create the change. It may frighten some and attract others, but fear of failure didn't stop people like Bill Gates of Microsoft or Ken Iverson of NUCOR.

BACK TO THE FUTURE

Before large corporations existed, people worked in small shops and businesses, farmers joined cooperatives, craftsmen created guilds, and many of us were self-employed in both unskilled and skilled endeavors. People worked close to their homes in their own communities. The trend is now to return to the community as large corporations relinquish their role as the principal source of work in the postindustrial era. According to the American Management Association, more than 12 million white-collar jobs have been lost since 1980. Companies have simply become too complex and expensive to continue to be magnets for all motivated workers, and even the best of companies have difficulty accepting new people with bright new ideas.

Where are all the workers going? People are again working in their homes and communities in roles that are highly untraditional compared to those in the corporate world. Workers of all types are again being asked to be broad problem solvers rather than the specialists that were in demand for the past twenty years. Virtual offices are sprouting all over suburbia, and a new generation of inexpensive office equipment has been developed that offers the home worker the same technical support that she would have at the office—without having to stand in line at the copier. Publishers, agents, stockbrokers, accountants, graphic designers, and consultants are among the many professionals who can now work at home or in a virtual office environment without being affiliated with a corporation and without commuting to big business centers. Advanced communications and information technology equipment can link them to customers and clients located anywhere in the world.

Both corporations and individuals need to begin focusing on the field of work, instead of labor and job markets, and see it as a reservoir for both the resources and opportunities that each requires. Neither can it be forgotten that the reservoir must be replenished to prevent its drying up. Workers will always be required, but they may no longer be funneled through the corporate personnel department. With less resistance to the change forces around us, we can better embrace third-order change. This means letting go of our dependency on a job while redirecting our focus toward work, ideas, and knowledge transfer. At the same time, companies must balance their focus so that their workers are viewed not just as overhead but as a resource for productivity and business growth. The end product will be less insecurity, more productivity, and greatly enhanced career satisfaction, which will allow us to better manage the forces of radical change—at all levels.

CHAPTER

3

Organization Building Amidst Radical Change

One of the most important things an organization can do is determine exactly what business it is in.
— PETER DRUCKER

For many entrepreneurs, the current climate of radically changing competitive conditions is a once-in-a-lifetime opportunity to launch and build new businesses. Unsuspected niches are revealing themselves in previously crowded markets. Technology breakthroughs are spawning entirely new enterprises. In the airline industry, emerging new markets are creating opportunities for carriers like TransAfrica Air and US Africa Air, both serving the newly democratic South Africa, while deregulation has given rise to Kiwi Air and Southwest Air. Cutting-edge telecommunications technologies are giving rise to promising companies like NEXTEL and Octel. An apparently unlimited market for specialty data-management services and their associated platforms has encouraged the emergence of hundreds of software developers and system networkers like User Technology Associates of Arlington, Virginia, and Profiles In Data, Inc. of Denver. As long as a stream of venture capital remains available, new biotechnology companies, like Amgen, Genentech, and Chairon, will continue to sprout in response to the demand for new cures for diseases.

In certain fields, it has always been relatively easy for entrepreneurial employees, even for dispirited refugees from impersonal corporate monoliths, to strike out on their own—offering specialty services that reflect enhanced customer support or improved products. This adaptation to niche markets is characteristic of the profusion of new, "boutique" financial services firms. Former bond traders, stockbrokers, and investment counselors now successfully compete with their old bosses: in less than a generation, mutual funds, once little more than a cottage industry, have grown into financial giants. Many of these funds were created by individual investment professionals who expressly intended to compete for investment dollars with larger equity trading firms. In the personal transportation industry, travel agencies, cruise lines, and air carriers are flourishing. Enterprise Rent-A-Car has been quietly growing into an industry giant by picking a niche where it would not directly compete with Hertz and Avis. Of course, information technology and its application may continue to offer the most fertile ground for startups.

Business ventures need not be born in an eccentric dreamer's garage. As large corporations downsize, they often spin off entire divisions or even small business units that are insufficiently contributing to overall profitability. These are not simply downsized business units but self-sufficient corporations like Genicom, a spinoff from GE and Sears Payment Systems now known as SPS Inc. Many are minibusinesses available for a few million dollars to venture capitalists or former managers located within the existing business unit. A leveraged purchase of these companies is possible for almost anyone who is both interested and gutsy. Despite generally negative attitudes toward expanded regulation, it frequently stimulates the growth of businesses that can ensure industry compliance. Regulatory consulting on the environment, medical and workplace safety, and hazardous waste transportation and disposal is a rapidly burgeoning service sector.

Nonetheless, the radically changing and seemingly chaotic marketplace also is studded with land mines that can destroy a promising business before it gets off the ground. Health-care reform may soon shrink the financial pipeline that has traditionally sustained emerging biotechnology and specialty medical-product businesses. The speed of technological innovation also can render an "indispensable" product obsolete before a new company establishes its customer base. The marketplace is fickle, and customers will quickly change suppliers for a better or cheaper mousetrap.

Globalization of markets is posing an interesting set of problems for new manufacturing businesses. Potential competition from foreign producers may go undetected until it is too late for a business to react effectively. At the same time, opportunities to enter promising foreign markets may prove too difficult (because of regulatory barriers), distant, or expensive to crack. Neither is it sufficient to examine only consumer markets when considering overseas expansion. Labor markets also must be factored into the equation. While the dollar has shrunk somewhat, it is still relatively expensive for an American manufacturer that uses American labor to compete with companies employing Asian or Latin American labor. For these and other reasons, a developing company needs to undertake as much change planning as any mature business. Unlike a mature business, however, the newcomer must tread the tightrope of the marketplace with a far smaller safety net that exposes a much larger fraction of business assets.

THE SHAPE OF BUSINESS CHANGE: THE BUSINESS CHANGE CYCLE

The *Business Change Cycle* represents a natural ebb and flow that every business encounters. In fact, entire industries experience these tidal forces. Business enterprises are dynamic systems— occasionally unpredictable, highly complex, and very difficult to plan for or manage. When these characteristics combine with the volatile change forces loose in the marketplace, as well as a temperamental regulatory climate, leaders of new businesses soon find themselves sailing a tumultuous sea without adequate charts. For this reason, it helps when corporate skippers can systematically measure, evaluate, and interpret their organizations' evolution and functioning over time. The Business Change Cycle is designed to provide that assessment and direction.

Some readers may view this tool as just another organizational life-cycle theory or model, which it is not. The most relevant aspect of traditional life-cycle theory, as compared to the Business Change Cycle, is that both postulate developmental cycles that emphasize the ongoing and rhythmic nature of an organization's development and functioning. This may be the only characteristic that the Business Change Cycle shares with life-cycle theories.

Organizational life-cycle models are a powerful and relevant *theoretical* construct, with many prominent academic advocates, including Ichak Adizes of UCLA, John Kimberly of Yale, Robert Miles of Harvard, and Noel Tichy at the University of Michigan. Nevertheless, there are several important and significant differences between life-cycle theory and the Business Change Cycle:

- Theories and models can provide only representations of the actual business world that are then viewed through a set of lenses or filters by an audience residing outside the marketplace. The Business Change Cycle, on the other hand, is a natural product of the business world or system that is being examined.

- Life-cycle theory tends to anthropomorphize the business organization by conceptualizing it as a living, breathing organism. The Business Change Cycle views the company as a complex system of people, business practices, technological processes, and market forces.

- Some life-cycle proponents go so far as to attribute psychological qualities to the business organization. These psychodynamic qualities are used to help explain behavior, relying on loaded terms like *neurosis, infancy, dysfunctionality, pathology,* and *family.* When this psychological model is superimposed on the business organization, it becomes the focus for discussion and debate. In contrast, the Business Change Cycle

utilizes business terms to explain the functioning and performance of the business organization—a vocabulary familiar to
business professionals. It sheds light on the subject rather than
creating mystery.

- Life-cycle theories tend to appraise business organizations on
the basis of one or two dimensions—such as internal functioning or political forces. Utilizing a three-dimensional
framework, the Business Change Cycle plots business functioning along axes of performance (that is, growth and development), operational and cultural functioning, and the
impact of change on the organization (see Figure 3.1). The
Business Change Cycle "sticks with the business" as long as it
exists, right to the point of failure. It provides a constant
developmental framework for evaluating the business organization, regardless of where the organization currently is situ-
ated in its Business Change Cycle. This allows companies to
tailor change initiatives or turnaround strategies to fit current
change conditions.

FOLLOWING A COMPANY THROUGH
THE BUSINESS CHANGE CYCLE

The Business Change Cycle is best understood by following it from
the bottom left of Figure 3.1, up the change curve, and through
the visioning and standardization stages to its apex. All business
leaders seek to continue their company's growth and development without experiencing the change phase of the Business
Change Cycle. Admirable as this goal is, few if any, companies or
industries are able to avoid the change phase. To do so would be to
avoid change itself. As a company moves down the right side, or
change side, of the cycle, hyphenated arrows extend from each of
the four change stages that represent potential turnarounds for
the company from each stage of the change cycle. Most companies
find a way to achieve a turnaround at one of these stages. Inherent in turnaround is the ability to understand and manage the

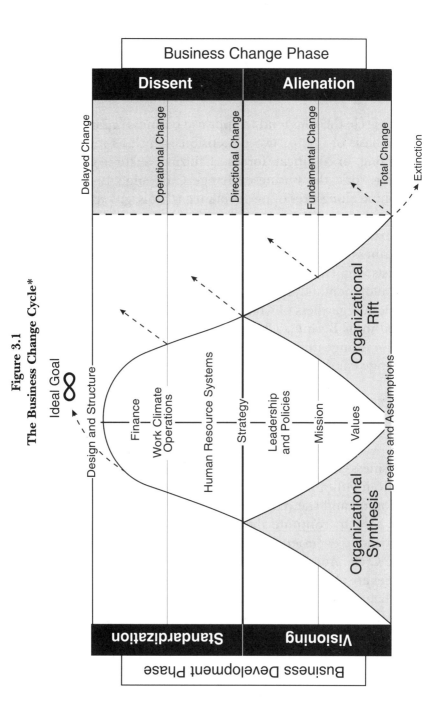

Figure 3.1
The Business Change Cycle*

© JEROME H. WANT 1990. REVISED 1994.
* Change cycle reads from bottom left (visioning stage) to apex of curve through alienation stage to bottom right corner.

48

changing needs of the culture of the company—*dissent* or *alienation*—and the increasing complexity of problems and breakdowns within the business at each change level. These will be discussed in further detail in Chapter 4. Companies that fail to successfully manage change eventually move toward extinction at the bottom right tail of the curve. This also is the dismal destination for companies that surrender to merger partners.

Business Visioning

It is easy to forget that every large corporation began as nothing more than an idea in someone's imagination. Ford, Watson, Olson, Galvin, Westinghouse, Gates, and McGowan may have started small, but they marched toward the future with ideas that quickly outgrew their desktop origins. These innovators also shared a high threshold for risk, a quality that is essential for successfully launching any business. Gordon Moore and Robert Noyce founded Intel long before there was any demand for their chips. Mitch Kapor actually started Lotus Development in his garage, and Bill Gates dropped out of college to grow his dream into Microsoft. What each of these pioneers possessed was a clear vision, supported by a strong set of assumptions about their product and the marketplace that told them how to grow their business.

THE VISION THING
A Case Study in Managing the Development Side
of the Business Change Cycle

A New England shipper of sensitive high technology equipment (I will call them AA Distributors) had been in business four years. Growth during the company's first two years was phenomenal. Third-year sales flattened, while profits

(continued)

evaporated—due largely to the expanded hiring (based on second-year performance) and increased capital investment required by the business. Fourth-year sales were declining, turnover was increasing, and expanding business with existing customers was proving difficult. A shortage of resources prevented the owners from pursuing major new customers for fear of not being able to serve them properly.

Eventually, workers were laid off, and others were being asked to accept a four-day work week. Fortunately, there were few problems within established distribution channels, and customers were generally satisfied. But volume was shrinking on most major accounts. AA's owners wondered whether they were experiencing the forerunner of another recession, but industry and government statistics indicated otherwise. Neither did it appear as though a competitor was suddenly undercutting them in the market. The owners meticulously examined the company's operations. They brought in outside consultants and satisfied themselves that there were no significant operational problems. They commissioned an internal audit of employees' attitudes. At the same time, they initiated a similar survey of their customers and prospective customers. Several themes began to emerge:

• Employees could not identify the goals of the company—aside from making money for its owners. Those who had previously worked for AA's competitors felt it was hard to see where their contributions fit in, since all decisions were micromanaged from the top. And no one seemed sure where the company was headed: "The owners never discuss their plans with managers." More significantly, the sales staff could not provide any reasons for targeted customers to drop their existing vendor for AA.

(*continued*)

- Interviews with AA's customers revealed they had signed up initially because of the shipper's low charges, their immediate availability, and their desire to help the new company get up and running. However, during AA's second and third years of operation, its charges quickly rose to match those of competitors. As the company grew, it found itself no longer able to offer customers special shipments on short notice. AA was being retained by existing accounts only as a safety valve for peak periods or backup when their principal shippers dropped the ball. There were no major differences reported between AA and its competitors in a crowded market, except that AA was still the new boy on the block.

The owners of AA decided to develop a major mission and strategy that focused on "sharing the company's vision with employees and customers." After identifying what they believed should be the vision and strategy for the business, they then assembled their employees to help "flesh it out." Of equal importance was the decision to convene a meeting with customers for the sole purpose of soliciting their ideas. They were especially interested in suggestions for how to implement the adopted strategy. Their customers and employees became their consultants and stakeholders in the business.

The owners were patient and decided to wait a full year before attempting to measure results. During that year, they continued to develop a process for "making the vision real" and for ensuring that their strategy would be effective. They personally wrote AA's first mission statement, and they incorporated a number of suggestions from customers into their strategy. Follow-up polling showed that employees were somewhat more committed to the company. They also showed an improved understanding of the company's mission and

(*continued*)

where individual jobs fit into the overall plan. But they still had little authority to resolve problems and implement improvements. While customers and employees could begin to see how the culture was changing, they still had trouble separating AA from its competition on the basis of service or price. The owners were still concerned.

In subsequent meetings with their customers, the owners discovered that customers wanted AA's managers and dispatchers to intervene directly to resolve problems. These employees were closer to customers and their needs than the owners were and could make decisions more quickly. It was also deduced from customers that AA could separate itself from its competitors by instituting a two-tier service option— a premium price for ultrafast delivery and special handling and a discounted regular service. Customers would have a choice, yet the two services would actually complement one another. Customers demonstrated their support for these options, as volume and revenue grew following their introduction. Employees were soon being called back to work. They were also given the opportunity to become more fully involved in daily operations. As routes expanded and new customers were signed up, workers concentrated on solving problems and improving service while the owners worked to expand the business and add value for customers. AA slowly became the shipper of choice.

This case study reveals the power of corporate visioning for the new business, especially when it is structured to include contributions from both the workforce and the customer. Donald Kehoe, a noted turnaround executive who has led both small and midmarket companies, cites the ability to examine and renew the corporate vision as a critical asset for the new and expanding company (Interview, September 12, 1994). Kehoe further notes the need for business founders to be flexible and prepared to modify or "migrate" the mission and strategy of the new business to meet changing market opportunities. Renewed visioning is critical in an ever-shifting competitive landscape. Leaders of emerging businesses have generally relied on an inside-out view of the marketplace. This perspective places the product or service being offered at the center of corporate thinking and planning. The AA shipping account shows how this two-dimensional perspective can be imbued with three-dimensional depth by linking the outside-in view of customers, as well as employees to the visioning process. I call this *wrap-around visioning*. It forces owners and managers to consider the identity and purpose of their enterprise from the viewpoint of all its important stakeholders.

The visioning phase is critical to an emerging company for several reasons (Figure 3.2). First and foremost, it is during this period that owners' basic assumptions, beliefs, and values about the business are established, tested, and operationalized. As operational issues and stresses begin to press in on the business, it needs to be able to signal to the marketplace the principal business aims of the company as well as its corporate identity. Successful visioning also communicates to new employees the standards by which the business will measure their performance. Finally, the company's leadership practices must move the business toward fulfillment of its mission and strategy, or they will develop haphazardly and leave the organization essentially rudderless. Eventually, this will force the founders and senior managers into a makeshift fire brigade.

Too many entrepreneurs side-step these vital organization-building issues because of a preference for and comfort in dealing with operational or product-development challenges. This occurs time and time again, even though it is much easier to implant a corporate vision as a living, breathing component of the business at this initial stage of development. Later often means never.

Figure 3.2
Visioning Stage
in Organization Building

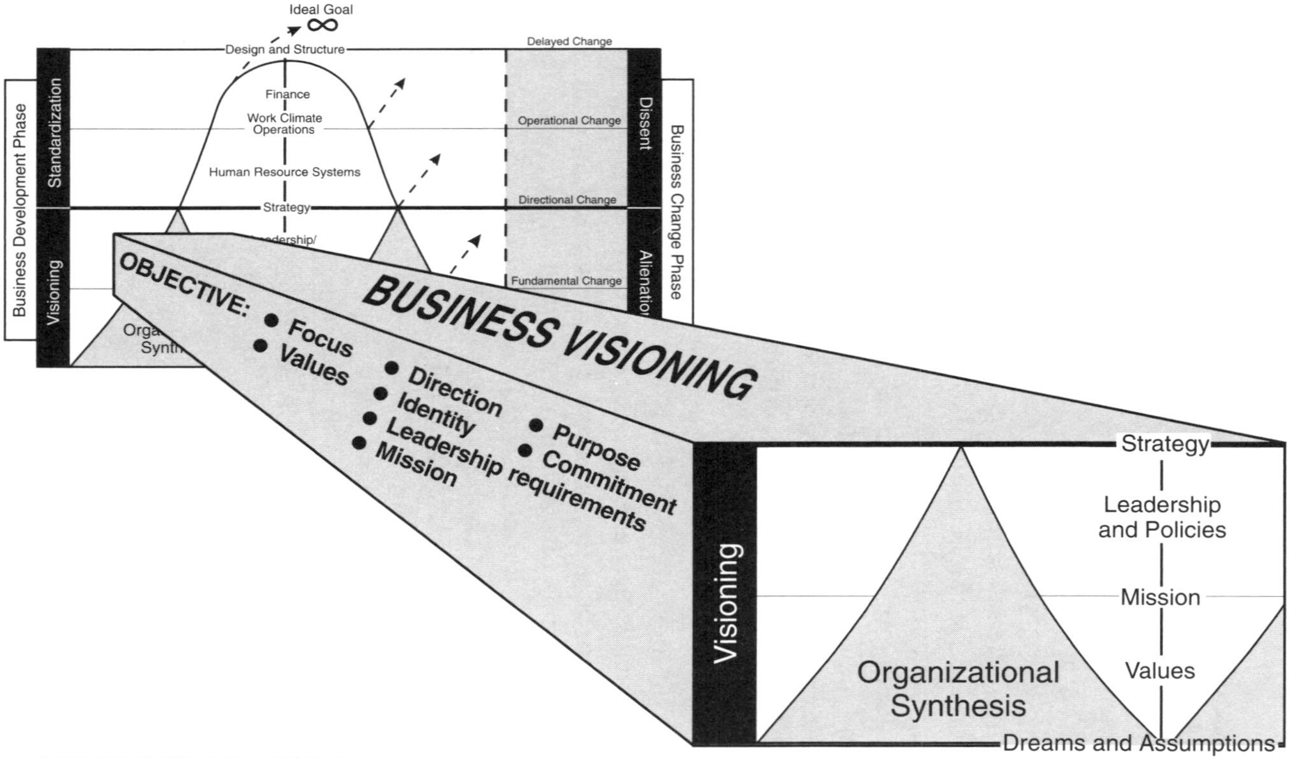

BUSINESS VISIONING

OBJECTIVE:
- Focus
- Values
- Direction
- Identity
- Leadership
- Mission
- Purpose
- Commitment
- Leadership requirements

Business Change Phase

Dissent | Alienation

Delayed Change
Operational Change
Directional Change
Fundamental Change

Ideal Goal

Design and Structure
Finance
Work Climate
Operations
Human Resource Systems
Strategy
Leadership/
Organizational
Synthesis

Standardization | Visioning

Business Development Phase

Strategy
Leadership and Policies
Mission
Values
Dreams and Assumptions

Organizational Synthesis

Visioning

© JEROME H. WANT 1991. REVISED 1994.

54

Business Standardization

Business standardization (see Figure 3.3) emerges from the natural need to formalize business operations and procedures so they will reliably and systematically support growing customer demand. On the positive side, this expanding demand tells managers that the critical mass that is necessary for sustained performance is being achieved. Standardization, and the infrastructure that comes with it, must be built on a sound business strategy—one that will actually work. It is likely to become the pivotal boundary that demonstrates that the startup business has successfully passed through its visioning stage and is now developing into a fully functioning business.

Too often, new businesses are caught up in a make-and-sell cycle. This can arise if the company has a novel product or service. It is particularly apparent in developing businesses that have ignored or undervalued the visioning process. Even when there is a formal strategy, it may be cast aside under the pressure to make, sell, and deliver products. Only when the inevitable slowdown finally occurs do managers start to look for reasons. At that point, a viable strategy can quickly turn around performance for the company. Strategy must be a functioning component of the business—not simply a printed plan. If the strategy is not actively at work in all areas of the business, then it is really a fiction like the tooth fairy. Inexorably, standardized functions and operations will break down, and precious financial resources will have to be applied in order to "fix them."

The key element in managing the change side of the business cycle is skillfully integrating changing business-development processes while maintaining operational and organizational continuity. A new company will eventually fail if it focuses exclusively on issues associated with the standardization stage and overlooks the visioning processes needed to construct a sound business foundation. All the managerial processes inherent in the developmental phase of organization building must be present and continuously balanced in order to ensure the success of a new

Figure 3.3
Standardization Stage
in Organization Building

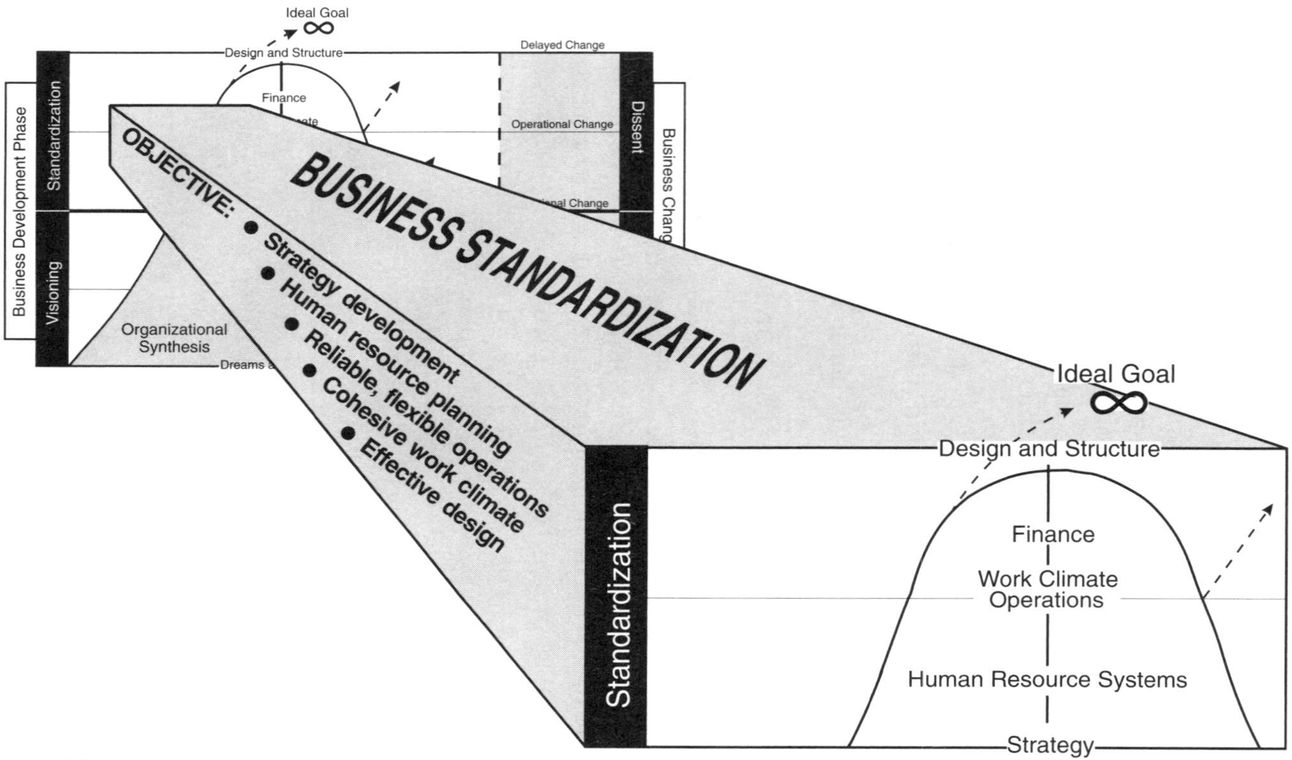

BUSINESS STANDARDIZATION

OBJECTIVE:
- Strategy development
- Human resource planning
- Reliable, flexible operations
- Cohesive work climate
- Effective design

Standardization

Design and Structure

Ideal Goal ∞

Finance
Work Climate
Operations
Human Resource Systems
Strategy

Business Change

Dissent

Delayed Change

Operational Change

Ideal Change

Ideal Goal ∞

Design and Structure

Finance

Organizational Synthesis

Dreams

Standardization Visioning

Business Development Phase

56

business. Chapter 4 examines this change side of the Business Change Cycle—how it is linked to the development side and the challenges and strategies associated with change.

LESSONS LEARNED FROM NINE OF TODAY'S SMALL BUSINESS BUILDERS AND THEIR COMPANIES

In addition to supporting many large corporations through my consulting practice, I've also advised a number of small business owners and their management teams. Since my engagements with these emerging companies have provided me with some of my most satisfying experiences and important insights, I believe it is worthwhile to share some thoughts and observations from their leaders. These tend to fall into the rubric of that old complaint, "If I had it to do over again, I'd probably do it differently".

I have included comments from nine leaders of small companies, ranging in size from $400,000 in annual revenues with five employees to over $65 million with more than a thousand employees. Seven of the nine are still managing their businesses, and all seven remain principal owners. One of the two remaining is a "Turnaround Executive", who is expert in growing a small business for its owners. The other has left the business he co-founded and developed to pursue his own independent consulting practice within the same industry. Six of the nine businesses are under ten years of age. They represent seven industries: information technology (two), transportation/shipping (two), advanced technology equipment (one), manufacturing (one), distribution (one), consumer services (one), and consulting (one). The issues were as follows:

Issue 1: As your new company began to grow, what was its greatest need?

Issue 2: What issues do owners of new companies most overlook in the first five years? What is the impact of these oversights?

Issue 3: What was the motivation or spark that started your business (examples: Opportunities offered by a changing marketplace, new technology, fortuitous timing, deregulation, divestiture, other)?

Issue 4: What is the principal cause of new company failure (within the first five years)?

Issue 5: Identify those qualities or characteristics of the new business founder or leader that most contributed to the success of the emerging business enterprise.

Issue 6: What is the biggest hurdle for most emerging companies on their way to attaining critical mass and sustained performance—that is, moving from the visioning stage to the business standardization stage?

Issue 7: What role has business visioning played in your company's development? Was there a formal visioning process from the outset?

See Table 3.1 for a compilation of responses, in abbreviated form.

Table 3.1
Polling of New Business Leaders on Organization Building
(*Most Frequent Responses*)

Issue 1: As your company began to grow, what was its greatest need?
1. Capital,
2. Marketing and advertising savvy,
3. The right people in the right place at the right time.

Issue 2: What issues do owners of new companies most overlook in the first five years? What is the impact of these oversights?
1. Defining a clear mission in the very beginning. *Impact:* Hampered ability to communicate the company's purpose or goals for customers, creditors, potential employees.
2. Securing the necessary capital for the long haul. *Impact:* Slowed growth cycle for business, inability to hire key people for business, taking on an unwanted or unnecessary business partner for their capital contribution.

(*continued*)

3. Controlling overhead. *Impact:* Cutting back on resources, people, marketing.
4. Willingness or ability to improve all processes in creating value.

Issue 3: What was the most common reason or spark that started your business? (Example: New technology, opportunities from the changing marketplace, fortuitous timing, deregulation, divestiture, other)?
1. Opportunities from the changing marketplace,
2. Fortuitous timing (being in the right place at the right time),
3. Having the necessary capital to start long-thought-of business,
4. New or unique technology or service offering,
5. Having a former employer or potential customer provide an opportunity.

Issue 4: What is the principal cause of new company failure (within the first five years)?
1. "Missing the market" (misjudging or incorrectly identifying where it is or what it needs),
2. Lack of capital,
3. Poor hiring,
4. Conflict between partners,
5. Inability to gain market recognition for the product or service,
6. Failure to control progress by timely and meaningful measurement of events.

Issue 5: Identify those qualities or characteristics of the new business founder or leader that most contributed to the success of the emerging enterprise.
1. Clear vision,
2. A commanding personality or presence that projects the company's image,
3. A good salesman or saleswoman for the product,
4. The ability to benefit from other people's ideas,
5. Tenacity.

(*continued*)

Issue 6: What is the biggest hurdle for most emerging companies on their way to attaining critical mass or sustained performance—that is, moving from the visioning stage to the business standardization stage?
1. Operationalizing the original company vision,
2. Developing a viable strategy that really works,
3. Recruiting enough of the right people who can take the business to the next level in its development,
4. Preventing customer demands from taking control of the business.

Issue 7: What role has business visioning played in your company's development? Was there a formal visioning process from the outset?
1. We waited too long to develop a vision for the company for everyone to share in;
2. The company mission kept us on track when things got out of control;
3. As market conditions and technology changed, the vision should have changed;
4. An early vision existed but was never formalized.

All nine small business leaders exhibit a high degree of intelligence, persistence, and, to varying degrees, impatience. All possess a genuine passion for what they are doing and exhibit exceptional self-confidence. In-depth knowledge of their marketplace was apparent among the majority, while several have been willing to seek outside assistance in order to better understand and capture market share. Five of the nine companies were created to fill an identified niche. Yet another created an industry or market niche that had not been previously recognized, which may be much the same thing.

Four of nine noted that fortuitous timing was a key ingredient to later success: they were in the right place at the right time. Seven of nine formerly worked for large corporations, and two were directly competing with former employers in the same market. Three out of nine were female. Two were in their thirties, one was over sixty, two were in their fifties, and the remaining four were in their forties. All of the companies remain in business and range in age from three to twelve years.

It would be misleading to point to just one or two critical failures or successes in summarizing what these small business leaders have learned and accomplished. The process for developing a new business is complex and often lengthy and cannot be fairly measured in just one or two years. Nonetheless, these leaders share successes in several areas:

- Encouraging innovation and experimentation,

- Soliciting ideas and advice from outside the business,

- Exhibiting tenacity (though not necessarily patience) on the part of the founder,

- Developing a clear mission (though this was often developed late in each business),

- Being in the right place at the right time,

- Having an opportunity to apply new or significantly improved technology or services,

- Finding a key individual to help grow the business.

Some of the common hurdles or impediments they experienced included:

- An unavailability or shortage of capital (especially from traditional lending institutions),

- Too little reliance on a formal vision to support strategy and marketing plans,

- Poor hiring decisions,

- Too much crisis management and too little planning,

- Too much reliance on the product's ability to sell itself,

- Insufficient change planning and anticipation of change,

- Tough competition,

- Waiting too long to define and capture a market niche,

- Uncontrolled growth of overhead.

The challenges presented by change are no less daunting or difficult for the small business than they are for their gigantic brothers and sisters. But with the right vision, small businesses can bring distinct advantages to the marketplace. Speed, flexibility, and innovation top the list of advantages. Even mistakes can be corrected more quickly, and at a lower cost, than is the case for corporate dinosaurs with a seven-layered, ninety-day approval process. Larger companies, on the other hand, can bring the financial resources and staying power that may be necessary to establish a place for a new product or service in the hearts and minds of customers.

Paul Hawken writes eloquently about the ecology of business, and while the analogy strains at times, there seems to be an appropriate and beneficial role for companies of all sizes: "There are and always will be predators, but just as surely there are and always will be ... partnerships that benefit even competitors. Finding that win-win niche is the key to sustainable growth and profitability" (*Growing a Business,* S&S Trade, 1988).

4

Strategies for Managing the Change Cycle: The Key to Performance

Dead battles like dead generals hold the military mind in their grip.
—Barbara Tuchman

Like most consultants, I like to tell war stories about the tough engagements I was able to capture, but occasionally, I prefer to talk about the prospects that got away. Once, I was called in by a former client who had been promoted from a corporate staff position to the presidency of a state telephone company. To his credit, he recognized the immediate need to "put some life back into the culture" of his newly inherited company. Anticipating little more than a two-year stewardship, he felt an urgency that he knew was not necessarily shared by his subordinates. A major issue was revenues, which had been on a steady decline due largely to the recession that gripped the entire state. A quick turnaround was unlikely. One consulting firm proposed a massive sales training program for the entire workforce. The goal was to rapidly transform the entire company into a more sales-conscious organization, both during phone contacts and in direct interactions with customers. This program proposed to enlist employees (union and nonunion) who were not normally assigned to sales positions. The program was packaged as "Get Out the Word."

My partners and I proposed a less immediate, more long-term, and ultimately self-sustaining process for developing the culture around specific change issues that would continue to impact the business. Many of these issues had to do with the culture itself, which had remained largely unchanged since the 1960s. Typically, new employees were recruited by friends and family members who were already employed within the company (the "family company" was a point of pride and key to the culture). The typical worker had more than seventeen years' tenure, and the company had been the *only* employer for nearly 60 percent of the workforce. In addition, the state was largely rural and had a narrow business base from which to build revenues. Many people who had lost jobs during the recession could not afford to maintain their phone service. That kind of environment rarely offers any quick fixes for the bottom line. The goal of my proposed intervention was to develop focused organizational competencies that could be applied to specific change issues utilizing teams of professionals that had the ability and commitment to succeed. Tangible results would start to be seen in one to two years, followed by sustained, long-term improvement.

When I learned that these competing proposals had been turned over to a committee chaired by the vice president of marketing and sales, I suspected that "Get Out the Word" would prevail over my proposal, and it did. Eventually, the phone company's bottom line turned around (due to substantial downsizing and an eventual economic recovery), but "Get Out the Word" did not deliver new revenues. Union employees, especially those not assigned to sales or customer service, adamantly resisted the sales-oriented training. So much pressure was placed on middle-management ranks to sell that normal operating issues were ignored. Flashy sales buttons disappeared from lapels after the first month. The sales approach created widespread alienation within the culture—not additional dollars. "Get Out the Word" also alienated large segments of the public that did not appreciate the company's sales hype. An already risk-aversive culture discovered that more of the same old medicine only produced greater risks. The realities about difficult change forces in the larger marketplace and an entrenched culture had been ignored. "Get Out the Word" didn't get the message.

WRONG PROBLEMS, WORSE SOLUTIONS: GUIDELINES FOR CHOOSING CHANGE STRATEGIES

This story about two competing proposals for revitalizing a company recounts a recurring frustration that motivated me to write this book: *Too frequently, corporate managers react to symptoms rather than to underlying problems.* As a consequence, they invariably reach for quick fixes instead of systematic *and* systemic solutions. The timing or promptness of results is a legitimate issue, but one of the roles of an effective manager is to manage time—to create the time that is needed to apply interventions effectively—and not to force strategies to fit an inappropriate or unrealistic time frame.

Get the Right Information

Far too often, erroneous assumptions are made by the CEO, division general manager, or executive team that is considering a change effort. Usually the information is based on their own internal grapevine or is shaped by crisis situations. An executive's own personal history and perceptions may influence his or her response. Prior to any intervention, a thorough audit of significant issues and business functions should be undertaken—strategy, leadership, operations, structure, culture, and human resources (see Figure 4.1). The most vital step is to develop accurate data about the change forces that are overtaking the business. The goals of the audit are twofold: to *gather information* while *eliminating bias* that can contaminate the planning process and misdirect subsequent action-taking steps. I am repeatedly dismayed by the widespread failure of businesses to initiate an organization audit

Figure 4.1
Functions of the Business

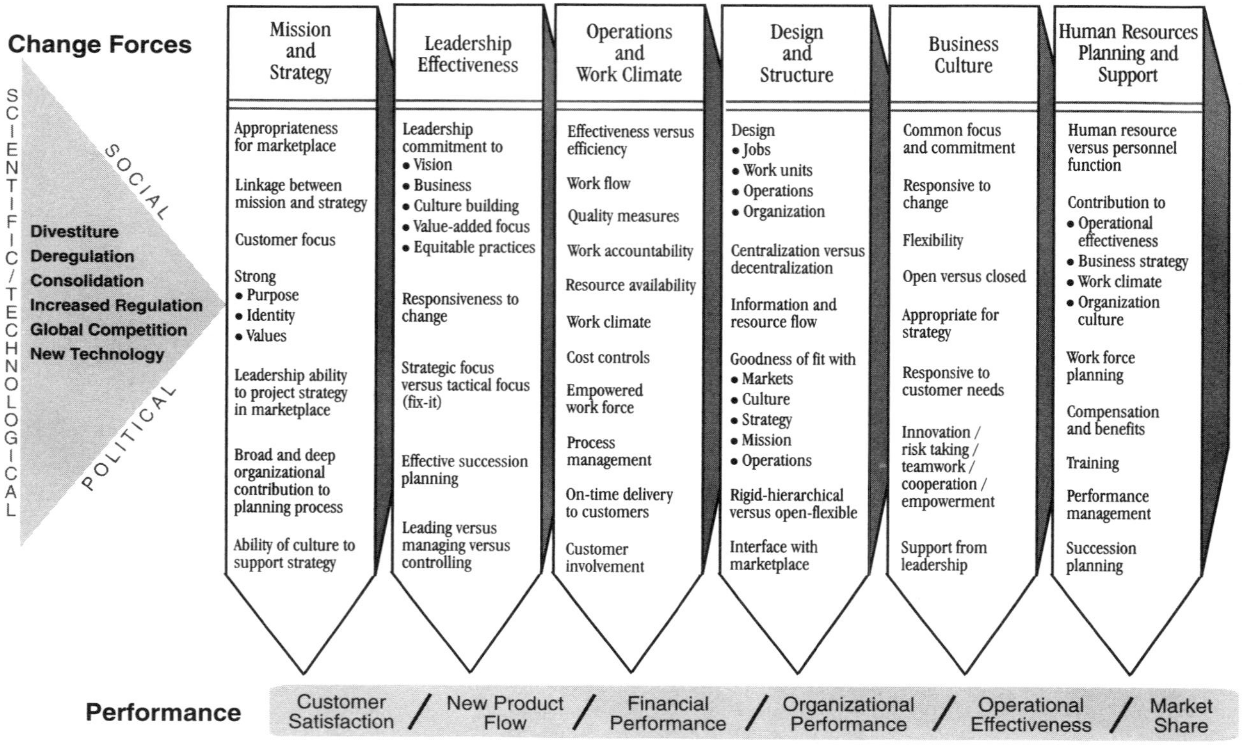

Change Forces

SOCIAL

TECHNOLOGICAL

POLITICAL

Divestiture
Deregulation
Consolidation
Increased Regulation
Global Competition
New Technology

SCIENTIFIC/TECHNOLOGICAL

Mission and Strategy	Leadership Effectiveness	Operations and Work Climate	Design and Structure	Business Culture	Human Resources Planning and Support
Appropriateness for marketplace	Leadership commitment to • Vision • Business • Culture building • Value-added focus • Equitable practices	Effectiveness versus efficiency	Design • Jobs • Work units • Operations • Organization	Common focus and commitment	Human resource versus personnel function
Linkage between mission and strategy		Work flow		Responsive to change	Contribution to • Operational effectiveness • Business strategy • Work climate • Organization culture
Customer focus		Quality measures	Centralization versus decentralization	Flexibility	
Strong • Purpose • Identity • Values	Responsiveness to change	Work accountability	Information and resource flow	Open versus closed	
		Resource availability	Goodness of fit with • Markets • Culture • Strategy • Mission • Operations	Appropriate for strategy	
Leadership ability to project strategy in marketplace	Strategic focus versus tactical focus (fix-it)	Work climate		Responsive to customer needs	Work force planning
		Cost controls			Compensation and benefits
	Effective succession planning	Empowered work force	Rigid-hierarchical versus open-flexible	Innovation / risk taking / teamwork / cooperation / empowerment	Training
Broad and deep organizational contribution to planning process		Process management			Performance management
	Leading versus managing versus controlling	On-time delivery to customers	Interface with marketplace	Support from leadership	Succession planning
Ability of culture to support strategy		Customer involvement			

Performance

Customer Satisfaction / New Product Flow / Financial Performance / Organizational Performance / Operational Effectiveness / Market Share process before commencing reengineering, corporate restructuring, or similar actions that impact the organization's larger ability to perform. The Big Six firms are noted for their reengineering and are attempting to position themselves as change consultants, but none seems to employ a systematic, organizationwide, bias-free audit process *prior to* reengineering. As a result, client sensitivities and strengths cannot be properly weighed, and major discrepancies are likely to occur between recommended strategies and the company's ability to employ them. Currently, this is an issue at one of the Regional Bell companies where their earlier planning for reengineering was far easier than their current implementation efforts.

In the 1980s countless corporations tried downsizing, TQM, just-in-time inventory management, and restructuring. No one strategy has worked consistently. Companies have continued to function or not function as they always have because corporate America continues to reach for what is popular, which is usually the latest magic bullet. Individualized, systemwide strategies designed to address real change issues are often avoided.

Consider the Depth and Breadth of Change

The depth and breadth of intervention are critical to change management. Singling out a small slice of the organization for change—dabbling with a division here or a department there—only increases the chances for failure and confusion. The small "laboratory" within the organization no longer knows how to coordinate with the larger, unchanged enterprise. Worse yet, it may encounter hostility to its own changed initiatives and appearance. This segment of the business becomes known as "the experiment." As it becomes alien to the main business because of its transformation, people within the unit become disillusioned and alienated—as do many individuals elsewhere in the organization. Eventually, the effort to change fails.

The 700 professionals of a corporate information systems function undertook a change effort that nearly crippled the entire corporation because no one outside the department was ready for change or understood what was taking place within the department. Most corporate information systems departments are centralized and bureaucratic. This one decided to flatten its structure and reorganize around project service teams—a good approach. Nevertheless, the entire corporation was twisting itself out of shape to satisfy the new requirements imposed by the new structure. Finally, after eighteen months, the change effort was halted, and the information systems department returned to its original operating structure.

Change needs to encompass an entire organization—all its functions, all staff and management levels, and all its diverse geographic locations. This is especially true when it involves a centralized function like information systems that impacts the entire organization. The same applies to culture and missioning, which are shared across an entire organization and not just segments. Most important, it must enjoy the fullest and broadest sponsorship of senior management. Without that commitment, it is seen only as the latest management exercise that will be swept out the door with a change in leadership.

Individualize Strategies

Specific needs and problems and particularly specific business organizations need individualized strategies. An approach that is widely perceived to have been effective in many other companies does not mean it will be effective for similar problems or issues elsewhere. If two companies have identical problems, there is no guarantee that the same intervention will prove successful, especially if they are in different industries. Consider two direct competitors in the consumer products industry—Colgate and Proctor & Gamble. To reengineer the value chain (continuous and integrated business processes starting with product development and ending with customer acceptance and satisfaction) in each of these giants requires different approaches given their different market niches, cultures, and scope of operations, to name but a few of their differences.

Commit Your Very Best People

The best results can be obtained only when you commit your very best people. Too often, people who have too much spare time or who have been identified for a possible layoff are committed to a change project by the boss. Every organization has its unofficial cadre of "project specialists" who do nothing but staff so-called special assignments. They become project experts but lose touch with the real operating issues of the business. Consequently, they become filters for any change effort and are no more representative of the internal culture than an outside consulting team would be. The highest possible level of commitment is required for any intervention, and for change involving systematic change management, nothing less than the CEO's commitment is adequate. This doesn't mean that the CEO merely signs off on the project or writes an announcement letter. Managers in the company should see the boss as being actively involved, and he should be prepared to commit a sizable portion of his time and thinking to the effort. Other officers and senior managers should be actively involved or step out of the way. Too often, a key group of executives will sit on the sidelines and quietly critique an engagement. When results are reported, they pounce to show how smart they were. I saw this happen once after the CEO and one of his key officers had reviewed, approved, and even edited a final consulting report before presenting it to the entire executive committee for their buy-in. To his credit, the CEO was always open to critical feedback, but the committee's attack on the report reflected their own executive-level subculture issues more than honest criticism. The CEO disbanded the meeting and found a more committed group of managers and executives to undertake the project.

MANAGING THE CHANGE CYCLE

All companies encounter change despite the best efforts of many to avoid or resist it. The American business landscape is littered with failed companies that resisted change. We forget, at our own peril, that American industry was born out of innovation and change. People laughed at Henry Ford for his automobile, and they scorned Bill McGowan for trying to introduce competition into the telecommunications industry. We will see in Chapter 8 how Thomas Watson and Ken Olson were criticized for trying to sell something called a computer that no one needed. By understanding how change impacts performance, managers can turn the business around rather than allow it to go into an uncontrolled nosedive. By understanding and adapting to change, businesses can gain competitive advantages over their competitors who resist change.

Organization Dissent and Performance

The change cycle does not simply reflect normal business success and failure. It provides a three-dimensional view of how change impacts a business's performance and its culture and proposes turnaround strategies that are required based on the type of change the business is experiencing. Without this integrated perspective of the *organization in change*, companies tend to oversimplify challenges, reach for simplistic strategies, and measure success by narrow, short-term results. These quick fixes fall short of helping the organization to manage change effectively. For example, how many companies have undertaken the painful process of restructuring and downsizing when, because they are at a level of fundamental change, the mission, culture, and leadership were the real sources of failure?

DISSENT

At this point, the Business Change Cycle will provide more insight into the relationship between change, business operations, and culture. The top right quadrant of the change phase (see Figure 3.1 on page 48) indicates that dissent will be the initial response of the organization's culture to change. Organization dissent will increase as the business experiences more change and proceeds down the change curve. Key components of the workforce or middle management will disagree with existing conditions or decisions, usually questioning their operational efficacy—how we make the product and serve the customer. Commitment to the larger business, its mission, and its leaders is still strong despite this dissent. In a top-performing, innovative culture or a customer-service-oriented culture, dissent is recognized as being necessary and constructive. In the former, it is a source of innovation and consensus building that leads to better ideas and products. In the customer-service culture, it helps keep the organization in closer contact with its customers. In bureaucratic and political cultures, dissent is many times suppressed or is even seen as disloyalty and as a threat to senior management.

DELAYED CHANGE

Delayed change represents a temporary suspension of normal business conditions. New strategy development and organization building are pointless *until the new rules of the game are made clear.* An example of delayed change occurred during the period of litigation between MCI and AT&T. AT&T and its emerging competitors were essentially frozen as they pursued their grievances over deregulation through the litigation process. Developing a new business strategy was pointless until a legal decision was rendered by Judge Harold Greene. The airline industry has twice faced delayed change in less than twenty years—first when the industry was undergoing deregulation and again during the Gulf War as the airlines had to be ready to surrender planes and pilots to the military. Such dramatic conditions need not be the only causes of delayed change. Often it is caused by such mundane or routine issues as a lack of key parts for an assembly-line conversion, an absence of competition, or repeated changes in management. Many times it is prompted by the introduction of a new product to see what its impact will be on the marketplace. This occurs in the information-technology industry every time a new software, chip, or computer is announced.

OPERATIONAL CHANGE

Operational change is the most common form of change (see Figure 4.2). All businesses eventually encounter operational change as they work to enhance production capacity or efficiency, improve cost controls, or increase timeliness of delivery. Productivity and efficiency are key to operational change. The foundations of the business—mission, leadership, strategy—remain solid. The culture of the business continues to be effective and committed to its mission and leadership. Nevertheless, there can be significant disagreement with some of the important decisions being made—*dissent.* As mentioned earlier, good corporate cultures are involved in the problem-solving and development process. Companies like Microsoft, Motorola, Intel, and the Saturn Division of GM are examples of companies that rely on workers and middle management to identify and resolve problems. In more traditional business organizations, the decisions are made from the top down.

Appropriate strategies are needed to satisfactorily deal with this level of change. Redesigning the corporation or a significant business unit or changing the culture would represent overkill and assuredly cause the operations of the company to suffer. As noted in Figure 4.2, operational problems or changes require operational remedies. If timeliness of production and management of resources are the issue, then just-in-time inventory management or a similar logistics approach may be appropriate. An effectively employed total quality management process should pay dividends when quality production on the shop floor is an issue. If people and process coordination are a problem, operations restructuring

Figure 4.2
Operational Change

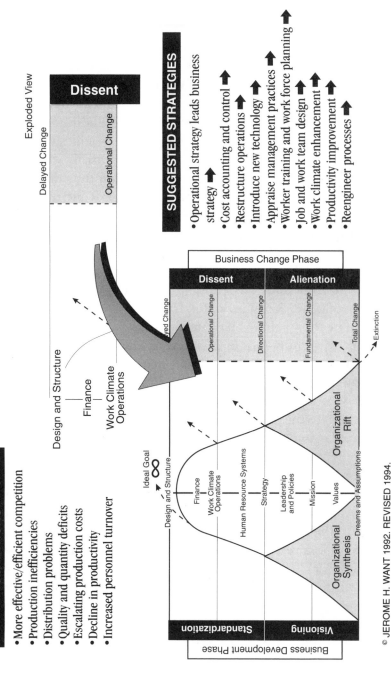

CONDITIONS
- More effective/efficient competition
- Production inefficiencies
- Distribution problems
- Quality and quantity deficits
- Escalating production costs
- Decline in productivity
- Increased personnel turnover

Dissent

Exploded View

Delayed Change

Operational Change

Design and Structure

Finance

Work Climate
Operations

SUGGESTED STRATEGIES
- Operational strategy leads business strategy
- Cost accounting and control
- Restructure operations
- Introduce new technology
- Appraise management practices
- Worker training and work force planning
- Job and work team design
- Work climate enhancement
- Productivity improvement
- Reengineer processes

Business Change Phase

Dissent | **Alienation**

Delayed Change

Operational Change

Directional Change

Fundamental Change

Total Change

Extinction

Organizational
Rift

Ideal Goal

Design and Structure

Finance

Work Climate
Operations

Human Resource Systems

Strategy

Leadership
and Policies

Mission

Values

Dreams and Assumptions

Organizational
Synthesis

Standardization | Visioning

Business Development Phase

© JEROME H. WANT 1992. REVISED 1994.
Note: Change cycle reads from bottom left (visioning stage) to apex of curve through alienation stage to bottom of right corner.

73

may be called for (not to be confused with corporate design and restructuring) or possibly process reengineering in more extreme cases. Poor communications and lack of cooperation may require work-climate enhancement. It is important to note that work climate is different from culture. Work-climate conditions may differ by work site. The work climate for the clerical staff at corporate headquarters' "mahogany row" may be quite different from the work climate on the shop floor, but they still share the same corporate culture. At a manufacturing company where management wanted to break down barriers within the culture, I identified a formidable wall separating support staff and managers from production workers and supervisors. Everyone thought that this separation was appropriate until I pointed out that upholding of differences between the two contributed to the increasing balkanization of the company. Work procedures and processes (work climate) should be differentiated depending on the needs of that immediate work environment. However, everyone within the company needs to share the same values, goals, commitments, and business identity—*culture*—to ensure a viable business.

The culture of the organization reacts differently when confronted by different change conditions. The dissent that arises during operational change conditions reflects employees' commitment to the business and to their bosses but disagreement with some day-to-day decisions. Sometimes, the reaction can be to a specific operational event or issue that seems to charge people. Given an opportunity, employees usually feel that they can apply their own solutions to problems and make a positive difference. New age corporate cultures and service-oriented cultures empower their employees to manage many change issues. Many of Federal Express's processes were developed by employees who were closer to the customer than upper-management was—and not through a traditional top-down cycle. In such an environment, there is a broad-based commitment to making operational-change initiatives work. Collegiality and open communications are essential. Workforce training is also critical for enhancing worker effectiveness, especially if new operating procedures need to be standardized across large segments of the organization. It's no accident that a company like Motorola is a leader in manufacturing quality since the amount it spends on employee training and education equals 4 percent of its total payroll, compared to the U.S. industry average of just 1.2 percent (*Business Week*, March 28, 1994). A well-trained and empowered workforce solves problems and makes money for the business.

Nonetheless, far too many businesses block employee input. In bureaucratic cultures, the power to act must come from the top before anything can be accomplished. In politicized cultures, a power struggle must take place before any change can be undertaken. Some cultures may never experience change, even at the operational-change level, but this status portends more serious problems and growing alienation within the organization.

DIRECTIONAL CHANGE

Directional change indicates that the company's business strategy is no longer working in the marketplace. This breakdown may develop for a variety of reasons:

1. Dramatically improved products or services from competitors,

2. Regulatory changes,

3. New technology breakthroughs by the competition,

4. New entrants into the marketplace, or

5. Poor leadership and the culture's inability to support the strategy

We will see in Chapter 11 how changing consumer demands are affecting the pharmaceutical industry through the growing power of health-care purchasing cooperatives—HMOs, PBMs, and PPOs. These relatively new purchasers/customers are dramatically changing how pharmaceutical companies price and distribute their products. This, in turn, is forcing a restructuring of the entire industry. Regulatory shifts have had far-reaching effects on the telecommunications, airline, and shipping industries. The demise of the cold war and shifting geopolitics are forging a smaller defense industry that is becoming more efficient and productive.

Directional change can also be attributed to major changes or failings inside a business. Many a business plan has failed because the company's culture was unable to support it. Innovative and dramatic strategies are not often successful if the culture of the organization is frozen, chaotic, or bureaucratic. Change in a company's leadership is another internal source of directional change. When George Fisher left Motorola to lead Eastman Kodak, it did little to the strategy (direction) or culture of Motorola. However, it did produce a major impact on Kodak's strategy, which was one of the benefits hoped for by Kodak's board. Other internal drivers of directional change can include an inadequately prepared workforce (a marketing team, for example, that is not prepared to introduce a new product to the marketplace), an ineffective distribution channel, or an underachieving production capacity. It is important that culture be prepared for shifts in strategy. Soon after the breakup of AT&T, several of the Baby Bells attempted to break out into competitive, nonregulatory businesses but were unable to overcome the ingrained behaviors of their AT&T bureaucratic cultures (neither did they enjoy the support of Judge Greene). They are now gaining the legal mandate to branch out, but it remains to be seen whether they have the ability to implement their new strategies, as we will see in Chapter 9 on the telecommunications industry. The banking industry has attempted similar directional changes since it has been allowed to offer the nondepository products formerly offered exclusively through the investment banking and insurance sectors. Their efforts have been largely unsuccessful for similar reasons: the cultures are too rigid; leadership was not prepared.

Organizational dissent continues to dominate culture during periods of directional change as it does during operational change (see Figure 4.3), but the level of dissent or disagreement is

Figure 4.3
Directional Change

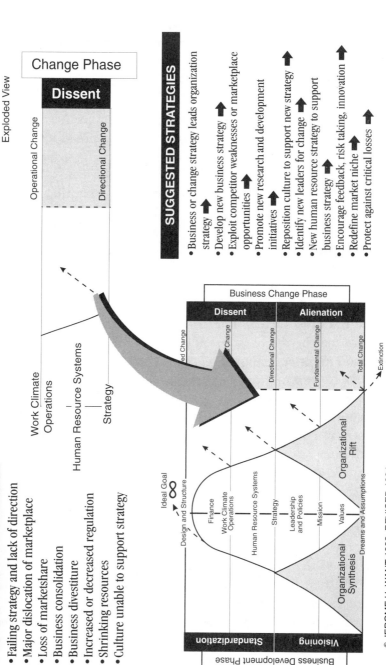

Change Phase

Exploded View

Dissent

Operational Change

Directional Change

Work Climate
Operations

Human Resource Systems

Strategy

CONDITIONS

- Failing strategy and lack of direction
- Major dislocation of marketplace
- Loss of marketshare
- Business consolidation
- Business divestiture
- Increased or decreased regulation
- Shrinking resources
- Culture unable to support strategy

SUGGESTED STRATEGIES

- Business or change strategy leads organization strategy
- Develop new business strategy
- Exploit competitor weaknesses or marketplace opportunities
- Promote new research and development initiatives
- Reposition culture to support new strategy
- Identify new leaders for change
- New human resource strategy to support business strategy
- Encourage feedback, risk taking, innovation
- Redefine market niche
- Protect against critical losses

Business Change Phase

Dissent   **Alienation**

...ed Change

...Change

Directional Change

Fundamental Change

Total Change

Extinction

Organizational
Rift

Ideal Goal

∞

Design and Structure

Finance

Work Climate
Operations

Human Resource Systems

Strategy

Leadership
and Policies

Mission

Values

Dreams and Assumptions

Organizational
Synthesis

Standardization

Visioning

Business Development Phase

© JEROME H. WANT 1992. REVISED 1994.

77

more prominent. People remain committed but openly question the strategy of the business or how it is being implemented in the marketplace. Many times this is a result of *how* the strategy was developed. Too often, senior managers make the mistake of retaining an outside consulting firm to write a new business plan, or they bury the strategy-development process in the internal planning department without gaining the widespread involvement of middle-management ranks. Since middle management is typically responsible for implementing strategy, it feels no affiliation with or ownership of these outside plans and is quick to spot the potential flaws at the operational (delivery) level. This is why consensus building to achieve broad-based buy-in is so important at the directional-change level. As is frequently noted, "No buy-in, no pay-off."

When turning around the business at this stage, it is especially important for leaders to demonstrate sufficient flexibility to tailor their actions to real-time conditions. The array of response options may be the broadest at this level for the organization (compared to other change levels), which is an advantage, but a broad array of response options also carries the increased likelihood of selecting and employing insufficient strategies. Directional change entails certain conditions, external and internal, that are threats to performance. *Turnaround strategies must be individualized and require a combination of business and human resource initiatives that are critical to performance.* Typically, selected strategies are often too narrow, too incremental, or insupportable by management and the larger organization. In a consulting firm survey of sixty-three companies valued between $300 million and $2 billion, only twenty-two (35 percent) reported that they felt that their business strategy was fully effective in the marketplace. Most of the dissatisfied respondents noted "execution" and "commitment/ understanding" as the reasons for failure.

Directional change is critical to a business because it serves as the *pivotal performance axis* for the organization between organizational dissent and alienation. On the development side of the change cycle, it serves as the boundary between visioning and standardization for the emerging or entrepreneurial business, but on the change side of the cycle, it reflects a critical difference between companies that are struggling to succeed and those that are struggling to fail.

The Impact of Alienation on Performance

FUNDAMENTAL CHANGE

Fundamental change reflects a major qualitative difference in the way the business is performing. Fundamental change indicates that the mission or the leadership of the business are failing (see Figure 4.4). People can no longer identify with the mission and are not committed to the company's senior management. The result is that breakdowns begin to occur, and the business is actually starting to fail (organization rift). While senior management may not yet recognize that the business is failing, it should recognize that pain is being felt within the organization as well as anxiety at the senior-management level.

Typically, employees begin to bail out, which puts added pressure on management. It can no longer count on the workforce to be there, and replacement hiring and training are expensive and time consuming. A few key executives may jump to the competition with ideas and initiatives that were previously ignored. Middle managers begin to retire in place and resist top-down decision making and directives: the bureaucracy takes over. Overall, the culture becomes less flexible, more conflict oriented, and more change averse. When companies at this stage offer early retirement to reduce staff levels, they almost always have more takers than they expect. Frequently, key people and their ideas leave, and the company must recruit to fill the gaps. This has happened at the U.S. Postal Service, where early retirement has decimated middle-management ranks and directly threatened operations. The same occurred with most of the phone companies as they downsized over the past five years. The new CEO of Scott Paper, Albert Dunlap, declared last summer that he will lay off large

Figure 4.4
Fundamental Change

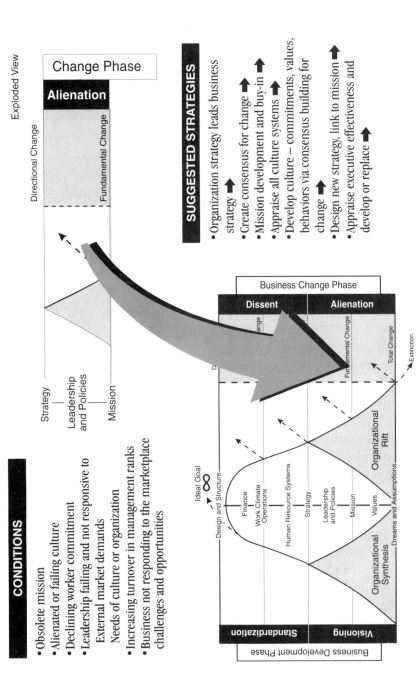

CONDITIONS

- Obsolete mission
- Alienated or failing culture
- Declining worker commitment
- Leadership failing and not responsive to External market demands
  Needs of culture or organization
- Increasing turnover in management ranks
- Business not responding to the marketplace challenges and opportunities

SUGGESTED STRATEGIES

- Organization strategy leads business strategy
- Create consensus for change
- Mission development and buy-in
- Appraise all culture systems
- Develop culture — commitments, values, behaviors via consensus building for change
- Design new strategy; link to mission
- Appraise executive effectiveness and develop or replace

Change Phase

Exploded View

Alienation

Directional Change

Fundamental Change

Strategy

Leadership and Policies

Mission

Business Change Phase

Dissent

Alienation

Fundamental Change

Total Change

Extinction

Ideal Goal

Design and Structure

Finance

Work Climate Operations

Human Resource Systems

Strategy

Leadership and Policies

Mission

Values

Dreams and Assumptions

Organizational Rift

Organizational Synthesis

Standardization

Visioning

Business Development Phase

80

numbers of existing employees who were wedded to the old culture before building a new culture. On the surface this seems laudable, but lack of selectivity will cost him key managers, expertise, and a great deal of time and money before any new culture emerges.

Changing the culture and gaining broad buy-in is critical. Mission development is an essential first step and, implemented properly, can help bring a company back together. Having the executive committee retire to a country club setting for a weekend to draft a new mission statement is not the right way to do this. We've all had a new mission statement or set of corporate objectives mailed to us from the CEO's office and wondered what it all had to do with us and our jobs. Instead, the CEO or executive team should implement systematic strategies for gaining broad and thoughtful contributions from employees throughout the organization. Every employee need not be solicited for ideas (though even this may be accomplished now that computers sit on virtually everyone's desk), but representative departments and functions of the entire organization could be included. This broad involvement of the workforce has a powerful impact on people's feelings of commitment to the organization and its leadership.

Failed leadership is also reflective of fundamental change and may be the most powerful source of alienation within an organization. Overcontrollers rob managers of initiative and tend to smother good ideas. They also tend to foster the emergence of more overcontrollers down the line, resulting in an oppressive *bureaucratic culture.* Those who unceasingly use the corporate environment for political game playing or for even more predatory goals foster a heightened sense of alienation within the organization. These styles of leadership behavior speed up the change cycle and the company's decline.

Occasionally, a company's executive cadre can be developed through coaching, counseling, and training. This can be especially successful with the leadership of smaller companies, whose scope and size can contribute to the change process. With large, publicly traded corporations, neither the board of directors nor its shareholders may have the patience to wait out such a process. The alternative is to recruit new leadership, usually from the outside. When a company culture becomes entrenched and insulated over time, outside leadership can be a force for positive change. Recently, classic examples of this type of leadership change from the outside have been seen at General Motors (John Smith), Kodak (George Fisher), and IBM (Lou Gerstner). At GM, there was first a critical change in the chairmanship of the board and subsequently at the CEO level. At IBM, there was a subsequent change in key officers reporting to the new CEO. Nevertheless, this is just one necessary component for change at this level.

Fundamental change requires a different level of turnaround strategy because the culture is becoming alienated from the company's leadership and mission. New business plans by themselves don't work at this level of change because the organization is incapable of supporting them. Turnaround strategies must be comprehensive, be capable of penetrating to the point of dysfunction and pain in the business, and enjoy the advocacy of courageous leaders who are not afraid to embrace change. Organizational and culture development strategies must be successful before new business strategies can be expected to succeed.

TOTAL CHANGE

Total change indicates that the business is *failing* (see Figure 4.5). All business systems are failing, but more important, the original values and assumptions about the business have failed or are being ignored. The culture has become highly fragmented, excessively politicized, or predatory. In such cases, employees can no longer rely on the organization to function in a rational, predictable manner. Employee initiative and commitment succumb to the nonproductive, irrational environment.

Officers and directors are isolated from the culture and are insulated within their own subculture. Too often, they misinterpret that subculture as being the same as the larger business culture. Middle managers no longer identify with the values of the

Figure 4.5
Total Change

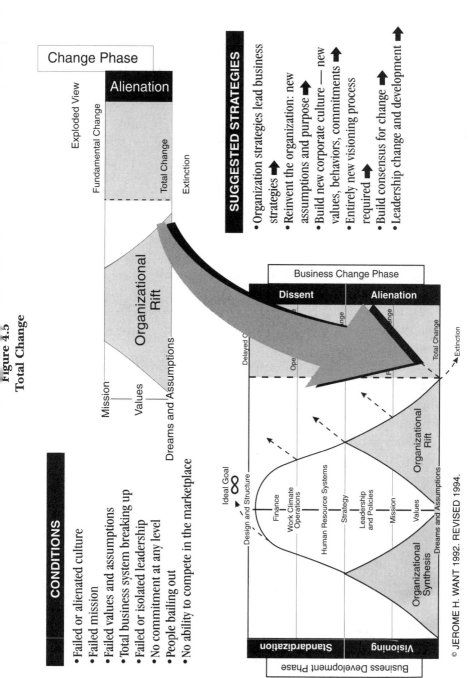

© JEROME H. WANT 1992. REVISED 1994.

CONDITIONS

- Failed or alienated culture
- Failed mission
- Failed values and assumptions
- Total business system breaking up
- Failed or isolated leadership
- No commitment at any level
- People bailing out
- No ability to compete in the marketplace

Change Phase

Alienation

Exploded View

Fundamental Change

Total Change

Extinction

Organizational Rift

Mission

Values

Dreams and Assumptions

SUGGESTED STRATEGIES

- Organization strategies lead business strategies
- Reinvent the organization: new assumptions and purpose
- Build new corporate culture — new values, behaviors, commitments
- Entirely new visioning process required
- Build consensus for change
- Leadership change and development

Business Change Phase

Dissent

Alienation

Delayed Change

Total Change

Extinction

Ideal Goal

Design and Structure

Finance

Work Climate

Operations

Human Resource Systems

Strategy

Leadership and Policies

Mission

Values

Dreams and Assumptions

Organizational Rift

Organizational Synthesis

Standardization

Visioning

Business Development Phase

83

business. Issues of trust, integrity, and reliability become daily stumbling blocks. Customers find that they can no longer rely on the business for goods or services and leave it for the competition. Creditors and stockholders can no longer rely on the business for a reliable return on their investment or their receivables.

Many business executives scorn the importance of values and flee from initiatives that focus on business values. Witness the fates of E. F. Hutton and Drexel Burnham Lambert as the original vision and values that each company was built on were cast aside by new leaders who used the business's resources to further their own personal goals. As we see in Chapter 12, the substitution of personal gain for the welfare of the larger business directly contributed to their failures. The Jett fiasco at Kidder Peabody and the broker scams at Prudential Securities and Merrill Lynch were more of the same, but at a broader middle-management level than was seen earlier at Hutton and Drexel Burnham Lambert. Unethical conduct was being institutionalized across the cultures of an entire industry.

Companies also fail because they simply have been mismanaged. The collapse of Macy's is an example of poor management combined with dangerous overleveraging. Others—such as the defense industry, where nearly half the companies have been swallowed up by their competitors—discover they can no longer compete in a shrinking marketplace. In Chapter 7, we see the consequences of how outdated leadership and unchanged airline industry culture have collided with a radically changed business climate.

Total change can also be a function of planned change, consolidation, or turnaround. One of the classic examples was the creation of Primerica Corp., a giant financial services corporation created in the mid-1980s out of American National Can—a traditional manufacturing company. It failed when it could not cope with the stock market crash of 1987 and was taken over by Sandy Weill, a savvy Wall Streeter (some would say a Wall Street shark). Originally accustomed to a more predictable manufacturing setting, the new enterprise had neither the skilled management nor the culture to cope with a radically changed environment on Wall

Street. In the 1970s and 1980s, the steel industry had to consolidate from its inability to compete with foreign producers and the modern, small steel producers. The recent consolidations in the defense industry are examples of planned change born of necessity.

Whether it is planned or unplanned, total change reflects the most serious challenge to a business's survival. Chrysler and Harley Davidson are conspicuous examples of companies that successfully managed the challenge of total change. True, government intervention was initially required for each in the face of predatory foreign competition, but Vaughn Beals (Harley Davidson) and Lee Iacocca (Chrysler) recognized the need to totally remake their companies—their culture and leadership, as well as strategy and operations.

SEPARATING CHANGE STRATEGISTS FROM THE TACTICIANS

At a superficial level, we all understand the distinction between strategy and tactics. The former is a multilayered set of plans and behaviors designed to win a war, to achieve a desired market share, or to start up a new business. The latter are the specific actions and behaviors required to win particular battles—to improve operations, enhance production processes, or introduce a new product or service. Everyone reading this could write their own similar definitions, supporting them with examples out of their own experience that would unambiguously contrast the two terms.

This conceptual familiarity often seduces us into believing that we can differentiate one from the other. But after nearly twenty-five years of corporate and consulting experience, I have learned that this is a false assumption (see Figure 4.6). In the heat of competition and crisis, executives will most reflexively reach for symptomatic relief. Fixing a problem until the next quarterly earnings report or until one's own retirement or transfer to another job is always a more attractive alternative than the advocacy

Figure 4.6
Strategic Versus Tactical Interventions

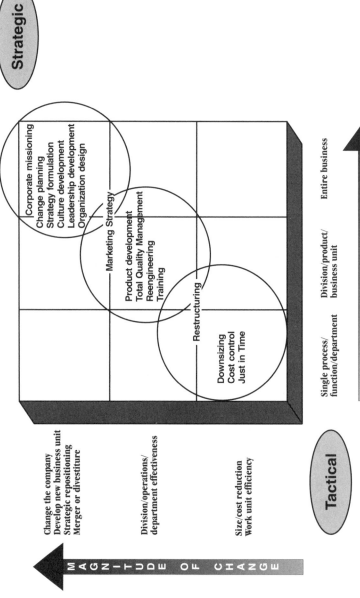

86

of fundamental, systemwide change. This is especially true if one cares to survey the battlefield from the ranks of middle management, which usually has a more intimate view of the battlefield and the results of a particular "strategy."

Without executive commitment to strategic revisioning that includes a comprehensive understanding of change—its direction and its impact on the competitive environment and the organization's ability to compete—tacticians will continue to masquerade as strategists. And each apparent victory will contain within it the bad seed of a later, more devastating defeat.

CHAPTER

5

Corporate Culture: Keeping Pace with Radical Change

What we need . . . is a new "paradigm"—a new vision of reality; a fundamental change in our thoughts, perceptions and values.
—FRITJOF CAPRA

I was once asked if I could categorize the business leaders I've worked with, based on their ability to understand and manage their companies' corporate cultures. I don't recall that my answer was either profound or succinct, but, after reflecting on the question, I realized that when company leaders are forced to deal with corporate culture, they generally fall into one of three categories:

- I don't know,

- I don't know how, and

- I don't care.

The last group is the easiest to work with since you can just walk away. However, when personally committed, the first two types of business leaders can make for immensely challenging, frustrating, and, ultimately, very satisfying clients.

IT'S THE CUSTOMER, STUPID

Business executives seem able to cope with a cornucopia of issues that most of us have difficulty understanding, much less mastering, including return on investment or equity, stock buybacks, quarterly earnings, inventory writeoffs, amortization of debt, leveraged buyouts, debtor-in-possession financing, and more. The subject of corporate culture, however, elicits a markedly different response that rarely keeps executives working at their desks past normal business hours. It simply doesn't register on the radar screen.

One exception is Tom Labrecque, chairman of Chase Manhattan Bank—one of our oldest, largest, and most conservative financial institutions. Stanley Schrager, senior vice president of human resources at Chase, will tell you that a customer can't have a discussion with Labrecque without listening to his description of the bank's vision and newly emerging culture. Labrecque is intent on transporting every employee into this new corporate landscape. For Chase, its emerging culture and vision (essentially synonymous at the bank) begin and end with the customer (interview, September 29, 1994).

Corporate culture is the set of behaviors and beliefs that enables a business organization to bring value-added services to customers in return for financial gain. Other CEOs who have diligently worked to make corporate culture an integral component of their businesses include Bob Haas at Levi Strauss; Harvey Kelleher at Southwest Air; Bruce, Jack, and George Nordstrom at the retail chain that bears their name; Leonard Hadley at Maytag; Philip Knight at Nike; and Bill Gates at Microsoft.

Companies are beginning to see that there is a direct link between their internal corporate culture and the marketplace—the customer. Poor product support is often the result of a misfocused business culture that doesn't value the customer. For many years, this was the case at apparel manufacturer Levi Strauss. In the 1960s and 1970s, Strauss was immensely profitable and could dictate terms to its customers (retail stores). In the 1980s, this arrogance caught up with the company as competitors began to match their products in quality and price while providing better service (such as on-time delivery of products) to their customers. The financial consequences for Levi Strauss were predictable, as profits plunged along with market share. In 1984, Strauss found itself with excess idle capacity that necessitated the closure of twenty-one plants and the dismissal of 6,000 workers. It was the first major layoff in the company's history, and it was painful for everyone involved.

In 1985, the Haas family resumed its control of the company and, under Bob Haas's leadership, set about rebuilding Levi Strauss around its original values. Haas believed that the *psychological contract* between the company, its workers, and its customers had been broken. A new emphasis was placed on teamwork, trust, leadership, diversity, and ethics. According to Sue Thompson, the company's human resource development director, Levi Strauss had become overreliant on its computer technology in serving customers. People, rather than printouts, are now expected to serve as the contact point with customers (interview, October 17, 1994). Throughout Levi Strauss, it is routinely expected that workers will not only work, but that they will provide ideas and criticisms while working together in cooperative teams that will better serve their customers. The result has been seven straight years of record growth and profits at Levi Strauss. Strauss recognized that the culture of a business is not transparent to the marketplace—a lesson that many companies have yet to learn.

THE COMPANY'S BLACK HOLE

During a meeting with a client, an executive once referred to his organization's corporate culture as the "black hole" of the company. For him, it seemed both an enigma and the locus of blame for the company's failures. I kept wondering whether the black hole wasn't sitting in front of me and whether I could keep from being sucked in. As I continued to work with this company, I realized the black hole was a real issue for employees, and I could see managers were ingeniously avoiding it. That they were even partially aware of culture as an issue put them well ahead of many other companies.

No company can hope to steer its way through changing competitive conditions without understanding its own culture and knowing how to change and improve it. Just as production lines and marketing departments must adjust to competitive challenges, so must a company's culture. In the first chapter, I defined culture as the collective belief systems that people within a company hold about their ability to compete in the marketplace, as well as how they act on those belief systems. If employees, but especially a company's leadership, fail to share a common understanding about their culture, then the organization is intrinsically handicapped.

I have observed that corporate cultures fall into a hierarchy consisting of seven major categories (see Figure 5.1): *predatory, frozen, chaotic, political, bureaucratic, service,* and *new age.* Most companies evidence political or bureaucratic cultures. But, as with politics, when it comes to categorizing a particular corporate culture—to a large extent, perception is reality. We respond to companies on the basis of our own appraisal of their internal values and goals, as well as their ability to perform. These appraisals are usually shaped by experience. Specific behaviors that are directed at us by a company and its employees tell us what and who we're up against. These external evaluations are generally far more accurate than any mission statement or management objective. Therefore, polling data can be useful in assessing the congruence between corporate visions and their actual performance.

Consequently, I surveyed former clients and colleagues from across the country (totaling seventy-eight respondents) to determine whether entire industries give rise to a characteristic culture. This survey was not the basis for a formal empirical study, but the

Figure 5.1
Hierarchy of Corporate Cultures

responses are revealing. While I firmly believe that every company and its culture is unique, regardless of industry, some interesting patterns emerged that may support the notion that industries, as well as individual companies, foster uniquely identifiable culture profiles. Certainly, within each industry, one can find stars and exceptions. Table 5.1 lists the most frequently mentioned industries within each culture category, based on the responses of the seventy-eight evaluators.

Table 5.1
Industry Identification with the Hierarchy of Corporate Cultures

Sample Industries	PREDATORY — Punitive/Alienating	FROZEN — Gridlock/Denial	CHAOTIC — Fragmented/Unfocused	POLITICAL — Retaliatory/Balkanized	BUREAUCRATIC — Procedural/Rigid/Regimented/Authoritarian	SERVICE — Customer Focus/Individualizing/Quality	NEW AGE — Innovative/Egalitarian/Consensual/Changing
Airline	Example: Mafia	Insurance (66)	Airline (32)	Example: U.S. Congress	Utility (62)	Computer company (48)	Software development firm (54)
Association	Wall Street firm (67)	Bank (47)	Publishing (29)	Hospital (73)	Bank (40)	Semiconductor (40)	Semiconductor (52)
Computer company	Advertising (60)	U.S. Postal Service (39)	Software development (18)	Large university (71)	Regional Bell company (38)	Small professional service firm (37)	R&D firm (25)
Environmental consulting, engineering	Large professional service firm (49)	Foundation (31)	Advertising (12)	Large professional service firm (26)	Pharmaceutical industry (30)	Long-distance phone company (30)	Manufacturing (18)
Semiconductor	Hospital (26)	Credit agency (28)		Media/Entertainment (16)	International oil company (27)	Small university (19)	Pharmaceutical (18)
Software development	Airline (14)	Tobacco (16)			State/federal government (24)	Package delivery (14)	
Pharmaceutical		Property management (15)			Airline (21)	Manufacturing (12)	
Small university, college		Airline (11)			U.S. Postal Service (20)	Association (10)	
Large university		Association (12)			Manufacturing (20)		
Advertising					Large university (18)		
Credit reporting agency					Railroad (14)		
Mortgage company							
Wall Street firm							
Property management							
Insurance							
Utility company							
Tobacco							
Large professional service firm							
Large retail chain							
Distribution company							
Publishing							
Small professional service firm							
Food processing							
Hospital							
State or federal government							
Village government							
Media, entertainment							
International oil company							
Regional Bell company							
Foundation							
R&D firm							
Long-distance phone company							
Manufacturing							
Railroad							
Delivery							
U.S. Postal Service							
Other (specify)							

Note: Respondents may assign each industry to multiple categories and may assign multiple industries to each category. N=78.

Predatory Cultures

Predatory cultures contribute the least to business performance, as well as to employee productivity, customer satisfaction, and marketplace effectiveness. Predatory environments are punitive and alienating to employees and often to customers. Being on the "right" team is critical to survival or advancement for employees and frequently determines the quality of service extended to customers. Many times these distinctions are made on the basis of being different or bringing a different educational, ethnic, or job history to a project or to the larger organization. Whistle blowers never last long in predatory cultures. Companies that are overwhelmed with customer complaints retaliate against the customers. According to our respondents, this predatory culture is best exemplified by Wall Street firms and advertising agencies. Hospitals ranked third, and professional service firms (such as law firms and consulting firms) also scored high on the respondents' list.

Predatory cultures seem to have few rules, assumptions, or commonly shared values that bind people together. Rarely does a widely shared vision exist within the company. Career advancement is tied to a mentor or protector, and when mentors leave (as frequently occurs), subordinates or an entire team may leave with them. Internal struggle, even sabotage, continually buffet the organization's day-to-day operations. Chapter 12 on Wall Street shows how the predatory culture of a once admired Wall Street firm contributed directly to its demise.

Predatory cultures may also exploit their customers. Again, Wall Street is a good example, as evidenced in the improprieties and fraudulent practices uncovered at Prudential Securities, Merrill Lynch, and Kidder Peabody. The collapse of the thrift industry was also directly related to predatory practices adopted by a new breed of owners who consciously disregarded the traditional charter around which savings and loan associations were established. This shift of purpose was engineered in order to underwrite speculators in other industries (Wall Street and real estate) who required low-cost capital for their self-serving schemes.

Predatory cultures are rarely changed from inside. Financial failure or external pressure (regulatory or legal) are the only routes to reshaping this kind of culture. Frequently, the business fails, as seen on Wall Street at Drexel Burnham Lambert, Kidder Peabody, Hutton, and Shearson Lehman. Only after John Gutfreund was forced out of Salomon Brothers, following federal charges of fraud, could its chairman, Warren Buffet, initiate a culture change process. Lavanthol and Horwath, a Philadelphia accounting and consulting firm, failed as a consequence of improper practices by several audit partners, which had gone unnoticed within the larger partnership. The culture of L&H's partnership was famous for its turf wars and failure to monitor the conduct of its members.

The collapse of Shearson Lehman Brothers, briefly the second-largest securities trading firm on the street, can be traced directly to its culture. The company was expanding primarily through mergers and the acquisition of other firms that could create an overnight Merrill Lynch. The turf wars between formerly independent firms rarely ceased, and Shearson could never unite around a broadly shared business focus. The company never made money, and its parent, American Express, eventually sold Shearson Lehman to Sandy Weill, who had originally sold it to AMEX. Today, regulators are taking an even closer look at all financial institutions, largely because of their propensity to defraud investors and their tendency to self-destruct. Kidder Peabody is the latest Wall Street firm to go out of business due to failed values and leadership—culture. The Prudential has been exposed for fraud in both its insurance and securities business. If predatory cultures could be compared with certain animal species, they are creatures that will eat their own young.

Frozen Cultures

Frozen cultures are paralyzed by gridlock. This may stem from a companywide aversion to risk taking, an aversion that usually emanates from the top, or to an inflexible or balkanized structure. It can also result from stagnant economic conditions or the absence of significant competition. Managers wait for permission before they act. New ideas rarely float up or out and can do so only through prescribed channels. Stepping outside of one's chain of command, department, or function is not tolerated—regardless of the merits of a suggestion. Going around the boss can quickly end a career.

The insurance industry was identified by more than two-thirds of the respondents as most representative of a frozen culture. Banks, foundations, the U.S. Postal Service, property-management companies, and the credit-reporting industry were also singled out, together with the tobacco industry. Airlines were placed in this category by several evaluators. Once again, there are stars within each of these industries that may operate counter to the prevailing view. For instance, in the credit-reporting industry, Equifax has long been known for its responsiveness to customers and consumers and also is sensitive to changing market conditions.

Even under extreme pressure, frozen cultures resist change and deny the need for retrenchment. The principal obligation of management is to maintain the status quo. This resistance to change extends to regulatory and legislative intervention. The insurance industry is notorious for its lobbying clout—clout that is used primarily to resist even the suggestion of reform. Tobacco companies are equally adept at delaying, watering down, and otherwise compromising attacks on their practices. The American auto industry of the 1970s and 1980s could correctly be categorized as frozen. Certainly, consumer demand for quality cars did little to change the industry, and corporate cultures at the Big Three remained unchanged until very recently. Only when Japanese auto makers began to capture significant portions of the U.S. market did the Big Three recognize the need to change. Even then, it took Chrysler's threatened failure to drive home the need for change.

Chaotic Cultures

A chaotic culture is potentially more productive than frozen or predatory cultures, justifying its higher placement on the hierarchy. Nevertheless, chaotic business cultures continue to be weak performers and make frustrating work environments. They experience difficulty sustaining performance, act unpredictably with both employees and customers, have difficulty focusing, and rarely can respond to competition in a sustained and coherent manner. To a considerable degree, chaotic cultures resemble predatory and political cultures, except that they usually subscribe to a well-defined mission. They just can't walk their talk.

Publishing, airline, and software development companies were most frequently identified as having chaotic cultures. Large numbers of respondents also placed Wall Street firms, ad agencies, and hospitals in this category. An underlying contributor to the chaotic culture is the lack of common focus between major disciplines or groups of professionals within the organization. Frequently, the creative and editorial staff of a newspaper or magazine comes into conflict with those responsible for the publication's bottom line. In a hospital, conflict between the administration and the clinical staff is never far from the surface. Chaotic cultures have difficulty competing or responding to change. Selected leaders within a chaotic organization may recognize the need for changing the culture, but they are unable to marshal sufficient political support to embark on a change initiative. Other managers may echo the need for change, but they won't take any risk to achieve it.

The structure of the chaotic organization is constantly changing. The companies are famous for introducing countless new flowcharts and reorganization schemes. Consequently, communications and decisions are undertaken in an environment characterized by perpetual turmoil. Priorities change with little rationale or predictability. Therefore, turnover is high in chaotic cultures. Worker loyalty is fleeting, as employees remain with the company only for selfish motives (notoriety, compensation, promotion).

The marketplace quickly picks up on the chaos, and customers begin to shun the affected companies, as seen recently at Digital. This was also evident at both Eastern and Continental Airlines. The outcome for Continental has been a diminished airline that was once known as the Cadillac of the industry. Today, following two bankruptcies, Continental is struggling to reorganize itself not just financially but by redesigning its operations and culture.

Political Cultures

Most of us have had more firsthand experience with the political culture than any other. The political culture transcends organizational size or industry and is found with equal frequency in both the manufacturing and service sectors. The internal jockeying for influence, resources, position, and promotion dominates the agendas of companies with politicized cultures. These organizations are balkanized by competing factions, disciplines, practices, and agendas. Retaliation, exclusion, deal making, and turf warfare are normative behaviors.

Hospitals and large universities were most frequently identified with political cultures. Large professional service firms, including legal and consulting firms, were a close third in this category. The Big Six auditing and consulting firms are well known for their factionalism. The media and entertainment industry, state and federal governments, and foundations were also frequently assigned to this category. In political cultures, the whole never equals the value of its parts. Separation, individuality, and hero building take precedence over the needs of the larger organization. Political organizations often appear to be specialized, as one portion of the whole achieves dominance over its internal rivals. In law offices, and certainly in consulting firms, a particular practice area or specialty may dominate the identity or priorities of the firm. In universities, a flagship department will receive more financial support than others and will, in turn, become a stronger magnet for students and researchers.

Bureaucratic Cultures

Bureaucratic cultures seem to exist in nearly every industry. They are capable of turning compliant customers into consumer militants. There would be fewer Ralph Naders in the world without bureaucracies. The bureaucratic culture places the prompt fulfillment of customer needs below the needs of bureaucracy. To be fair, bureaucratic cultures are usually constructed around the need for systematic and verifiable procedures to check, monitor, and oversee safety practices or strict financial accounting. As a result, we find utilities, bank, phone companies, and the pharmaceutical industry heading the list of bureaucratic cultures. Each of these industries is closely regulated. In addition, the U.S. Postal Service, mortgage companies, large universities, and retail chains were frequently identified as bureaucratic, along with the federal government—the mother of all bureaucracies.

In bureaucracies, jobs are fragmented around layered procedures and processes that are part of the checking, monitoring, and double-checking process. This, in turn, smothers innovation and problem solving. The regulatory bureaucracy of government exists to protect the public welfare. In response, utilities, pharmaceutical companies, airlines, and phone companies establish their own internal bureaucracies to ensure compliance with these external requirements. Problems arise when the bureaucracy spreads to other aspects of an organization's operations and customers are subjected to bureaucratic "administration." Bureaucracy is even found in businesses that experience little regulation. In those cases, it is intended to protect the company from itself—to reduce costly mistakes that will erode customer confidence, product vitality, and company resources. *Nonetheless, bureaucracies seem to carry an inherent propensity to mold behavior so that it serves procedures rather than people and their productivity.*

Bureaucratic cultures are never lacking for a mission, which stands in contrast with the other cultures we have discussed. People within the organization usually know why they are employed and what they are expected to accomplish, although they may not have a clear understanding of the larger process or business. The mission may be outdated, but the organization will continue to justify itself against that mission.

Service Cultures

Service cultures are focused on serving the customer. Strategy, structure, systems, product development, and operations all start and end with the customer. In a true service culture, "If you are not serving the customer, you better be serving someone who is" (K. Albrecht and R. Zemke, *Service America,* Dow Jones Irwin, 1985). Improving the quality of products and services is a continuing objective in the best service cultures. Companies like Whirlpool, Crate & Barrel, 3M, Motorola, MCI, Giant Food, TriNova, Nordstrom, Control Data, McDonald's, Federal Express, and Deluxe Check never forget who is ultimately paying their bills. Readers will note that a number of these leading service providers are manufacturers. Consistently successful production companies know that making and selling the product is not enough. They have to customize products around the customer's needs as practiced at Motorola, 3M, and Control Data. At Crate & Barrel, employees and store managers undergo months of training before being assigned to a store. It is no coincidence that companies like AMEX and GM have stumbled, given their commodities orientation and lack of service to the customer. Motorola customers are frequently part of a product development team and many of 3M's products are created in direct response to marketplace needs. Deluxe Check has a reputation for lightning fast delivery and accuracy.

Even more important, the product must be supported and serviced after the sale. This is not just a matter of repairing the occasional defective product but an opportunity to add value to the product. The business that cannot do this is little more than a commodities venture. A good example of a commodities broker transformed into a high tech service company is Packard Bell.

This computer clone manufacturer had trouble shaking its record of poor-quality products. This reputation was reversed by finding out directly from customers what they actually valued in a low-cost, high-quality product. In addition, Packard Bell has expanded its distribution and sales network to include traditional retail distributors like WalMart, which customers prefer over the specialty computer stores.

Interestingly, the manufacturing sector received little recognition in the service category among our respondents, possibly because the larger, more prominent producers, such as autos and steel, have been slow to shed their commodities identity and most consumers have little need to interface with a producer of large durable goods. The computer and semiconductor industries were rated as having the highest service-provider cultures, along with small, professional service firms. Close behind were long-distance phone companies and the package delivery industry. Regardless of industry, companies with strong service cultures share several common commitments or behaviors:

- *The customer is integral to the mission.* Eloquently worded mission statements rarely exist in top service companies; instead, the customer-centered focus of the business speaks for itself through reliable service to the customer.

- *Strategy and operations support the service mission.* The mission is more than a slogan. It is a business driver that is actively supported by a service strategy—not just a business strategy—that helps organize all business operations around serving the customer.

- *People are empowered.* Professionals who serve the customer are more than mere complaint handlers. Their roles are valued by the company. They are empowered to access company resources to solve problems for the customer. They put customer needs ahead of company or production convenience. In the very best service centers, like Nordstrom, Giant Food, and FEDEX, everyone is a customer-service provider. There is one paramount goal for maintaining close contact with your customers: it helps the business identify change trends in the customer's needs, desires, and preferences.

The New Age Culture

The new age corporate culture combines innovation with a strong commitment to the customer. It also fosters an egalitarian and democratic workplace along with a top-to-bottom readiness to anticipate, and thereby benefit from, changes in the market. The new age culture also embraces the ethical treatment of employees and customers.

I use the term *new age culture* because these behaviors embody the requisite qualities for success in the evolving new business age we are entering. Today, only a handful of companies evidence the characteristics of the new age business culture, but the trend is irreversible. We can expect to witness the transformation of existing companies, as well as the emergence of new companies organized around the values and behaviors of the new age business culture. The overwhelming majority of survey respondents placed computer firms, software development companies, semiconductor, and R&D-based technology companies in the new age category. This may indicate that, in the minds of our respondents, advanced technology is a necessary ingredient for the emergence of this new style of corporate culture—that technology drives culture change. This presumption is more readily understood when we observe that newer companies like Microsoft, Intel, and Sun Microsystems seem to exemplify the new age culture by setting new standards for product innovation, workforce effectiveness, and service to the customer.

Other companies, like Nike, Kiwi Airlines, Johnsonville Foods, and Levi Strauss also demonstrate characteristics of the new age business culture, yet none of these companies is built around exotic new technologies. Not all new age cultures depend on cutting-edge technology for their innovation or success, although a disproportionate number of fast-growing technology companies may come to symbolize the new age culture, since they are likely to be the principal source of job growth in the future. New age cultures are usually a challenge for the outside observer or the new employee who may be accustomed to a rigidly hierarchical work setting. Structure, hierarchy, and titles are less evident and are usually replaced by autonomous work teams with a limited life based on a particular product or process. Neither is decision making caught up in a deep or rigid chain of command. Fluidity, lack of formal structure, and even confusion may be evident in different areas of the organization. Ownership of new ideas is shared by the team and the larger organization. Worker initiative and commitment to the company's success is apparent throughout the business.

The new age culture integrates features of the service culture in a number of areas, especially in its commitment to the customer and the empowerment of the workforce. The new age culture is unique, however, for its ability to translate innovation into business performance, as well as for its ability to anticipate change, even to create it. Businesses with new age cultures are also magnets for the very best talent in the labor market. Needless to say, they experience low turnover and high levels of worker and customer loyalty.

OVERCOMING BARRIERS TO CULTURE CHANGE

Changing a company's culture may be the most difficult challenge that senior managers can face. Much of the challenge comes from having to overcome an entrenched culture that will no more stand aside than a fortressed army awaiting an attack. Culture change involves nothing less than changing the attitudes, beliefs, values, commitments, and behaviors of everyone in the organization (see Figure 1.1 on p. 18). This can be threatening to a lot of people at every level within the organization, but the tools and processes exist to ensure the successful change of the culture.

Where to Start

Where to begin culture change is as important as *how* to do it. On this issue, academicians, culture change consultants, and corporate organization development managers come from two schools of thought: bottom-up and top-down.

The bottom-up approach assumes that success is not possible without first gaining a broad-based buy-in from the operational core of the business. Depending on the company and its style of leadership, this may be appropriate. It can be particularly useful with employee-owned companies where management naturally turns to the workforce for direction. It can also help in cases where managers and service providers face very different demands, creating separate subcultures. A good example is a major theme park where consultant Bob Spencer, of the Institute for Human Development, has successfully strategized with park employees about the issues of worker empowerment and customer service. In this case, specific change strategies for workforce behaviors, commitments, and values would naturally apply to both employees and their supervisors who interface with park customers. It would not necessarily be pertinent, however, for executives at headquarters. Bottom-up culture change can also be effective in flat organizations where there is a small middle-management cadre and senior managers are more closely involved in operational decision making.

Top-down change strategies imply the need for sponsorship from the top, which is certainly true for most organizations. This approach is appropriate for business cultures with a layered or deep management hierarchy. In bureaucratic, chaotic, or frozen cultures, sponsorship from the top helps to melt resistance. Top-down strategies are almost always necessary in privately held companies and especially in family-owned companies. In these cultures, everyone is naturally looking "up" for permission and direction. Therefore, it is important for the CEO and her executive staff to assume ownership of culture-change initiatives before directing others in the organization to tackle the change process. It is very helpful for senior management to articulate expectations and to then exhibit these new behaviors so that middle management can see, "It's OK. It's safe!"

Barriers to Culture Change

THE WRONG SPONSORSHIP

Culture change is highly complex and sensitive. Since it will inevitably encompass the entire organization, it requires the highest level of sponsorship—the CEO. Management at Johnson & Johnson actively monitors and supports its culture with an annual audit that is promoted by Ralph Larsen, their CEO. Without this endorsement, the culture-management process could not succeed. Nor can its implementation be delegated to a subordinate officer. Too often, the CEO signs off on the audit or change process, only to disappear until problems develop. This can spur failure. The CEO cannot (and should not) be the project manager, but his presence and active sponsorship should be felt and seen throughout the process. The CEO's personal commitment to the change process can overcome pockets of passive resistance that may exist in the business.

BALKANIZATION

Many times, balkanized cultures are in the most need of change. Balkanized divisions and departments within a company may resist involvement, especially if their leaders (department manager or division officer) feel threatened by the change process. At times, the CEO may have a contender within the company who resists proposed changes. It is well to remember the analogy that many corporate structures are like feudal systems that masquerade as hierarchies. Here, again, the CEO's sponsorship and leadership is required to overcome the resistance.

"WE HAVE NO TIME: THE COMPANY IS IN TROUBLE"

Companies struggling to survive are almost always unwilling to examine or change their cultures. Management doesn't recognize the long-term benefits that can be derived from culture building. More important, they do not understand how the corporate culture—if ignored—can be a significant detriment to the company's survival. Contrary to popular belief, there is a direct link between culture and business performance as demonstrated in studies by University of Michigan's Noel Tichy (*Managing Strategic Change,* Wiley, 1983) and later by Harvard's John Kotter and James Heskett (*Corporate Culture and Performance,* Free Press, 1992). In more immediate ways, culture can be measured by its impact on defects on the assembly line, accuracy in store checkouts, timeliness of product delivery from the distribution center, and employee turnover. A careful appraisal of the culture during periods of stress and challenge can reveal the true *character* of the organization, as well as its ability to compete.

"WE HAVE NO NEED: THE COMPANY IS DOING FINE"

Companies that are making money feel no need to tamper with things: "If it ain't broke, don't fix it." Many times this attitude is more pronounced for the company that has successfully emerged from a bankruptcy or downturn, falsely believing that the improved revenues and profits reflect an improved culture as well. Nonetheless, existing profitability is not a measure of future success or of the culture's long-term viability. Consistently top-performing companies—like ALCOA-Tennessee, Nike, Levi Strauss, Intel, Hewlett-Packard, Johnson & Johnson, and Whirlpool—always keep culture development at the top of the agenda.

ADDICTIVE BEHAVIORS WITHIN THE CULTURE: HIDDEN LAND MINES

Barriers to culture change are erected through patterns of addictive behaviors. I have borrowed the phrase "addictive behaviors" from Anne Schaef and Diane Fassel (*The Addictive Organization,* Harper & Row, 1988) because it so thoroughly captures the problems associated with most business cultures today. Understanding the behaviors of an organization and its individuals is critical to comprehending the larger social context in which it will be necessary to formulate change strategies. While most people associate *corporate culture* with a faceless system or mass of workers, the term also refers to how individuals within the workplace conduct themselves and interact with coworkers and subordinates. These interactions inform the individuals within the social system about what is acceptable behavior, thereby creating barriers to change or opening the door to new behavioral options as the case may be.

Politics as Usual

With the exception of the U.S. Congress, no system or organization is more political than the corporation. Business is characterized by game-playing, deal-making, and constant political maneuvering. For many managers, the game itself is as important as anything else. For still others, the optimum outcome is acquired power and advancement. Money or the advancement of the company may be almost incidental.

Obsessive-Compulsive Behavior

Obsessive-compulsive behavior reflects an inability to abandon the status quo. In bureaucracies, obsessive behaviors may develop around slavish commitments to outmoded procedures, outdated strategies, or long-dead missions. In predatory and political cultures, on the other hand, a compulsive reliance on power exercised by a means of intimidation may dominate behavior. An obsession with work and long hours is worn like a badge by workers in some organizations. I have noticed that many engineering and research firms are heavily focused on process and detail, which is, to some extent, understandable. But this obsession can blind a work unit or the entire company to larger business issues and objectives affecting its business and culture, especially if it invades other functions of the company that interface with the marketplace, thereby requiring a different mind-set and behaviors.

Punishment as a Tool

An excessive reliance on punishment is most often seen in predatory and political cultures, but retribution can be practiced in any corporate culture. It is less often seen in the service and new age cultures. A mean-spirited and punitive environment evidences a fundamental mistrust and degrading of individuals, as well as a deep skepticism of coalition and team building initiatives. The fear of punishment kills any chance of risk taking or knowledge transfer between employees. Reliance on intimidation by a key executive involved in the culture-change process can destroy the entire effort. Unless this behavior is changed first, the fine words will ring of fraud.

Projection of Blame

As finger-pointing becomes more widespread in the general population, there should be no surprise that more and more employees are taking this behavior with them to the workplace. Rather than accepting blame for mistakes or inappropriate behaviors, it is increasingly common to project blame back onto the boss, co-workers, customers, or even the company itself in order to escape personal responsibility. On many occasions the business is responsible. Widespread force reductions have overloaded many employees, while saddling inexperienced workers with tasks for which they have received little or no training. Projection of blame develops and persists when there is no outlet for the individual to express his frustration. The result can be disastrous for an organization when no one is prepared to take responsibility for their actions. The benefits of accountability and commitment are never realized by the business.

Ethical Convenience

When individuals in an organization feel they have the option of acting unethically, even if this permission is available only under special circumstances, it portends the eventual failure of the business. Unethical behavior can involve outright theft from customers and suppliers, or it may involve more subtle treacheries such as "cooking the books" or "reinterpreting" sales figures. More subtle forms of duplicity involve the revision of history, the creation of "personality conflicts," or the destruction of a co-worker's or competitor's reputation. The fabrication of a personality conflict has been a favorite weapon of choice to justify the dismissal of a subordinate or colleague who no longer "fits in." Fluid ethical standards undermine the workforce's sense of trust, risk taking, and commitment to the organization—all necessary ingredients for business success.

HOW TO CHANGE CORPORATE CULTURE

We should keep in mind that most corporate cultures are always changing to some degree. They are truly dynamic. *The key is managing the change process to fit changing competitive conditions*, as well as the needs and capabilities of the culture. You will see in several of the industry chapters in Part 2 how the failure to proactively change the culture has prevented companies, even entire industries, from meeting their business objectives.

Create Sponsorship at the Top

Sponsorship from the CEO is critical to success, even when the strategy calls for a bottom-up change process. If people are expected to change their behaviors, commitments, and belief systems, then they must be able to see that the top of the organization—the leader—mandates it and is exhibiting his own changed behaviors. Some organizations aptly call it "walking the talk." Most important, the CEO must actively encourage and sanction an open environment that promotes communication and feedback.

Establish Alternative Qualities and Standards for the Culture

Convening focus groups and seminars is not enough to change the culture. The organization has to know where it's going and what is expected of the culture. New and revised qualities and behaviors must be tailored to the goals of the business, while the processes and empowerment for changing the culture must be widely dispersed throughout the organization (see Figure 5.2).

Identify Natural Change Leaders

Natural change leaders are those who are not only committed to change but are excited by the process and have ideas that can propel the process. They have a keen awareness of the implications of change for their organization. Natural change leaders may be found at all levels of the organization. Many times, it may be the squeaky wheel who has rarely been given an opportunity to contribute in a significant way. Natural change leaders should be identified within all levels of the organization.

Communicate, Communicate, Communicate

Don't keep the change process a secret. That only creates anxiety. Help people throughout the organization to understand the steps they are expected to take, as well as the desired outcome from

Figure 5.2
Qualities of Corporate Culture

New Age/Innovative Cultures	Frozen or Failing Cultures
Customer (market) orientation	Product and procedures orientation
Asks "Why not?"	Asks "Why?"
Asks "What can we do?"	Asks "How can we do it?"
Leadership focused on organization	Leadership focused on structure
Attracts and keeps good people	Recruits and loses people
Asks whether new employee can be productive	Asks whether new employee's personality fits in?
Mistakes of commission (ask forgiveness, learn, move on)	Mistakes of omission (ask permission, displace blame, avoid)
Courageous and proactive leadership	Controlling, incremental, reactive leadership
Open to risk taking and new ideas	Risk averse, relies on conventional ideas
Noisy, open, self-critical	Quiet, closed, self-promoting
Focuses on value added	Focuses on profits and losses (margins)
Encourages open and democratic work environment	Promotes closed, authoritarian work environment
Anticipates change	Resists change
Acts strategically and dramatically	Acts incrementally and conventionally
Facts and results dominate decision making	Politics dominate decision making

these behaviors. Whenever possible, solicit input from employees and key managers for improving the process, particularly warnings about any hidden land mines.

Build a Broad Consensus for Change

Consensus Team Building™ is both a concept and a specific intervention process to be undertaken with groups of employees. A company's culture can change only through organizationwide consensus building. People must agree about existing cultural values, business conditions demanding change, and the shape that the future culture should take. Without this broad-based buy-in, the new culture will never evolve. Contrary to popular belief, consensus building does not prevent constructive criticism or divergent thinking. I initiated this process in an organization known for its encouragement of contrary opinions, and, in the beginning, managers were afraid I was going to suppress the expression of diverging opinions. But after I explained the process (and changed its name), participants were more trusting. They found that to achieve consensus, you must first air diverging opinions and concerns. They also learned that convergence of goals and commitments was crucial to collective success. For those managers who continue to believe that corporate culture is a nebulous, unmanageable condition, definite signs can be found that will indicate it is changing. The culture is changing if:

- A dialogue has emerged that questions the prevailing culture;

- New behaviors have emerged that run counter to the prevailing culture and are becoming pervasive throughout the organization;

- New values and commitments have emerged that support the new behavior; and

- Commitment to the organization for its success and performance prevails over a commitment to the organization for the security or benefits it provides employees.

The culture is *not* changing if:

- Old culture behaviors, values, and commitments persist under changed conditions, crises, or challenges; and

- New culture behaviors are isolated and are not spreading throughout the organization.

The goal is to achieve a pervasive change in behaviors and commitments throughout the organization.

Reinforce Ethical Standards

The change process should reinforce the "rightness" of ethical conduct, both within and outside the organization. This may be the narrowest line we walk in the business world. People need to hear that ethical conduct is *required* by the organization—not just desired—and that it will always be safe to consistently apply ethical standards in one's endeavors. The marketplace demands it.

Assess Change Through Bias-Free Processes

Change can be measured and should include qualitative as well as quantitative measures. This will help ensure bias-free data gathering while providing everyone in the organization with feedback on their collective progress, as well as a compass for the direction they need to take.

GOALS FOR CULTURE CHANGE

The paramount goal of culture change is improved performance. If a business is to successfully respond to changing competitive conditions, its culture must be capable of supporting shifts in strategy and employee behaviors. In light of the unprecedented level of radical change that American business is experiencing today, the evolution of corporate culture must become a priority for many businesses that have formerly ignored the subject. Simple survival may depend on it. Other objectives of the culture change process should include the following:

- *Creating a performance-driven culture* that is responsive to changes in the marketplace and that values even higher levels of performance is imperative. Ultimately, culture is about the competitive success of the business.

- *Building flexibility into the culture* is critical if a company is to swiftly respond to changing market conditions. Managers and employees have to be accepting of and responsive to change, redirecting their thinking and energies as the competition changes. In a global marketplace, this is especially important.

- *Creating widespread worker empowerment* will assist those within the culture to identify the shifts necessary to effectively respond to competitive change. Management will have to demonstrate greater faith in the ability of its workforce to recognize and solve problems on its own. Companies can no longer rely solely on direction from above. Senior management is many times too far removed from actual change and its demands and is not always able to act quickly enough.

- *Encouraging reasonable risk taking and innovation* will be needed to elicit the break-through ideas, service, and products that a company requires to compete in a faster-paced, more challenging business environment. Change is coming at too fast a pace and from too many quarters to place all key decision-making responsibility in the hands of a tiny group of executives. New ideas need to percolate up from the larger culture. More important, granting permission to act on these ideas means that mistakes must be accepted so long as they flow from reasoned judgments and evolving processes. *We fail our way to success.*

- *Instilling a strong sense of values throughout the culture* is a serious responsibility that has often been overlooked by many businesses. This is not merely a question of how individuals act toward one another. It also refers to how and why people are rewarded by the company. Too often, corporate boards have been rewarding CEOs for downsizing their companies following several years of financial losses. DEC's CEO, Robert Palmer, and several of his key officers were awarded huge bonuses and salary increases after "surplusing" thousands of workers by 1994. This followed several years of astounding losses and a glaring failure by Palmer and his lieutenants to turn the company's fortunes around. In two of the last three years, AMOCO's chairman, H. Laurence Fuller, achieved profits only by laying off employees—nearly 20 percent of his workforce. Fuller was rewarded with a bonus and pay increase after the downsizings of 1992 and 1994. Despite the damages of the Exxon *Valdez* affair, and the subsequent bungling and denial by Exxon, its CEO, Larry Raymond, was rewarded with stock and cash bonuses. Similar rewards were distributed to Roger Smith by GM, even though the company was rapidly losing market share to its competitors. This standard of conduct at the top does little to instill a strong sense of values and equity throughout the larger culture.

There was a time when the largest paychecks and bonuses were awarded to those who took the greatest risks. Today, workers and middle managers are shouldering the risks—without the rewards. Russell Ackoff (*The Democratic Corporation,* Oxford University Press, 1994) notes the necessity for recognizing the actual stakeholders and not just the shareholders of a business. Without this recognition, there is no sense of equity and fairness in the workplace, diminishing individual commitment to the business. By ignoring the contribution of all the stakeholders, the directors of a company make the company more vulnerable to eventual failure.

The importance of corporate culture is too easily dismissed because it is simultaneously too big and too "soft" a subject for easy discussion. Culture includes everything from company history and heroes to logos and informal dress codes, as well as unspoken attitudes about diversity in the workplace, problem solving and risk taking, the role of research and development, the importance of seniority, and the centrality of the customer. Each and every business represents a unique case, brimming with hundreds of contending personalities, and much to understand. But certain patterns and certain principles can be identified. It is not a mere conceit that corporations are treated as persons under the law. Just as each of us is a product of our past experiences, companies are also products of their experience, some good and some bad. Nothing, it seems, is predestined, except for change. Its inexorable demands cannot be avoided. Therefore, corporate cultures must continue to develop and change if their companies are to change and perform within a radically changing business environment.

PART II

Change in Seven Critical American Industries

CHAPTER

6

American Manufacturing: Still Competing on an Uneven Playing Field?

JOHN E. DANIELS
Vice President, Mercer Management Consulting

Since the mid-1970s, leaders of American manufacturing companies as well as labor unions have lamented their loss of markets to foreign competitors. They have been quick to point out that the playing field has been slanted against U.S. companies that tried to compete in overseas markets while foreign competitors were allowed to capture significant shares of American markets. In selected industries, those unfavorable conditions may have been true for a while. Certainly, U.S.-made electronics, computers, and autos have been shut out of Japan, while Japanese autos and motorcycles captured significant shares of the American market. Governments in countries like Korea, Belgium, and Taiwan subsidized production overflows in steel, which allowed their companies to dump overflows in the United States at prices well below their costs. In addition, several countries also had the opportunity to leap-frog the United States after World War II with new state-of-the-art manufacturing plants aided by American know-how.

However, in many cases, the American government stepped in

to protect vital industries long enough for them to regain some of their lost markets while retooling for a more competitive global environment. Harley Davidson and Chrysler were recipients of direct financial aid from the government, and U.S. quotas were placed on foreign steel imports for a decade. Just last year, the Clinton administration pressured the Japanese government to ease the restrictions on Motorola wireless communications products.

In reality, I believe the *uneven* playing field probably never existed. It was a soothing myth, much like the imaginary missile gap of the 1960s. Instead, the competitive landscape in worldwide manufacturing can more accurately be described as being a *bumpy* playing field, with advantages and disadvantages developing like shifting sands. Until recently, many American manufacturers had no desire to learn how to play on that bumpy field, but that attitude has changed as American companies learn the new truths of global competition.

Americans overlooked the fact that foreign competitors also have had to play on the same bumpy playing field. Asian producers always have had to cope with competitive differences, such as paying for high transportation costs to ship their products to the United States and coping with wide gaps in the currency-exchange rate. Even though the Japanese are now producing autos in the United States, a large portion of these autos are being built here for shipment *back* to Japan because of their higher labor costs and aging workforce. Foreign manufacturers now experience new challenges, which include a dramatically cheaper dollar that makes foreign-made products more expensive in comparison to American products. Even American companies that flocked to Mexico for its cheaper labor market quickly found that the education and productivity of the Mexican worker lags far behind that of the American worker. In addition, American companies found that the absence of a sophisticated distribution system in Mexico makes it difficult and costly to ship products back to the United States. Recently, in recognition that the grass may not be greener on the other side of the fence, Motorola closed plants in Mexico and Germany and replaced their manufacturing capacity with plants in the United States and Scotland.

NEW RULES FOR A BUMPY PLAYING FIELD

American manufacturers have been quick to embrace downsizing and efficiency improvement schemes that, once implemented, did little to create sustained performance improvements. In fact, many companies continued to lose market share despite these initiatives. With downsizing came the loss of core competencies and capabilities, which undermined the ability of companies to develop and support effective business strategies. As Jack Welch of General Electric was fond of saying, "A company can boost productivity by restructuring, removing bureaucracy and downsizing, but it cannot sustain high productivity without cultural change." In Chapter 1, Jerry Want makes a strong case for scrapping traditional fix-its and replacing them with the broader, vision-led strategies that are needed in the current climate of radically changing business conditions. During the current period of global business change, sustained performance will be possible only if American manufacturers employ a different business focus. With the scrapping of traditional fix-its, an increasing number of high-performing companies have adapted a holistic view of productivity by focusing on a set of business levers and the linkage between them to address changing business conditions as shown in Want's Business Change Cycle (Figure 6.1). To sustain improvement, each of these levers must be addressed in an integrated manner, recognizing that design and strategy were the easiest levers to pull, while culture is the most difficult to change. Effectively managing radical change can be achieved only by addressing each of these levers through an integrated process (as advocated by Want in Chapters 1 and 4). *A holistic view of performance improvement is needed in order to achieve a truly successful result.*

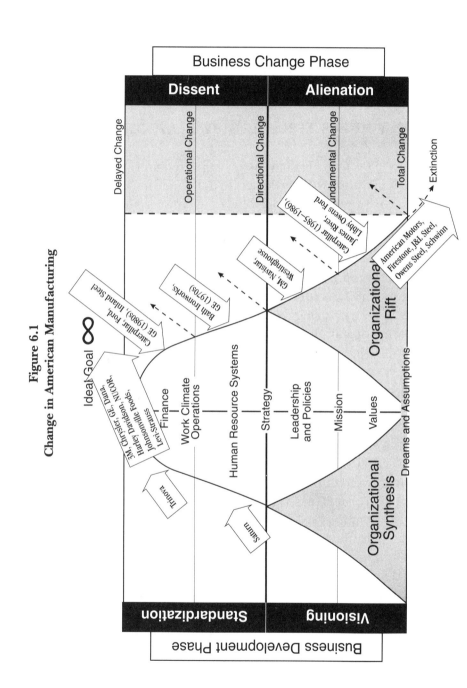

Figure 6.1
Change in American Manufacturing

124

To tackle performance improvement in a holistic manner, organizations must become more adaptive and develop critical skills they may not now possess. These skills include managing complexity with flexibility and simplicity, creating a clear customer focus, managing through holistic business strategies, redirecting the culture through worker empowerment, and cultivating labor–management cooperation. Each of these capabilities is required as a foundation for improved performance in a changing business climate.

Managing Complexity with Flexibility and Simplicity

Jack Welch expanded his thoughts on cultural change by relating improvement to profitability and simplicity. He enjoys telling the leaders of GE's business units that their destiny is linked to swiftly managing complexity and fully comprehending the complex differences between managing an enterprise yesterday as compared with managing it to meet the demands of tomorrow. If you want to be faster, you must be simpler. Welch was one of the first *Fortune* 500 leaders to recognize and deal with the inherent perils of complexity for the business organization. Even after recognizing the problem, however, too many companies still retain complex hierarchies that are a product of their growth during the 1960s and 1970s. In the 1970s, Westinghouse undertook a massive study of manufacturing organizations to determine the ideal size for manufacturing plants. It found that plants staffed with no more than 300 people were the ideal size for a manufacturing organization because larger plants generated exponential growth in complexity. A lower staffing level promotes efficiency, coordination, and internal cooperation and promotes a focus that is critical to sustained business success. *Complex management hierarchies are an unnecessary and ineffective way to manage organizations.*

Creating a Clear Customer Focus

The benefits of a customer focus far outweigh economies of scale. I am convinced that *most* of today's *Fortune* 500 drift from their stated business focus. Successful smaller companies have recognized that strategic focus is critical to growing a successful business. The same is true for large, mature enterprises. As many large manufacturers embraced downsizing in the 1980s, they sacrificed focus to restructuring. Work units and divisions had fewer people, but the business was not less complex, and people at all levels lost focus on where the business was headed. For many years, AT&T was the epitome of a massive, monolithic structure that made it nearly impossible for employees to see how they were linked to the customer. It was an organization that was entranced by its own complexity. A decade-long downsizing contributed little to its organizational need for focus. Now AT&T is regaining its focus and competitiveness through reinvented and relatively autonomous business units that are focused on their specific customers and the processes that add value for those customers.

Until recently, manufacturing managers retained an excessive commodity orientation that kept them from innovating and customizing for the customer. The downsizing and efficiency frenzy of the 1980s only increased managers' micro thinking where macro thinking was needed. Foreign manufacturers like Electrolux and Volvo have been famous for maintaining focus at all levels of the organization, and the leading Japanese manufacturers are equally respected for translating focus into captured markets. Today, 3M, Harley Davidson, TriNova, General Electric, Black & Decker, NUCOR, and the *new* Chrysler Corporation are just a few of this country's manufacturers that are making focus pay off. *Focus on the customer and on the processes that add value to the customer generates improvements that far exceed economies traditionally obtained through downsizing and restructuring.*

Managing Change Through Holistic Business Strategies

Before Jack Welch's ascendancy at GE, it, too, was a company that functioned more as a commodity business. Complexity, micro thinking, and centralized, top-down planning were pervasive characteristics of the culture. Under Welch, GE management has moved away from these traditional structures. Instead, it places a premium on remaining nimble, flexible, and adaptive. Every GE business unit understands that it must be first or second in its market if it is to survive. To do this, all performance levers must be understood and used, and strategic market segmentation and specific customer needs must drive business strategy. Consequently, holistic, macro management has replaced micro thinking throughout GE. Downsizing is no longer viewed as a panacea but is regarded as a blunt tool of last resort only: it is just one of the many tools in the tool kit to be used when needed. Each business unit is viewed as an integrated system of tailored processes, part of a larger business environment—not just a piece of the GE federation.

To the outside world, another leading holistically managed company, 3M, looks like a company that develops and sells commodities. It keeps launching a dizzying array of products for both the consumer and industrial markets. However, within the company, a concerted effort is made to avoid the thinking of a commodities-driven business. To internally differentiate itself from others, 3M sees itself in a much broader way and regards itself as a technology-driven business. Over time, a unique culture has been created and nurtured that heavily stresses outpacing the competition through innovation. Rewards and recognition are based on innovation and value-added contributions. Those general and administrative functions such as finance, purchasing, legal, and human resources are necessary but secondary organizations that are not allowed to interfere with the product-development and manufacturing processes. Again, the focus is on linking R&D, manufacturing engineering, process engineering, production, and customer satisfaction into a unified set of holistic processes. *Business strategies created with a holistic view of the corporation provide clearly differentiated advantages.*

Changing the Culture Through Worker Empowerment

Too many companies wait until they are facing their imminent collapse before they act. When the survival reflex kicks in, companies invariably downsize, which is followed by more downsizing. Many times, it is couched in terms of *reengineering* or *right sizing,* but the outcomes are always the same.

Scott Paper is a recent example of a large manufacturer that waited too long to deal with change and then was confronted with failure. Using the Business Change Cycle, it seems clear that Scott is struggling with total change—failure of mission, culture, and leadership as well as business strategy. And alienation will build as the company downsizes. Scott's new CEO, Al Dunlap, indicated that the purpose for downsizing was not simply to cut costs but to eliminate the former culture through layoffs (*New York Times,* September 4, 1994). While this strategy may not fully incorporate a holistic approach to saving the business, it could help as Scott takes the first steps toward changing its corporate beliefs, values, and behaviors.

Although this is a high-risk approach, the demand for immediate action is apparent. The problems at Scott Paper did not occur overnight but have been the product of years of incremental tinkering linked to a commodity focus and micro thinking within the business. Scott Paper may well survive, but after a year or two, a real risk exists that its core competencies will dramatically shrink along with its market share. Other production companies that have faced or are facing fundamental or total change have included International Harvester (now Navistar), John Deere, GM, Westinghouse, and IBM.

A company's culture is not quickly changed through downsizing or reengineering and is not just eliminated. Downsizing eliminates jobs, people, and their *competencies*—not work or complexity. Neither does it erase turf battles. In contrast, delayering changes individuals' exposure to work and helps to reveal the real leaders within the culture while preserving core competencies. Even better, empowering allows the workers and managers to solve problems for themselves.

In the 1970s, GE had nine layers of management hierarchy that functioned much like a government bureaucracy—blocking and checking decisions rather than empowering actions. Many decisions were made by corporate staff, not the business managers. Today, many GE businesses function with four management layers, and they are driving for a still flatter organization. The key is *empowerment*. Empowerment is the most important action that a company's management can take to change the culture and, at the same time, improve productivity. When people within a work environment are truly empowered, the culture changes and performance improves. These are the qualities found in the very best U.S. manufacturing companies. People can speak and work without fear of reprisal. They also can take reasonable risks and quickly become more innovative on behalf of the company. Failure, by itself, is a sufficient deterrent against imprudent behavior. Managers must also keep in mind that the 1960s' challenge to authority is starting to become the norm in American business. Some of our largest companies—like Sun Microsystems, Levi Strauss, and Microsoft—are being led by people who reached maturity during the 1960s. Worker empowerment is required in a customer-focused organization because it places decision making at the closest point to the customer (see Figure 6.2).

The ultimate goal in changing the culture through worker empowerment is the establishment of high-performance teams. However, as many companies have found, team-based organizations are difficult to establish. Significant investments of resources and time are required to achieve success. Many organizations that attempt to establish teams have abandoned the effort without recognizing that the business and its employees must pass through three phases before they can produce high-performing teams. These phases are shown in Figure 6.3. *Positive change is driven by empowered workforces and high performance cultures.*

Figure 6.2
Vision-Led Strategy

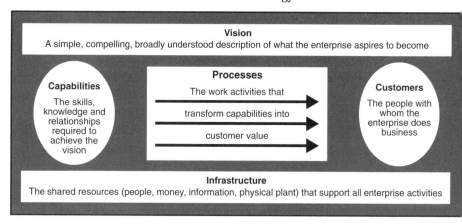

Figure 6.3
High-Performing Team-Based Organizations

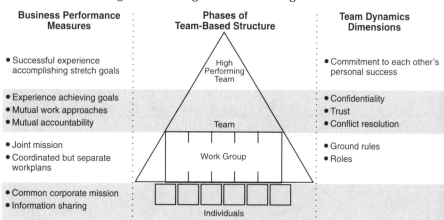

Building Labor–Management Cooperation

Critical to any resurgence of manufacturing in this country is improved cooperation between labor and management. Labor–management problems can be traced back to the Industrial Revolution, when workers were seen simply as extensions of their machines. The Taylor school of industrial management reinforced that notion with its principles of division of labor and the breakdown of work into micro steps. Employees lost their ability to see the outcome and the value they were adding to the product, and their pride and sense of ownership in the quality of the product vanished. This was clearly evidenced at the Big Three auto makers in the 1970s and 1980s and contributed directly to their loss of market share to their Japanese competitors. This long-term climate of mistrust and adversarial posturing cannot be remedied overnight. However, trust can be systematically established over time to foster a common focus and commitment.

Building this new trust can best be accomplished when management empowers the workforce to participate in defining the product and processes, while encouraging a freer hand to initiate independent action on the shop floor. Where unions exist, they must be integrated into the focus and strategy of the business. In Germany, labor has long had permanent representation on the boards of most companies. This is now being duplicated with quiet success by the Big Three auto makers. At Bath Ironworks, a major ship builder for the U.S. Navy, management and labor are working together to design the transition to nondefense production. At Johnsonville Foods, a sausage manufacturer, labor is now responsible for hiring and the appraisal of worker performance. At Titeflex, a highly regarded hose and fitting business, supervisory foremen have been replaced by technical assistants who support work teams and production processes rather than giving orders. At Saturn, employees participate in work-process design to ensure that processes are fully adding value for the customer.

Nonetheless, workers need to stop whipping management for all their problems. Instead, they should strive to add value for the customer from their experience with work processes. Many of the challenges that company managers and directors face are beyond immediate resolution, since most companies have limited resources. Even in our most conservatively run corporations, management has changed significantly from past traditions, and working conditions are now vastly improved. We also see workers willing to take ownership of their efforts, and in some cases (e.g., Wheeling Pittsburgh Steel, Avis Car Rental, and several airlines) even buying their companies—something that was almost inconceivable twenty-five years ago. *Increasingly, labor–management cooperation creates employees who are assuming ownership for processes they help design and run.*

Developing the Right Leadership

I have referred to GE's Jack Welch in this chapter, but he is not the only leader from the manufacturing sector to set new standards for leadership. Andy Patti of the Dial Corporation, Howard Selland of TriNova, Black & Decker's Nolan Archibald, and Frank Iverson of NUCOR represent a new generation of leaders who are not just reinventing their companies: they are revolutionizing American manufacturing.

Libby Owens Ford was primarily a supplier of glass to Detroit's auto makers. In the 1980s, LOF management recognized that glass was becoming a commodities-driven business, which typically has diminished opportunities to set prices for products, particularly since the producer's ability to add value to the product is limited. Believing that future success meant adding value to customers, LOF divested itself of the glass business and created TriNova. After selling off the glass business, TriNova pursued three different market segments, so that it could add value to the final product while gaining more control over pricing. Under the operational leadership of Howard Selland, TriNova strengthened its position in hose and fittings, plastics, and hydraulic power devices. As the business began to prosper, these three product lines were also integrated in various, innovative ways to add customer value. This allowed the business to reduce internal seams and barriers while promoting innovation and cooperation. These changes have enabled TriNova to continue serving an industry it understood—automobile component manufacturing.

Today, TriNova is a major supplier to each of the Big Three Detroit auto makers, U.S. transplants like Honda, Mazda, and Toyota and other auto makers worldwide. Company leadership developed the foresight to see where it had to go to prosper—not just strive. Howard Selland had the presence to see the company's future under a different set of competitive change conditions. An effective leader copes with a bumpy playing field—what Jerry Want calls managing change.

To ensure lasting success, change management must be installed before change forces begin to erode a company's ability to compete. Business leaders who successfully manage the bumpy terrain of competitive change do more than watch for potholes in the road. They also recognize future opportunities that a company can utilize for its own competitive advantage. This new age leadership attitude is also building a better generation of middle managers who *coach, counsel, teach, build resources,* and *develop people.* These are the foundations of holistic business management. *Effective leadership has been the missing element in the old management axiom of planning, implementation, organizing, and motivating (POIM).*

THE FUTURE OF AMERICAN MANUFACTURING

The future of American manufacturing is here. Manufacturing companies are chasing labor markets as well as consumer markets to all parts of the globe. Competitive markets have become too broad or too crowded for many companies, requiring them to narrow their focus to niches or segments. Breakthrough technologies have radically altered production processes and employment patterns. Added to these normal dilemmas are the challenges of ever-changing international trade agreements and fluctuating currency values. The CEO of one internationally focused company quipped that he needed his own commerce and state departments.

Based on these types of developments over the last decade, some would argue that the future entails more automation, increased reliance on high technology assists like robotics, international alliances between companies, divestiture of less important business components, and continued workforce reductions. That is only a partial and not very accurate picture of changes in contemporary manufacturing because it puts the focus on internal company considerations. The real future for manufacturing lies in focusing its efforts on the customer and ensuring that all organizationwide efforts are concentrated on adding maximum value for the customer. Responding to changing customer needs with *speed, simplicity,* and *self-confidence* will be the key to winning in the future.

The Workforce of the Future

Manufacturers are immersed in a period of radical change—a period of uncertainty and considerable discomfort. Plants are being closed, consolidated, merged, and acquired. The net effect seems to be the loss of jobs and manufacturing capacity across the country in almost every sector. The great majority of those companies that have closed found that they were no longer competitive. Owners did not possess the commitment or resources to invest in improved plant and manufacturing processes to meet their competition.

Some jobs did go overseas, creating a painful employment void at one end of the labor market. For example, semiskilled and unskilled jobs in the textile industry have migrated overseas where labor costs are lower. Other jobs have been lost to increased automation, especially in heavy industries like steel and autos. Many of these jobs, however, were the most arduous and dangerous and generally added little direct product value. These unsatisfactory tasks, most would contend, should be done by robots and other automated work aides. But even with automation, we should constantly work to upgrade skills and worker competencies so that we can develop and migrate the larger workforce instead of placing workers on the unemployment rolls. Eventually, the walls that separate labor and management will have to come down to ensure success in a global market. As that happens, both the company and its workers will benefit.

A New Management Approach

History clearly tells us that manufacturing enterprises must focus on adding value and thereby differentiate themselves. Although commodities businesses have less opportunity to differentiate by adding value, it is evident that value can still be added in many cases. U.S. agriculture has demonstrated that the application of technology and ingenuity can offset an uneven playing field created by low wages and excessive government subsidies elsewhere. 3M has been very successful in differentiating their tape business through the application of processing and adhesive technologies, especially in their transparent tape products. Consumers are willing to pay a premium above the "yellow tape" products (original Scotch Tape products). 3M and the U.S. agricultural industry are successful because they focus on processes that add value even though they reside in commodity segments.

To take advantage of the synergies and efficiencies that value-added processes can engender, many manufacturing organizations are developing a new process- and customer-focused management model that Mercer Management Consulting calls Horizontal Management™. Leading organizations such as Boeing, Ericsson Electric, General Electric, Honeywell, Intel, Volvo, and Xerox are replacing outdated management models with this new management model. In the industrial age, when change was infrequent, communications a challenge, and markets close at hand, centralized, vertical management was the preferred model. Today, however, companies complete in globalized, informationalized, customized marketplaces where change is rapid and continuous and the ability to adapt and learn is the key to survival. Experts agree that Horizontal Management™ represents the best solution for bringing all business levers into play in a holistic, integrated way. Horizontal Management™ inspires and enables people to work together—to respond quickly, flexibly, and creatively to customer needs in an emerging global marketplace (see Figure 6.2 page 130).

Five principles characterize the horizontally managed organization:

- The enterprise serves its customers through horizontal processes. Such processes are a key element in an integrated model for conducting business and adding value where all work is part of a single process designed to satisfy customer needs, business processes translate customer preferences to define the value of work activities, and process management is driven from the top as a means to build and execute strategies.

- Process owners, teams, and individuals are driven by customer accountabilities. Process owners are responsible for developing, deploying, and improving process to meeting customer needs.

- Processes are the focal point for decision making and organizational infrastructure. Day-to-day business operations are driven by a full process perspective.

- People possess the attitudes, skills, and behaviors required to sustain a horizontal enterprise. Personal characteristics reflect the realities of life in a dynamic, process-driven work environment.

- Information enables successful horizontal integration and adaptive learning. A systematic approach to capturing and applying knowledge enables continuous improvement of processes.

For manufacturing enterprises, the choice today is not *whether* to change but *how* and *when*, and evidence is mounting that Horizontal Management™ can be a powerful force for company success. Sideliners will not escape: change will knock them off their benches as they lose customers, employees, and market share.

In summary, complaining about playing on an uneven field may be an interesting way to pass time, but winners will recognize their disadvantages and create and develop compensating advantages that lead to profitable growth. Significant growth opportunities exist in every industry, including manufacturing, but growth will profit only those enterprises that are competent at managing radical change.

John E. Daniels

John Daniels is a vice president for Mercer Management Consulting, where he specializes in serving the manufacturing, aerospace, and transportation industries in the areas of organization analysis, operations strategy, and operational effectiveness. Among his many clients have been the 3M Corporation, Borg Warner, TriNova, Aeroquip, and the Dial Corporation. Mr. Daniels has held a variety of operational management positions at General Electric Company and was director of worldwide operations for an industrial medical laser company. He earned his bachelor of science degree in electrical engineering from the University of Massachusetts.

CHAPTER

7

The U.S. Airline Industry:
Bailing Out After Deregulation

NICHOLAS J. RADELL
Vice President and Director, Airline Industry Practice,
Mercer Management Consulting

ALAN E. SCHNUR
Principal, Towers Perrin & Company

JAMES G. PURVIS
Senior Vice President, Human Resources,
Westin Hotels International

"There are two tragedies in life—one is to not get your heart's desire—the other is to get it" (*Man and Superman,* Heritage Press, 1962). G.B. Shaw may have been thinking ahead to 1978 and the deregulation of the airline industry when he penned this phrase. A unique convergence of political forces placed most of the principal actors firmly in favor of airline deregulation when Congress debated the issue in 1978. Despite the reluctance of labor, travel agents, industry management, business flyers, and editorial writers, congressional Republicans and the Carter administration enthusiastically embraced a liberated marketplace. Deregulation of the U.S. airline industry was intended to promote competition, thereby expanding choices available to the traveling public. Deregulation was touted as the catalyst that would improve the way airlines served the public. Sixteen years later, the airline industry appears dazed and confused in the face of a growing chorus of complaints from its customer base.

Interestingly, the average price per mile of air travel has fallen in a fairly constant and predictable way since 1950 (see Figure 7.1). Until 1978 these savings were primarily driven by technology improvements, including the introduction of wide-body jets in 1969. After deregulation, this decline continued largely due to more efficient operations driven by competition. Despite this apparent success, the reality of air travel has been that these statistical savings are experienced by the public in an unpredictable and impenetrable morass of discounts, alternative fares, and ever-changing travel rules. Regular business travelers frequently find themselves sitting next to a student or senior citizen with the same

Figure 7.1
Decline of Airline Prices Due to Technology
Improvements and Increasing Competition

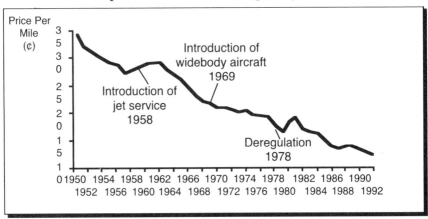

Note: Prices adjusted for inflation, 1992 dollars.
Source: DOT. Courtesy of Mercer Management Consulting.

travel itinerary but purchased at a fraction of their own fares. Saturday night layovers, connecting flights rather than nonstops, and carry-on trips that allow you to throw away the back half of a ticket have become routine tactics for the budget-conscious traveler.

On the plus side, many might agree that service—as narrowly defined by the airlines in terms of on-time departures and arrivals, as well as the error-free handling of baggage—is actually improving. But overall customer service provided by U.S. airlines has remained mediocre at best and is arguably eroding on short-haul flights where food service is disappearing and flight attendant crews are shrinking. As for customer choice, deregulation has resulted in more similarity than differentiation between carriers. Fares are comparable, if not identical, within the same route, and the "flying experience"—from contact with a reservation or travel agent at the beginning of the trip to baggage pickup at the end—is pedestrian and forgettable.

Deregulators forecast that a world of fierce competition would create significant changes in pricing and service. Airlines were expected to embrace the opportunity to satisfy the long-suppressed needs of the flying public. The marketplace would justify itself through the operation of Adam Smith's "invisible hand," and a happier public would be better served by airlines freed to outmaneuver and outperform their competitors. For the most part, these changes have not and do not appear likely to occur as the industry, as a whole, continues to move in lock step. Although passengers hear the obligatory assurance that "We're glad to have you flying with us today because we know you have a choice of carriers," too frequently their experience tells them they are neither valued nor appreciated.

Conceptually, deregulation of the airlines constituted a legislative extrapolation from a few isolated, but successful, experiments in the trucking and taxi industries during the early 1970s—most of which had been attempted at the state or local level. Although all are forms of transportation, this is where any similarity ends. The dynamics of trucking and taxis are very different from those of airlines. The former are characterized by low capital entry, independent owner operators, and relatively small public risk. Airlines, on the other hand, are vast corporate hierarchies with huge capital investments that demand massive cash flows. Deregulation represented a leap into uncertainty and not just a measured tactical redirection.

More than fifteen years after deregulation, the airlines have found the competitive marketplace to be far more challenging and complex than they ever imagined. Significant, proactive change—which is the essence of marketplace competition—has been avoided throughout the industry. Ironically, it's not that airline executives don't want to change or that they have failed to recognize the need for change. Instead, they find themselves unable to produce needed behavioral change in their cultures and their management teams. The absence of organizational flexibility and capacity for cultural change within airlines is severely limiting most carriers' ability to compete successfully in the new, deregulated marketplace—a marketplace they are finding increasingly global in scope and competition.

INDUSTRY CONDITIONS UNDER REGULATION

Structure and Competitive Conditions

Much like public utilities, U.S. airlines were protected from the pressures of competition prior to 1978. In that insulated environment, management's primary objective was the provision of safe, reliable air travel at a reasonable price. Carriers enjoyed the luxury of developing highly structured, hierarchical organizations that divided up the market among themselves in a system of government-determined gentlemen's agreements. There were no true national airlines. Even the largest systems were basically regional or specialty carriers that linked with one another through major gateway cities. Airlines concentrated on serving one or two of the five major traffic corridors (see Figure 7.2).

Figure 7.2
Major U.S. Air Traffic Flows

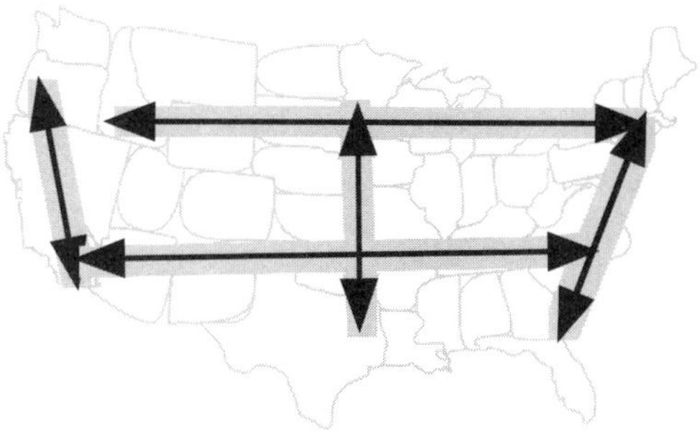

Route	Estimated % of U.S. Air Travel
N-S East Coast	30%
N-S West Coast	20%
N-S Central	10%
E-W Northern	20%
E-W Southern	20%

Source: DOT. Courtesy of Mercer Management Consulting.

This created inherent inefficiencies since demand fluctuated seasonally within each corridor, but these costs could be passed along in fares.

Airlines operated within a remarkably simple economic system. They were guaranteed profitability if they flew safely and avoided inordinate mechanical problems and their associated delays. Performance was barely measured, customer satisfaction was largely ignored or presumed, and competition was essentially nonexistent. With federal route protection, bottom-line performance was rarely a concern for airline management. Life on mahogany row was good. Rewards were high for senior managers—substantial power and unlimited, free travel extended between carriers as an executive courtesy. Without competitive threats, there was little need to create new services, products, or management systems. The challenge was to maintain safety, reliability, and reasonable cost.

At times, the traveler had it good, too. Fares on selected routes were low—$19 between San Francisco and Los Angeles with a seat assignment, and a similar fare on the Eastern corridor shuttle. Flights were frequent, even into outlying markets, and carriers like Pacific Southwest (PSA), Western, and AirCal were able to create unique identities and loyal customer bases. The regulated environment created a growing market for air travel through a combination of decreasing fares with safe and reliable service. Curiously, airlines appeared more distinctive—even more interesting—to the public prior to deregulation than they do today. Few who flew PSA will soon forget airplanes painted with smiles under their noses or flight attendants wearing hot pink miniskirts and Jackie Kennedy–inspired pillbox hats. Braniff, Western, People's Express, and others seemed to possess actual personalities.

Even some of the larger carriers were able to differentiate themselves in the marketplace by creating a unique public image. Pan Am, for example, targeted its advertising around a vision of air travel as adventure. Their Clipper Class service, which harkened back to the days of amphibious aircraft, promised passengers the luxury formerly reserved exclusively for the wealthy. Not surprisingly, during the carrier's final days, employees openly wept for "the loss of the only airline devoted to keeping the romance of air flight alive." The number of successful carriers, the rapid advance in aircraft design, and the growing demand for air travel suggested to many that the industry was ripe for deregulation.

Some consolidation was expected, but this Darwinian winnowing would benefit only the fittest. Competition had made America great, and deregulation would make the airline industry great as well. Airlines would seize the opportunity provided by open competition to lower fares, improve service, and expand routes. To the contrary, deregulation has not helped make the domestic airline industry great. Rural markets have lost jet service, and attention to customer needs has been replaced by the concept of the flying bus.

Industry Culture: The Paramilitary Mind-Set

In hindsight, it should have been obvious that organizational and behavioral change would be difficult to achieve in an industry where inflexibility, restricted patterns of communication, risk aversion, and uncomplaining conformance were highly prized traits. It should have been obvious, but it wasn't. These rigid corporate cultures have resisted much needed change and will continue to undermine the likelihood of consistent profitability in a deregulated market. This characterizes the frozen culture, according to the hierarchy of corporate cultures discussed in Chapter 5. Additional bankruptcies, predatory mergers, and a rising tide of red ink will continue for some years as consumer irritation grows.

Pre-deregulation airlines were dominated by managers and pilots with previous military service, and they drew on this military experience to guide them as they constructed organizations designed almost exclusively to provide safe and reliable air travel. These hierarchies were paramilitary in structure, personnel, and operating style. Like the military, airline management created multiple layers of supervision. It was not uncommon, for example, to find twelve levels of management with each layer having just a handful of direct reports and well-defined spans of control. Bureaucracy was the order of the day. This structure created a caste culture that instinctively blocked both innovation and the introduction of necessary cost efficiencies.

This top-down management style reflected a faith in control, authority, and procedure. Former astronaut and military officer Frank Borman best exemplified this martial approach to managing when he was CEO of Eastern Airlines. Orders were given, and immediate compliance was expected. Employees soon learned that suggestions were not desired, individual initiative would be punished, and obedience was always the order of the day. This resulted in an exaggerated internal focus. Without significant external competition, airlines became excessively focused on internal issues over information access, resources, and power. As long as the planes flew safely, attention was rarely paid to customers or other carriers.

Management created work environments intolerant of innovation, risk taking, and feedback. Rules and procedures governing employee conduct were exhaustively defined and strictly enforced. Safety performance was viewed as the natural product of a highly compliant, closely supervised, and risk-averse culture. Consequently, with the exception of stewardesses, who were viewed more as decoration than contributors to financial success, an employee's value to the organization grew only through longevity. Seniority was rewarded and, in many ways, defined an individual's stature in the company. Thus, respect for and unquestioning loyalty to management, rather than personal initiative, were recognized and rewarded. The corporate culture differed little from that observed in the civil service.

These characteristics contributed to an often hostile relationship between management and labor. Communications were poor and tended to focus on the basics of working conditions, pay, and benefits. In keeping with the paramilitary mind-set, management operated from a philosophy that labor was merely a commodity that could be readily replaced when it objected to established procedures. This attitude thinly disguised a prevalent disdain for working men and women best exemplified by Frank Lorenzo's open hostility for workers at Continental. Carl Icahn had little understanding of the industry when he purchased TWA, and he subsequently used the airline essentially as a financial asset to be sold off piece by piece. This chasm between management and its workforce eventually proved to be a substantial barrier when airlines attempted to reduce costs, improve efficiency, and maintain profitability.

Given these dynamics, is it any wonder that most airlines were poorly positioned to grapple successfully with the challenges and opportunities presented by deregulation? Freedom, it turned out, could be a terribly overwhelming challenge for those who were new to it—particularly those who resisted it. The key to success for any organization entering a competitive environment is behavior change. Indeed, if a company is to perform differently, its people must behave differently—both its managers and its nonmanagement employees. Open communications, a focus on customer needs, the willingness to bend rules and to do "whatever it takes," performance feedback, and easy access to executive decision makers are necessary ingredients to success. Airlines had few, if any, of these attributes when their newly deregulated world dawned.

Ideas originated at the top, but only after months, even years, of review and comment. Employees rarely had the opportunity to generate ideas and pass them up the line. These barriers alone, would have prevented any company from succeeding in an environment where creativity, speed of decision making, and customer focus were essential to success.

INDUSTRY RESPONSES TO DEREGULATION

In the minds of many, the airline industry swiftly transformed an opportunity into a widespread calamity—for themselves, their employees, and the flying public—in the decade that followed deregulation. Permitted to operate on a wider playing field, with greater potential rewards, carriers soon discovered that economic failure was the dark side of deregulation. By 1990, virtually every airline was losing money on a historical scale. Unfortunately, executive management acted in ways that tended to alienate rather than attract airline employees and the flying public.

Aggressive cost cutting programs were launched throughout the industry. Downsizing—via furloughs, layoffs, early retirement incentives, and restructuring—eliminated millions of dollars in overhead. Smaller communities watched their service diminish as low traffic and marginally profitable routes were quickly eliminated. Support services were consolidated into larger centers, and technology was used to improve the productivity of backroom functions. In some cases, these functions were transferred to competitors or independent service bureaus. Inflight meals were reduced in size and quality. Where union rules permitted, airlines froze pay, reduced crews, and increased workloads. This attempt to "save our way to profitability," as many employees sarcastically described these cost-cutting strategies, produced a few positive and just as many negative effects on service and bottom-line performance.

Congestion at ticket counters and gates has increased as fewer agents handle larger traffic volumes. Reservations queues require longer waits, and a single booking may take as long as thirty minutes while agents examine the myriad options available among literally hundreds of competing tariffs. Despite their fear of biting the hand that feeds them, the American Society of Travel Agents has grumbled about the "irrationality" of fare structures "which cry out for reform." Customer service has been reduced to a first-come, first-served process that discriminates against connecting and business passengers.

Hubbing also began to dominate the industry following deregulation. Carriers established a series of "hub and spoke" connections modeled on the Atlanta operations of Delta airlines. This concept grew rapidly, and soon there were competing hubs scattered across the country. Hubs generally offered operational economies in terms of efficient use of personnel and equipment. Workloads could be flattened, and the mere presence of the hub allowed a carrier to increase its local market share by as much as 10 to 20 percent. The favorable economics of hub operations were largely dependent on an airline's success in capturing origin and destination traffic between a hub and its spokes. This traffic would prove vulnerable to point-to-point competitors like Southwest Airlines. Over time the geographic centrality of a hub has become a major criterion for its success.

Another response to deregulation, and one that was predicted by industry analysts, was *expansion via acquisition and merger*. Notable examples include Continental's purchase of Frontier, New York Air, and People's Express, American Airlines' acquisition of AirCal, and USAir's takeover of Pacific Southwest and Piedmont.

This "buy your markets" approach to expansion, a trend that was prevalent throughout other segments of the economy during the 1980s, has yet to prove successful for airlines and has led to more than one spectacular collapse. The consolidations that failed can be traced to differing underlying miscalculations, but all were characterized by a poorly developed corporate strategy.

Pan Am's acquisition of National Airlines as a hub feeder to its international gateways sounded like a good idea and has since worked for others, but Pan Am never really seemed to know what it needed or wanted from its junior partner, and both partners withered. This mismatch was excused by Pan Am as a poor fit. In reality, it was a classic case of poorly executed strategy, inattention to new culture and mission requirements, and incremental decision making by management. For Pan Am, it resulted in total change and failure, as reflected on the Business Change Cycle. USAir's purchase of Piedmont and PSA involved the integration of widely divergent cultures. USAir extinguished the maverick qualities that had attracted customer loyalty at Piedmont and PSA, reaping little long-term benefit from the acquisitions. Today, US-Air's culture deficits continue to hold back the airline's performance as the company perpetually struggles with fundamental change. Delta's decision to purchase Pan Am's European routes proved another serious mistake. It paid too much for them and had little understanding of how to operate them, and their profits suffered catastrophically as a consequence. Braniff's international expansion eventually doomed this popular carrier to the bankruptcy courts and oblivion.

Several of the upstart deregulated carriers also badly mishandled expansion in the 1980s. Midway Airlines' decision to expand to Philadelphia, outside their Midwest base, was premised on the expectation that Eastern Airlines would soon collapse. Instead, Midway found itself lured into a crippling fare war, while also attempting to reconfigure their aircraft with the addition of first-class seating. This created a substantial drain on capital that pushed Midway into bankruptcy. People's Express decided to go toe-to-toe with American, United, and Eastern without possessing a fully developed marketing structure or adequate slots for their planes at critical airports. The major air carriers struck back with frequent flier initiatives and the full array of discounted seven-, fourteen-, and twenty-one-day advance fares. These innovations virtually neutralized People's price advantage and changed the face of air travel for the public.

Frequent flier programs, initially started by American Airlines, were a genuinely brilliant premium for regular air travelers. The marginal cost to carriers was negligible, as little as $17 for a round-trip ticket, while the value to customers is high. Polls show that frequent flier miles are second only to cash as currency in the underground economy. And they take some of the sting out of canceled flights, weather delays, Saturday night layovers, and mis-routed luggage. With so many flyers cashing in on frequent flier miles today, airlines are taking a second look at how to manage the program.

WHAT IS GOOD SERVICE?

Service is defined very differently by the airlines and their customers, perhaps a unique divergence for a service industry. The industry continues to measure its performance by on-time arrivals and departures, together with the accuracy of baggage handling. Safety, of course, remains a central value. But customers take these measures for granted, as a baseline expectation. They remain far more interested in the "quality of their total experience with the airline," from contact with reservations, through check-in, to the demeanor of flight attendants. And what they've learned to expect is some kind of a problem, which helps explain the high volume of carry-on luggage.

The customer-service issue is critical and isolates a serious flaw in the strategies of most domestic airlines. *What airline executives think customers want is, more often than not, different from what customers say they want.* Truly competitive organizations in other industries don't make this mistake. They recognize that customers are their lifeblood and then work feverishly with their employees to meet or exceed customer expectations. Research tells us that air travelers prefer different things on different kinds of flights. For a short haul (one hour or less), the primary concern is price. As the length of a trip extends, issues like amenities and leg room begin to take precedence.

This type of analysis has been receiving increasing attention and has created a successful market niche for Southwest Airlines. Southwest is fundamentally a short-haul, point-to-point carrier with exceptional on-time performance. Frills have been cut in favor of warmth and enthusiasm exhibited by its employees. With its pilot- and fuel-efficient fleet of Boeing 737s, limited backroom functions, low fares, Orca- and Lone Star-painted planes, and friendly, informal personnel, who are likely to joke on the intercom with passengers, Southwest has sent a shock wave through the industry. Indeed, it can be argued that Southwest is what deregulation was meant to be all about. Better yet, its bottom-line performance has been consistently profitable. Many recent Southwest Air passengers also note that the inflight atmosphere is one of a casual social gathering, as opposed to the sterile, slightly stifled feel of other airlines.

Globalization of the Industry

Like so many other industries, U.S. airlines are quickly evolving into global players. American, United, and Delta now fly to dozens of cities in Europe, South America, and Asia, and Northwest is expanding its service to other Pacific rim cities. Penetrating these overseas markets is just the first step as competition with state-owned airlines on their own turf is already proving to be a challenge. Typically, the state-owned airlines are well financed and able to provide superior service to their flyers given their subsidized status. Still, U.S. travelers bound for overseas destinations now have a greater selection of airlines from which to choose.

As is typical with market globalization, the wind blows in both directions, as more foreign carriers now are flying to U.S. cities.

To ensure their access to the U.S. market, foreign airlines are investing in U.S. carriers, as seen by British Air's half billion dollar stake in USAir and KLM Dutch Airlines' investment in Northwest. In addition, alliances have been formed between American and Canadian International Airlines, Continental and Air Canada, and United and Lufthansa to name just a few. These alliances and investments may not make the skies any friendlier but may increase the competition—on a global scale.

Two Ships Passing in the Night: American and United

Until 1991, United Airlines was the undisputed leader of the domestic airline industry, with 22 percent of the market to American's 16 percent share. In 1992, American surpassed United (United is now trying to make a comeback). American's emergence was no accident: it invested heavily in customer service and training, ancillary services, and the Sabre system. The Sabre system, created under Max Hopper's direction, is American's central reservation system, which has become a model for the industry. Over 55 percent of all flight reservations nationwide are made through Sabre.

American's investment in ancillary services was a bold stroke that would not have occurred in the regulated environment. CEO Bob Crandall saw the need to diversify services into *fixed-base operations* such as plane cleaning and airport services, which created an additional revenue stream for the parent company, AMR, through lower-wage, nonunion services needed by smaller regional carriers. In an industry known for tough management, Crandall, along with Frank Lorenzo at Continental, helped to set a new standard for toughness. The similarity between the two ended there. Unlike other industry leaders, Crandall has been adept at anticipating change for American and at keeping pace with customer demand for service reliability, when others have cut back. Crandall provided an environment that supported superior performance and held people accountable. Lorenzo's "strategy" was to simply squeeze the airline for more revenue: it squeezed

Eastern out of existence and forced Continental to function as a cut-rate carrier.

United's "Fly the Friendly Skies" advertisement became more a slogan than a reality. Its decline may date back to 1984 with a highly publicized confrontation between labor and management. The carrier has also been limited by its fleet. After deregulation, United moved to broaden its route structure overseas—despite an aging fleet with few planes that could accommodate transocean routes. Standards for performance slipped, debt grew, and labor-management conflict continued. Customer service became a serious problem.

Employee Ownership

Employee ownership, on the surface, appears to be an attractive way to enhance a company's business performance. Greater commitment and productivity, coupled with less waste, are anticipated outcomes of the transfer of company ownership to employees. Indeed, many organizations perform well in competitive environments after becoming employee-owned.

The key to success in an employee-owned business is whether the organization's new owners can think and act like owners. Can they strategize and implement programs and processes to outperform the competition? Can they forget the past and work together to improve performance? Will they make the hard decisions—especially those regarding employees—often required of management?

These and other challenges await United's new owners. Despite compelling advertising, can the same people who were out to break the company just ten years ago work together to make United a top performer today? Can their new owners forge a cooperative relationship with organized employees? Can they service the debt they have bought? Or will they fail like People's Express?

TWA faces an even steeper, uphill battle. While in bankruptcy, they have realigned their cost structure and reengineered their organization. Their debt load, however, is substantial, and they have yet to go toe-to-toe with low-fare airlines. They have also lost their tradition of good customer service once seen in their overseas routes. They appear to have made significant short-term changes, but will they be able to sustain this over the long term? TWA seems to be stuck at a level of change requiring total change management. Nevertheless, TWA's issues are surmountable and will hinge directly on the strength of its management and the cooperation of employees during the next few years.

THE WORKFORCE OF THE FUTURE

Airlines that continue to cling to their paramilitary operational style are in for the fight of their lives. Deregulation has forced their hands: *performance gains will be made by people*. Technology will play a role, but customer contact with employees will play a greater role in determining the fate of their airlines. The jury remains out on employee-ownership experiments like the United Airlines buyout. It won't be easy to shrug off decades of risk-aversive culture. One of the authors was recently informed by a United agent that his flight was delayed because of bad weather in Denver, a traditional and convenient excuse during winter months. A phone call proved this excuse false, and a few more questions revealed that the incoming crew had been scheduled on a canceled flight from Chicago, creating the delay. Such disingenuousness breeds customer contempt rather than affection for a carrier.

Successful managers will have to establish a collaborative relationship with their nonmanagement customer-service employees. Improved credibility with customers and employees is essential. The caste systems of old must be discarded in favor of team building and worker empowerment. Operational flexibility and speed of action and decision will be critical to success. In order to differentiate themselves from the competition, the successful airline will need to maintain a constant dialogue with its employees and its customers. This will be especially crucial as air travel becomes increasingly global in structure. Employees will need to establish a unique identity for their airline, one that will be attractive to their target markets. They will need to focus on beating the competition by manifesting an urgency about exceeding their customers needs—as compared to simply meeting them. Every employee will have to believe that his or her personal performance can make a significant contribution to corporate success. This attitude need not exist only in the employee-owned companies like United and TWA, which have just as much reforming to do as the others. This kind of airline will look and feel different both to employees and their passengers.

THE FUTURE OF THE INDUSTRY

In the short term it appears that a mix of hub-oriented and point-to-point carriers will share the American market. For one thing, airlines with significant capital investments in their hubs can't walk away from them. But they will need to vigilantly guard against a loss of traffic to their point-to-point competitors. One emerging strategy is evidenced by the development of Continental Lite and United's Shuttle service. It isn't clear at this point whether this tactic of building an airline within an airline can work, but it demonstrates a newfound initiative within the industry.

Other carriers are diversifying into nonflight subsidiaries like computer services and consulting. American Airlines' Sabre system has been a significant money-making component in the company. These subsidiaries, in turn, are selling services back to the parent as well as to its competitors. Serious consideration is also being given to "unbundling" airlines and contracting out traditional in-house services like aircraft maintenance and passenger reservations. Such strategies obviously carry profound implications for existing corporate cultures. Carriers also are facing up to the slow growth characteristic of a mature industry.

U.S. enplanements stabilized around 470 million in 1987. Although the market can be stimulated by unusual fare reductions like the 1992 American–Northwest fare war, it has tended to return to a steady state once the cheap fares are discontinued. This maturation of the market was obscured by a recession, and airlines continued to order aircraft in hopes of a return to historic growth rates of 5 to 6 percent. Throughout all this turmoil, however, the Big Three carriers—United, American, and Delta—have increased their marketshare from 51 to 58 percent. A significant portion of this increase has occurred in international markets, where these airlines hold a cost advantage over their competitors.

Looming on the horizon is the possibility of a marketplace revolt by *Fortune* 500 companies, which purchase $26 billion dollars a year in travel services from U.S. airlines. Many of these companies are beginning to argue that airlines are subsidizing occasional and vacation travelers out of fares paid by corporate travel departments. Much as the telephone companies long subsidized local service from business account revenues, deregulated airlines have offered discounts to seniors, students, and the leisure travelers while the business traveler often pays premium fares. This customer dissatisfaction has coalesced into the Business Travel Contractors Corporation (BTCC) led by Kevin Mitchell, a former vice-president at CIGNA who managed the insurance company's $30 million travel budget.

With $3 billion a year in purchasing power, BTCC is demanding an overhaul of the entire pricing structure for business travel. It has approached the Federal Trade Commission for authority to negotiate standard unified fares directly with carriers in 1995. BTCC advocates an end to frequent flier programs, travel agent overrides (bonus commissions for steering business), and fares based on the number of miles traveled. These proposals won't be popular with business fliers, but they may prove popular at the home office. It does mean that the airline industry will remain in a state of flux and change into the foreseeable future.

All of this adds up to an industry experiencing widespread fundamental change when measured against the Business Change Cycle (see Figure 7.3). Missions have been long outdated, and company cultures have been sacrificed to cost-cutting and effi-

Figure 7.3
Change in the Airline Industry

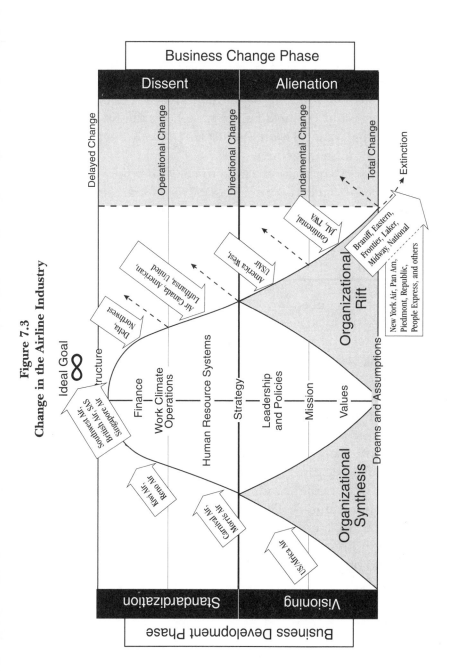

ciency improvements. No air carrier has been spared from declining worker dissatisfaction and commitment, excessive management turnover, and internal battling. The executive suite is no longer a comfortable place to reside as the results of failed leadership practices continue to haunt the industry. For many carriers, total change and business failure have been the final solution—through open competition but just as surely through short sightedness and mismanagement.

Today's survivors have no time to celebrate, since they quickly could become tomorrow's next loser. Traditional remedies of cost cutting, reliance on technology, and continued consolidation have been taken to their limit. Neither should the recent return to profitability by some of the industry's carriers be interpreted as a justification for those short-term tactics. For now, the improved economy is the rising tide that lifts all ships.

Air carriers need to better manage change—*to change themselves*—their leadership practices, cultures, missions, and strategies (see Table 7.1). Innovation and more open communications must become ingrained in the business. A new set of core capabilities for managers and executives must be created and operationalized. Turning responsibility over to a union has to be more than transferring debt. The union-owned carriers, as rigid bureaucratic organizations themselves, must be prepared to examine and change their cultures to serve the flyer just as the others must. Technology gains are becoming more incremental, and globalization of the industry will create new challenges as well as new opportunities. The airline industry can no longer take fifteen years to figure out how to deal with the last change cycle. It must begin preparing for the next wave of change now if it is to stay ahead of the change curve.

Table 7.1
**Required Change Strategies for
the Airline Industry**

Criteria	Objective
Mission or vision	Clearly defined around alternative standards for performance, behaviors, unique identity and values; requires broad organization input and buy-in
Corporate strategy	Clearly defined strategy and commitment as low-cost producer, differentiator, or niche competitor
Route structure	Hub or route strength or dominance with alliance synergies
Cost structure	Fundamentally low or reengineered cost position relative to current or future competition
Customer service	Realized performance standards to reflect customer needs and desires, not industry desires
Leadership qualities	Less authoritarian or dictatorial promoting more risk taking and open communications among management
Culture	More innovative, open, and cooperative; less internal battling and segmentation between professional groups, union and management; rewards for performance to organization
Organization structure	Flatter promoting more bottom up communications and cross-functional cooperation
Labor-Employee relations	Positive labor relations; wage, benefit, and work-rule provisions that support competitive cost structure
Information systems	Strong management information systems to support decision making such as computer reservations and field management systems

Nicholas J. Radell

Nicholas Radell is a vice president in Mercer Management Consulting's transportation practice, where he directs the firm's international aviation practice. In his thirty-eight-year career, Mr. Radell has advised the leaders of numerous airlines around the globe on such issues as organization planning and developing, management evaluation, strategy implementation, and operations. Prior to joining Mercer Management Consulting, Mr. Radell was a director of Towers Perrin & Company. He also managed the central region transportation and manufacturing practices for Cressap McCormack and Paget, the general consulting division of Towers Perrin. Mr. Radell earned his M.B.A. from the University of Michigan.

Alan E. Schnur

Since coauthoring this chapter, Alan Schnur became the senior vice president of human resources for the Robert Mondavi Winery. During his consulting career, he consulted to a number of airlines, including Continental, American, Cathay Pacific, and Air Alaska on issues related to culture change, organization planning, and leadership development. Previously, Dr. Schnur was a principal with Towers Perrin & Company, and he was a manager and consultant with the Hay Group. He earned both his master's and doctorate degrees in psychology from the University of California, Berkeley.

James G. Purvis

James Purvis is senior vice president of human resources for Westin Hotels International, where he is responsible for all worldwide human resource services. Previously, he served in a similar capacity with ALCOA, and he was vice president of human resources for Eastern Airlines. He graduated from the University of Notre Dame and holds an advanced certificate in languages from the University of Insbruck.

The Information-Technology Industry: A Revolution in Progress

LAWRENCE J. BOLICK
Vice President, Cambridge Technology Partners

ROUJA BRZOZOWSKI
President, Arbicon Consulting

THE CONSTANT RESTRUCTURING OF AN INDUSTRY

In a period that will be known for its radical change, information has become the primary raw material of the age, driving commerce and industry much as coal and iron ore drove the industrial economies of the nineteenth and early twentieth centuries. Increasingly, key industries depend on the rapid availability and use of information. Securities firms rely on market data feeds, the modern analogs of the stock ticker, to provide a window into financial activities taking place around the world. Grocery stores shape their inventory and speed checkout lines by relying on bar code readers to identify and price shoppers' purchases. Manufacturers closely manage inventories of raw material and finished goods by analyzing information from their distribution channels and manufacturing lines. Airlines rely on information from customer bookings to efficiently design their route systems and schedules. These and other industries have adopted computer and telecommunications technologies and services to facilitate their information-dependent activities.

The introduction of this information technology became an avalanche of activity over the last three decades, as entire industries sought the efficiency and competitive advantages promised by these technologies.

The impact on providers of information technology was no less dramatic. Companies once viewed as the bedrock of the American economy, such as AT&T and IBM, found themselves struggling to define their roles in this new world. Others, such as Sun Microsystems and Williams Telecommunications, sought to identify and attack nontraditional markets. Some, like Wang and Rolm, found themselves increasingly disconnected from a radically changing market and were incapable of making the transition to this brave new world of evolving technology and business change.

The Business Change Cycle captures the essence of the changes affecting the industry. From the evolution of new companies with new age visions like Microsoft and Cambridge Technology Partners, to older companies like DEC and IBM, as well as telephone companies like NYNEX and AT&T, corporations throughout the economy found themselves facing fundamental and, at times, total change.

CONVERGING INDUSTRIES AROUND CONVERGING TECHNOLOGIES

The demand for manipulating, storing, moving, and analyzing information during the last few decades has fueled dramatic growth among the suppliers of equipment and services that provide tools for information management. As indicated in Table 8.1, this information-technology industry can be viewed as the convergence of three previously distinct industries: computers, telecommunications, and information services.

Table 8.1
Information-Technology Industry

Information Providers

- Dow Jones
- Dun & Bradstreet
- McGraw-Hill
- Reuters
- Others

Systems Integrators

- Arthur Andersen
- Cambridge Technology Partners
- Cap Gemini Sogetti
- Electronic Data Systems
- SHL Systemhouse
- Others

Telecommunications Providers

Services	Software
• AT&T	• BellCore
• British Telecom	• IBM
• Comsat	• Novell
• France Telecom	• Retix
• Intelsat	• Others
• McCaw	
• MCI	*Hardware*
• Metro Fiber Systems	• AT&T
• NTT	• Codex
• NYNEX	• Hayes
• Wiltel	• Northern Telecom
• Others	• Others

Computer Providers

Services	Software
• ADP	• Adobe
• Arbicon	• Aldus
• EDS	• Lotus
• MicroAge	• Microsoft
• Motorola	• Oracle
• Others	• Profiles in Data
Hardware	
• Apple	• AST
• Compaq	• Cray
• DEC	• Dell
• Fujitsu	• Groupe Bull
• IBM	• Silicon Graphics
• Others	

Component Providers

• Alcatel	• Ericsson	• Motorola	• Siemens
• AT&T	• IBM	• National Semiconductor	• Toshiba
• DEC	• Intel	• NEC	• Others

Each of these industries has a unique history, but the need for their customers to better manage information has driven them toward a common destiny. For example, modern telecommunications equipment is often controlled by computers. Modern computer equipment and services depend on telecommunications that tie together geographically separate systems. And, finally, the services of information providers such as Reuters, which supplies news and financial data to customers worldwide, rest on complex foundations of information technology. We have computerized

and networked our society—from automatic teller machines
(ATMs) to computerized automobiles—and our increasing reliance on information technology, in turn, has helped shape the
industry that created it.

The information-technology industry exhibits many of the ever-
shifting characteristics captured by the Business Change Cycle
(see Figure 8.1). When first commercialized, many of the products
and services now regarded as staples of the industry encountered
limited success. In the 1880s, few individuals recognized the potential of a new device known as the telephone. In the late 1940s,
Thomas Watson, Sr., the visionary leader who shaped a conglom-
eration of business machine companies into the company we
know today as IBM, commissioned a study to size the market for
IBM's early computer products. The result: a projected market of
only seventeen computers in the United States. Decades later, Bill
Hewlett, one of the founders of Hewlett-Packard, sought to build a
product never before manufactured—the hand-held calculator—
only to be told that no market existed. Today, of course, tens of
millions of these devices are in use daily.

How has the information-technology industry changed as a
result? As the capabilities of these and other information technologies become more widely understood, a vision developed for
their use while suppliers developed organizations with the mission
and wherewithal to fulfill the vision. Today, the industry is undergoing even faster change. Formerly, these industries were linked
but not truly interdependent. They had separate and individualized business objectives and strategies to attain them. For example, telephone companies traditionally planned for thirty-year life
cycles, seeking to move forward via laborious development of
consensus along a broad corporate front—regulatory, marketing,
engineering, financial, and so on. Computer and electronics companies moved much more quickly, seeking to gain initial advantage in a market and then translate that early advantage into a
dominant market share.

As these industries continue to converge into the information-
technology industry, the traditional rules have begun to change.

Figure 8.1

Change in the Information-Technology Sector

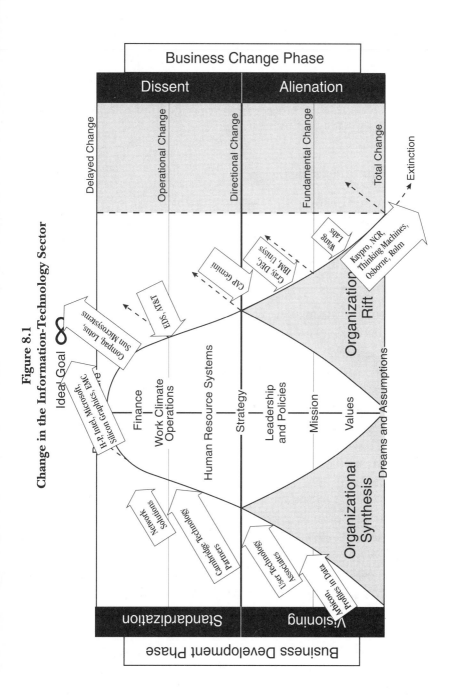

165

Being first to market no longer leads to dominant market share, as Motorola discovered when its 68000-series microprocessors had to compete with Intel's 8080-series microprocessors. Nor will telephone companies enjoy the luxury of thirty-year planning cycles, as evidenced by the explosive growth of cellular telephony since its inception in the mid-1970s.

The Computer Industry

The electronic computer, as we know it today, was born during World War II as engineers sought more accurate and efficient means of plotting shell trajectories and other battlefield conditions. The Electronic Numerical Integrator and Computer (ENIAC) was one of these efforts. Developed at the University of Pennsylvania, ENIAC served as the wellspring for a host of subsequent innovations—as well as corporations. From its infancy, the industry's development has been based on radical change.

Large computers, known as *mainframes*, emerged from the technological success of ENIAC. Companies with roots in office and consumer products sought to design and market their own mainframes. By 1965, one supplier of business equipment—IBM—had captured nearly two-thirds of the market. The business vision behind IBM's success included a salesforce knowledgeable about the business environment in which their computers would operate and capable of acting as consultants as well as salespeople. IBM products became the de facto standard in the data processing industry. The choice of conforming to IBM's direction or risking further loss of market share discouraged many early competitors, who merged or sold their computer operations.

Dissenters were lurking in the industry, however. The mainframe computer served the needs of corporate functions like accounting but were generally too expensive and too difficult to program to serve the needs of engineers and scientists. In 1957, a young visionary named Ken Olson formed a company to address this need. Digital Equipment Corporation (DEC) and the *minicomputer* industry were born, and DEC went on to impose its own technology as a de facto standard on this new segment of the industry.

Today, of course, IBM and DEC are both grappling with even more change. IBM, lulled into complacency by decades of fat profit margins on its mainframe computers, began to ignore customer needs by substituting its own solutions for those of the customer. The customers, on the other hand, increasingly viewed the mainframe as an expensive anachronism in the emerging world of personal computers (PCs). Encumbered by an "old think" culture, IBM failed to react with a coherent strategy that could cope with the radical change that was overtaking IBM and saw its revenues fall and losses mount, resulting in a new chairman and wholesale replacement of its senior executive staff. In the context of the Business Change Cycle, IBM was undergoing fundamental change. Managers found themselves striving to redefine the company's culture and mission to recapture the creativity and flexibility that had enabled it once to solve customers' most difficult technology problems—a characteristic that enabled the company to dominate the computer industry in the first place. Later in this chapter, the IBM case study details some of the company's failings that led to its recent struggles.

DEC is undergoing a similar but, in some ways, even more severe transformation. Stung by substantial losses a few years after posting record earnings, DEC said good-bye to its founder, Ken Olson, and sought to transition its revenue streams from the profitable but aging VAX line of minicomputers to the new Alpha microprocessor. A successful transition depended heavily on two assumptions that were beyond DEC's control: (1) the rapid market acceptance of Microsoft's new Windows NT operating system software, which would run on the Alpha products, and (2) the availability of application programs to run on the Alpha machines from non-DEC software development companies. Both proved slow to develop, leaving DEC customers with aging computers, high maintenance costs, and plenty of alternatives available from DEC competitors. Consequently, DEC is now a company struggling with fundamental change—no longer sure of its mission, products, or how to satisfy customer needs. Productivity per employee lags behind even IBM. Customers have difficulty ascertaining the advantages DEC brings to their businesses. To survive, DEC will be forced to become a very different company—smaller, more targeted at individual markets, and infused with a culture much more entrepreneurially focused.

At the same time that IBM and DEC are struggling, competitors such as Hewlett-Packard and Compaq have emerged from their shadow. In recent years, entrepreneurial thinking at both companies has led to a string of notable successes—in Hewlett-Packard's case, the explosive growth of its laser printer business and strategy, together with a successful gamble on retooling its product line, using relatively unproved reduced instruction set computing (RISC) technology. Compaq has updated its products around a new mission to dominate the PC market. They have successfully accomplished this with lower-priced products, improved distribution channels, significantly lower overhead, and a reenergized culture. However, only a few years ago, both companies were experiencing a period of profound directional change: strategies were not working and needed redirection.

Want's culture cycle of *visioning, standardization, dissent,* and *alienation,* as evidenced in the Business Change Cycle, has become a hallmark of the computer industry as new technologies, markets, and competitors continue to emerge. The advent of the personal computer and its simpler technology in the early 1980s sparked an explosion in the number of companies designing, manufacturing, and selling their own computer designs. Only two of these designs emerged to set the standards for the personal computer: IBM-compatible PCs and the Apple Macintosh. Well-recognized names in the personal computer industry, such as Altair, Kaypro, Franklin, and Osborne, have disappeared. Now we are seeing the emergence of the Power PC as an attempt to break the Intel-Microsoft stronghold on the marketplace. Trends and emerging changes building in the gigantic consumer electronics marketplace, such as the shift to digital video and related software, will shape the future of the computer industry into the next century.

In the early 1980s, a group of electrical engineers unhappy with their work environment left a company known as Shockley Semiconductor Laboratories to start a new firm named Fairchild Semiconductor. Fairchild became the progenitor of numerous successful Silicon Valley firms, including Intel Corporation, the world's leading manufacturer of microprocessors. Shockley's loss became Intel's gain. Change and dissent, however it is generated, can promote the vitality of an entire industry—and of individual companies—when it is properly channeled.

The Telecommunications Industry

While its history predates the information-technology industry, telecommunications has become inextricably linked to the transfer of information. After Alexander Graham Bell, the two most influential players in the industry have been Bill McGowan, the visionary founder of MCI, and Uncle Sam. The latter has played a significant role through a century of industry regulation, first sanctioning and overseeing the largest monopoly in history and then breaking it up. The industry's slow development and avoidance of risk and innovation—mainstays of the information-technology sector—can be directly attributed to the regulatory climate it grew up in. McGowan, more than anyone else, was responsible for breaking the AT&T monopoly, while setting a new standard for innovation and visionary leadership that was more typical of leaders in the information-technology sector than were his counterparts in telecommunications.

Where it once utilized electronics, today the telecommunications industry is increasingly driven by microprocessors, software, and computers—the guts of information technology. As it shares more of the same technology that is being used in information-technology and media industries, it moves closer to merging business interests around that shared technology. Sprint has merged with three cable companies to provide one-stop shopping for telecommunications, home entertainment, and information transference. MCI is positioning itself to be a pipeline for conveying information between business customers. The cellular sector has taken off only since the refinement of microprocessors, and now all of the regional Bell companies and AT&T have purchased cellular companies. Telephone companies are positioning themselves to be the pipeline for *all* information and data regardless of its content or form. Eventually, wired telephones will be replaced by cellular and digital technology.

Still, there are challenges and pitfalls as telephone companies move toward mergers and joint ventures with information-technology and media companies. There could be clashes around differing cultures and leadership styles as already seen between Bell Atlantic and TCI, with their ill-fated merger plans. As existing companies merge around technology, their successor companies will be required to rethink their positions on the Business Change Cycle, while building entirely new cultures and standards for performance.

The Information-Services Industry

Companies that collect, analyze, and distribute information—information-service providers—have emerged in a variety of industries. Dun & Bradstreet and McGraw-Hill market information to a diverse array of businesses. Their modus operandi: collect data from a variety of sources, organize the data into massive computerized volumes known as *databases*, slice the databases in various ways to suit the needs of various types of customers, and distribute the information in convenient ways. D&B customers, for example, can retrieve credit ratings of individuals and businesses from its databases in paper format, in electronic format, or by touchpad telephone. Reuters, on the other hand, has its roots in the news and telegraph industry. Julius Reuters established one of the first international telegraphic newswires in the mid-1800s, when he interconnected incompatible telephone networks in Europe by using carrier pigeons. In the 1960s, Reuters recognized that its network could be used to distribute information other than news and began disseminating price quotes on U.S. securities for European customers. Today, 90 percent of Reuters's revenue is generated from the delivery of financial information.

The Dow Jones Company, publisher of the *Wall Street Journal*, has also recognized the trend toward computers and telecommunications technologies for the collection, processing, and delivery of information. Dow supplemented the *Journal*, which peaked in terms of circulation in the late 1980s, with an electronic data delivery service known as DowVision. This service provides customers with electronic access to information and computer programs operating at Dow Jones's computer center—all in a package customized to the user's needs.

Information-service providers have emerged across a broad range of industries, including banking, advertising, manufacturing, construction, and transportation. The common thread is a growing reliance on information technology to support the collection, analysis, and delivery of data while providing the flexibility to adapt to rapidly changing market conditions. *As the convergence of the computer, telecommunications, and information industries continues, increasing change will be inevitable, and the ability of organizations to adapt will become critical.*

Signs of increasing adaptability are already beginning to appear. In the face of a growing desire, customers conveniently interconnect computers purchased from multiple vendors. IBM, the once-dominant manufacturer, has apparently abandoned a decades-old philosophy of supporting interconnection only with other IBM products. It is now enhancing the capacity of its products to exist in multivendor environments. AT&T acquired NCR Corporation, a midsized computer manufacturer, in an attempt to grow its computer business—domestically and globally—more rapidly than would have been possible by relying solely on internal development.

As a consequence of these external changes buffeting the information-technology industry, information-services companies find themselves positioned at various and unfamiliar locations on the change cycle. Newspaper publishers find themselves struggling with directional change issues. Circulation in many geographic areas has peaked, and competition for advertising revenues is keen, forcing these companies to consider alternate distribution channels, such as broadcasting and electronic access. Video store chains find themselves in a period of operational change. As high-capacity networks (conceptualized as the information superhighway) become more widely available, video information will be delivered directly to individuals' homes— eliminating, in large part, the need for the neighborhood video rental store. Nevertheless, the computer manufacturing sector has undergone the most painful change, as witnessed at Wang, UNYSIS, DEC, and most especially IBM.

IBM AND THE CHANGE CYCLE
A Case Study of Radical Change for the Industry Giant

Not so long ago, if you referred to the information-technology industry or to computers, you really were talking about IBM. Some would say that Big Blue became irrelevant as the industry grew exceedingly complex and diversified. Many ask whether the industry has actually passed IBM by. IBM is not the only hardware producer to stumble: the entire sector has had problems. Nevertheless, Big Blue's troubles have been the most visible because of its:

• Huge loss of marketshare and revenues, and

• Arrogance and refusal to anticipate changes that were transforming the industry.

Virtually every major computer manufacturer has experienced losses in recent years—Digital (DEC), Cray, Apple, Hewlett-Packard, and even Compaq. Compaq has made a spectacular turnaround, and time will tell whether Apple, DEC, and Cray can do the same. Even Dell has had its problems, despite its meteoric emergence in just a few years. Nevertheless, the big bets are now being wagered on whether IBM can save itself from becoming irrelevant.

Many people don't understand why hardware companies have encountered problems while the software side of the industry has prospered. Microsoft grows by leaps and bounds, while Lotus Development appears to have recovered the innovative magic that once made it the leader in its sector. Software development is an art. It is labor-intensive, intellectually complicated, creative, and proprietary. In essence, software cannot be reproduced or modified easily, and it is copyrighted. It is copyrighted because it is easily duplicated. Computers, however, are easily cloned through reverse engineering, and IBM's products were the first to be cloned since they were once perceived as the Cadillac of the industry. Eventually, with more products on the market and in light of the growing dominance and importance of software to the industry, computers became a commodity. Software development and systems integration have become the sexy products. Consequently, profit margins at Big Blue began to plunge.

CORPORATE CULTURE AT IBM

When Jerry Want talks about the impact of business culture on long-term performance, IBM can serve as a laboratory. Certainly, being the biggest and the best for so long contributed to IBM's current problems—and its famous arrogance. Certain critical qualities were closely associated with IBM's culture, and it is those corporate qualities or characteristics that contributed to its recent failures:

* *Focus* For years, IBM has been internally focused. The universe of computers was centered at Armonk, New York,

(continued)

and IBM saw no need to develop an external focus. Big Blue controlled the industry; denial prevailed. When it finally became necessary to look beyond its own backyard, it found it couldn't. IBM lost the ability to focus on changing business conditions as it became nearsighted.

- *Decision making* Like many large, complex organizations, decision making was top-down and heavily influenced by internal politics. Dispersion of ideas, experimentation, and feedback at the local site was not encouraged or rewarded by the organization. Those with the most clout were more successful in getting their ideas an audience, and they were more likely to win support. Fact-based decision making was too often ignored, along with proactive thinking and action taking. "If it wasn't invented here, it doesn't exist" aptly applied to IBM management.

- *Rigid structure* IBM's rigid organizational structure was legendary. It was highly bureaucratic and centralized. Departments and functions were created like silos—ringed off from many other functions, inhibiting cross-functional communication, collaboration, and easy interaction. As a result, centralized governance was the rule—*reflecting the mainframe mentality.* The business was truly postured to be defensive and reactionary. Interestingly, IBM's PC business was originally created as a separate strategic business unit (SBU) in Boca Raton, but as it gained market share and importance, it was pulled under central IBM control. Innovation in the company structure to accommodate new ideas and market challenges was frowned on: "We're the best. We have done this for twenty years. Why change?"

When we apply Want's hierarchy of corporate culture, IBM exhibits the characteristics of three types of cultures: *political* (balkanized), *chaotic* (fragmented and unfocused), and *frozen* (grid-locked, engaged in denial). It was this characteristic of being frozen that contributed so significantly to IBM's decline.

In an eleventh-hour move, Akers and the board decided to break up IBM into a number of semi-autonomous SBUs, but the move proved too little, too late. Developing separate viable cultures requires a great deal of time, as well as systematic planning, if it is to succeed. IBM did not have time and already faced problems with a seriously fractured culture.

Clearly, we are looking at a corporation that is functioning at the fundamental change level on Want's Business Change Cycle (see Figure 8.1 on page 165). IBM's mission had failed—or more accurately, had been lost. Leadership failed as it lost its vision—its ability to foresee changing forces in the industry and to reposition the organization to respond to the changing forces. Smaller companies with fewer resources fail for the same reasons.

THE HOPE OF NEW LEADERSHIP AT IBM

All of this contributed to a culture of inertia, which is worse than arrogance in an intensely competitive climate. When Akers took command, he had several good ideas, and he could certainly see beyond the forest—but he couldn't see how to escape it. Only time will tell if Lou Gerstner can do any better.

Despite the initial concerns about him as an outsider unfamiliar with the business and its technology, this outside perspective may serve him and the company well, since IBM has traditionally been so insulated. Nevertheless, conventional turnaround management techniques will not suffice (and they didn't at RJR Nabisco—his last stop). A formidable salesforce and eye-popping new technologies made IBM

(continued)

great, but those qualities are no longer enough to ensure success. As other technologies have bypassed IBM's famous mainframes, alternative sales strategies of smaller competitors like AST and Dell (whose products are similar to IBM's) have neutralized IBM's army of sales professionals. Keep in mind that IBM was the first company to make millionaires out of its sales professionals. Now you can buy a Dell or AST computer out of a catalogue or over the telephone, and Compaq's computers will soon be available at WalMart. The IBM salesforce is still impressive, but the strategy—or its execution as Gerstner states it—may be obsolete.

CREATING BALANCE AND A SENSE OF DIRECTION AT BIG BLUE

During the past decade of market erosion and profit losses, the salesforce and management teams at IBM continued to be rewarded with high salaries and commissions. At the same time, operations and manufacturing remained somewhat overstuffed and gold-plated despite nearly 100,000 layoffs. Clearly, there has been an imbalance, and if Gerstner is to be successful in turning IBM around, he will have to restore a sense of balance and focus. To accomplish this, he has set in motion a surprisingly simple strategy that may be effective for IBM.

Gerstner plans to reinvent IBM into a more integrated information-systems company that will serve the marketplace with *hardware, software, systems-integration consulting,* and even *semiconductors*. It will become a one-stop supermarket for all its customers' needs. This may prove to be the proper course of action since there seem to be limits on the hardware business. It also means that its competitors will become more numerous and will be bumping up against Big Blue in all sectors of the industry. To accomplish this, Gerstner has noted that the culture must be remade: managers must start working with each other, and new ideas and new technologies must find a common arena for conceptual sharing and cross-pollination.

Defining a new strategy is relatively easy, and Gerstner aptly notes that execution is what is always hard to accomplish. Changing the culture may be even more difficult and will be crucial to the success of the strategy. Since IBM's culture has been gridlocked (frozen) for so long, changing it may be Gerstner's ultimate challenge. For now, he proposes no specifics on how he will accomplish this. Specifics are required if IBM is to return to sustained profitability and performance.

INDUSTRY DRIVERS

Four key drivers have and will continue to shape the information-technology industry: technological change, emerging markets, fierce competition, and governmental oversight.

Technological Change

Technological change raises the threat to well-established companies of being leapfrogged by younger competitors, much as the slide rule was rendered a relic by the hand-held calculator. Younger companies view technological change as presenting new opportunities—not challenges. The minicomputer posed a threat to the established idea of the mainframe computer (and thus to IBM), and the personal (desktop) computer now poses a threat to the minicomputer. Soon, portable computing devices may well threaten desktop computers. Indeed, this technological churning serves as the engine driving the entire industry—*nonstop radical change.*

Technology breakthroughs continue today. Personal computers are growing increasingly powerful and within a few years will be capable of recognizing their owners' voice and handwriting. The proposal by British scientists in the early 1960s to transmit information over strands of glass has blossomed into an industry of its own, with thousands of miles of this optical fiber crisscrossing America. The trend is continuing in the 1990s as optical fiber begins to extend from telecommunications networks to users' homes and offices. This ongoing change promotes the continued emergence of new information-technology products and creates opportunities for newly established companies to outmaneuver their more mature competitors. Sun Microsystems embraced the trend toward *open systems* early in its existence and designed compatible characteristics into its products. Sun's primary competitor at the time, Apollo Computer (the established market leader in 1983), needed to reengineer its products to meet the requirements of an open-system architecture, quickly losing its lead to Sun. By 1988, Apollo sold out to Hewlett-Packard.

Emerging Markets

Emerging market opportunities are being sighted by companies with an eye on the twenty-first century. Notebook computers that fit in a briefcase and recognize handwriting and voice instructions are likely to become an important market for computer manufacturers. Wireless communications, in the form of pocket-sized telephones and data communications products, will be another. Replacing the archaic public telephone networks in Eastern bloc nations offers another market opportunity.

The information-technology industry is also shaped by the needs of its customers, who are influenced by trends in their business environments. The emergence of the personal computer as an important business tool has led to the development of hundreds of software products that support business needs. These products range from word processors and spreadsheets to statistical analysis and mechanical design tools. Businesses are finding it necessary to integrate these established tools with mainframe-resident applications. This is creating the demand for improved open-system technologies. The search by businesses for efficiency and competitive advantage has also led them to increased reliance on influence over information-technology suppliers and their products. The globalization of industries and their constituent companies have driven information-technology companies to globalize in an effort to serve the needs of their customers. This broadens the talent base of their staffs. IBM and DEC, for example, operate sales and marketing organizations worldwide, but they also conduct significant research and development and manufacturing operations overseas.

Fierce Competition

Competition also exerts a strong influence on the industry. IBM blunted the early challenges of competitors like General Electric and Xerox in the mainframe computer market and effectively shaped that market in its own image. Today's march toward non-proprietary, open systems has forced IBM to play by rules other than its own for the first time. Competition in the information-technology industry will stiffen during the 1990s as entrepreneurial firms seeking to leverage new technologies in emerging markets find themselves clashing with the vested interests of older, established firms seeking to defend their market share.

Government Oversight

Government oversight also plays a role in shaping the future of the information-technology industry. The potential for government antitrust actions serves to maintain competition in the computer industry. Government oversight, it should be remembered, actually created the separation of long-distance carriers and local telephone companies seen in the U.S. telecommunications industry today. Prior to the divestiture of AT&T in 1984, New York Telephone and New England Telephone were subsidiaries of AT&T. Now, New York Telephone and New England Telephone are known as NYNEX. Today, some industry players are experiencing government scrutiny of their businesses. For example, Microsoft's dominance of important segments of the computer software industry has piqued the interest of government regulators in recent months. While they have confirmed predatory practices at Microsoft, regulators have stopped short of breaking it up, as some industry authorities have predicted.

OUTCOMES OF CHANGE

The challenges of the 1990s to the information-technology industry and its constituent companies are formidable, but the opportunities are equally impressive. Successful information-technology companies in the 1990s will share three keys to success: adaptability, ability to manage change, and the resources to deploy cutting-edge technology. And buffeted by the gales of change in the information-technology industry, all will find themselves confronting an unwelcome level of change on Want's Business Change Cycle. Most will find themselves challenged by the need for operational change. Others, such as newspaper publishers, likely will find themselves confronted by directional change issues where entire new strategies are required. Still others, such as telephone companies, are undergoing fundamental and, in some cases, total change.

Fortunately, innovative and visionary leadership models abound in the industry. Bill McGowan, a past chairman of MCI, led the company from its role as a Midwest supplier of private telephone lines to the second-largest long-distance carrier in the United States—generating much of the competitive and regulatory turmoil that shaped the industry in the 1980s. His tenacity and sense of regulatory possibilities in large measure restructured the telephone industry.

Bill Gates first heard of the availability of a microcomputer in kit form as a business school student in 1975. With his friend, Paul Allen, Gates wrote a programming language for the microcomputer that became known as Microsoft Basic. Gates runs the company (Microsoft) that grew from this initial product. He carried it to a position of undisputed leadership of the personal computer software market with a string of popular products shaped by a keen eye for industry trends and savvy business agreements.

Of course, not all leaders make the transition from entrepreneurs to corporate managers. Mitchell Kapor, visionary cofounder and chairman of Lotus Development Corporation, found himself unhappily burdened by the workload of managing product development, manufacturing, and sales. He recruited a consultant, Jim Manzi, to serve as president, thereby allowing Kapor to focus on product development. Subsequently, he severed all ties with the company. Steve Jobs led Apple Computer from a company based in a California garage to an innovative force in the personal computer industry. However, Jobs's vision for Apple conflicted with that of John Sculley, the chairman Jobs recruited to manage and grow the company. Jobs subsequently left Apple and founded another firm known, not coincidentally, as Next, Inc. Many other equally talented and innovative leaders are exploring the market. The more successful ones have an inherent understanding of change and know how to utilize it to their advantage. Those that do not may repeat the struggles of IBM.

Convergence

Driven by technological breakthroughs and the demands of the marketplace, the convergence of the computer, telecommunications, and information-services industries will continue in the 1990s and pose significant challenges—and opportunities—to the information-technology companies we know today. This convergence will take place in an environment marked by widespread deregulation of the industry, as well as by its globalization. We will also witness a consolidation or vertical integration of companies across industry lines—driven by technology convergence. Within the industry itself there is a blurring of hardware and software that will be accelerated if IBM and Apple are successful in standardizing the computers that they make.

New Corporate Structures

Businesses will continue to adapt information technology for diverse purposes, including perceived competitive advantage, management of increasingly dispersed organization, distribution of products and services, and intercompany, interindustry communication. Vertical markets are already emerging, which will pose a challenge for most companies. As a result, corporate managers are likely to see their span of control widened via the use of information technology, as the organizations they manage become broader and shallower. The industry itself is expanding with the emergence of service consulting firms (like ADP, MicroAge, and Arbicon) and companies that specialize in systems integration (like EDS and Cambridge Technology Partners), payroll management, and production processing (like EDS). Corporate reliance on a workforce skilled in the use of information technology will continue to grow, as well as the ability of corporations to quickly locate and transfer information and skills across national borders. Companies are finding that it is better and more cost effective to stick to the basics of the business while outsourcing noncritical and non-value-added functions such as payroll and building maintenance.

Information and Power

From a societal perspective, the decentralization of information-processing power, as exemplified in the personal computer, will represent another step in democratization. Information and the ability to use it increasingly will equate to power. There are potential dangers, however. Becoming overly reliant on the analytical tools offered by information technology can dull human instinct and creativity—by focusing the view on the forest while obscuring the view of the trees. Decreased interpersonal contact due to the use of electronic mail, video conferencing, and other information-technology tools may similarly dull sensitivity to differences in culture, language, and other human characteristics.

Potential dangers exist for society as well. What impact will future information technologies have on the makeup and well-being of society? An expansion of the economic schisms in society is possible—especially if schools fail to acquaint all economic classes with the power of information technology. Workers who do not have access to or mastery of information systems may be subjected to the whims of those who do.

THE WORKFORCE OF THE FUTURE

Losers and Winners

The information-technology (IT) workforce will change as much or more than any other, primarily due to changing technology and the proliferation of new technologies. As one generation of technology gives way to another, the workforce must adapt to the new technology or move on with the technology into obsolescence. Typically, corporate IT professionals have closely affiliated themselves with one specialty, product, or vendor, such as Cobol, mainframe, or PC. Now, however, they will need to know and be able to work with multiple technologies. Rather than retrain all IT professionals with new, expanded skills to match the new technology, corporate IT departments have responded by *warehousing* workers or by laying off workers. Frequently, IT departments will stack one layer of professionals on top of another as it brings in each new technology. The result is mass confusion, the sporadic utilization of talent, and the creation of an IT bureaucracy—the very condition that corporate IT functions were intended to help eliminate. The more recent practice has been to lay off large numbers of IT professionals and replace them with new workers with skills to match the new technology. Turnover creates excessive expense and downtime for recruitment and training. Neither does it foster a committed workforce if IT professionals know they are to be replaced with each new generation of technology. The biggest loser is the company itself, which can no longer rely on its IT department, especially when operations are affected by ever-changing IT systems. The successful IT professional will enlarge her knowledge base around enlarged and increasingly integrated technologies.

Vendor Wars

Vendor wars are creating a worldwide headache for users, whether they are PC users who work at home, corporate IT professionals, or the corporate user who is just trying to access e-mail. The proliferation of competing and incompatible software products is the cause. One day they may become more compatible; until then, the IT professional will have to learn to use *families* of software to expend their skills and to extend employment longevity just as people know how to drive more than one kind of car—not just a Chevy or Mazda.

Resistance to Change

Neither the industry nor the workforce has responded well to change. Managers are easily threatened, and the broader IT work-force actively resists change. In some cases, people with older skills are outsourced to companies that will continue to serve the company or other clients through older systems. This extends worker usefulness, though not indefinitely. As each technology fades, so must the workers and their skills.

A Profile of the New Information-Technology Professional

IT professionals will have to develop broader capabilities if they are to remain contributors. Those who are able to expand their capabilities around new technology while adding value to the business are likely to be in greater demand. In the past, corporate IT functions have built their own applications from scratch. Now they are buying and integrating products, which is more cost effective and less time consuming. It also permits the upgrading of components of systems, rather than requiring the replacement of the entire system. With this migration to modular systems, increasing numbers of professionals will have to become cross-functional and technical builders—integrators. This will include applications architects, applications developers, and applications integrators.

IT professionals will have to replace their former technology orientation with a strong service orientation. They will have to be able to solve problems, speak the customer's language (not just IT language), and understand broad business and market issues. As a result, interpersonal skills building and mission critical skills will be in great demand.

The corporate IT function will also change. The IT bureaucracy will be replaced by small, semi-autonomous work teams that will have stronger consulting skills and that will be supported by external consultants. Managers will also require broader skills and must become facilitators and supporters of subordinates. Just as internal consultants from human resources, logistics, and planning range through the organization serving various clients, so must the IT consulting team. This also will require that businesses redefine how they compensate, organize, and manage IT professionals so that they are organized for the contribution that they make. Clearly, changes in technology will drive change in the industry and within corporate IT functions. The information-technology workforce will have to keep pace with both.

The dangers are real, but information technology will increasingly shape our world. The challenge will be to channel the use of this technology in directions appropriate to national and societal goals. Understanding the cyclical nature of the industry—the stages within its change cycle—will provide an important tool with which to direct the future of the information-services industry and of our world.

THE INDUSTRY OF THE FUTURE

The change cycle applies to the companies comprising the information-technology industry, as well as to the larger industry itself. All players in the industry are affected by business, technical, and other change drivers that create an environment of challenges and opportunities. Few predicted the declines of IBM and DEC. As the 1990s continue to unfold, all players will find themselves confronting change—some more desperately than others.

Once identified as a backwater industry known for its eccentric leaders and marginal products, the information-technology industry has become an indispensable tool for American business, while growing into a giant, diversified industry. Brilliant scientists, engineers, and entrepreneurs can no longer drive and manage a company indefinitely. Their startup companies must quickly seek to acquire broadly based business skills. The technicians that shaped individual firms, as well as the industry, during its formative stages now must yield—or metamorphose—into business managers. On the other hand, firms that once relied primarily on marketing savvy must increasingly integrate research and development into their business operations. The challenge for managers in the 1990s is not to attempt to suppress worker dissent and alienation but rather to harness it. Thus, successful leaders in the 1990s will be those able to assess ideas that lie outside the mainstream—recognizing those ideas with value, while fostering their implementation.

The future will belong to those companies that are intellectually and culturally flexible enough to grasp it. The Business Change Cycle provides a valuable tool by which to measure progress in this constantly changing world. Business managers in the information technology industry should place it in their toolkit for the 1990s.

It is not inevitable that every company must undergo the kind of painful changes now going on at IBM. Nevertheless, all the conditions and phases of change depicted in the Business Change Cycle seem to apply to the information-technology industry. The history and development of so many other industries have been obscured by time, but that is not so with this industry. We can still remember the birth and development of companies like Lotus Development, Sun Microsystems, Dell, Apple Computer, and Microsoft, and their founders are still young and are generating new ideas and technologies, even if under a different logo. For that reason, their progression along the Business Change Cycle carries even more meaning.

Brilliant scientists, engineers, and entrepreneurs cannot guide a company indefinitely. Startup companies must acquire broad business-based capabilities that will allow them to address a full range of business components. Kapor knew that he was not cut in this mold and fired himself, while Dell wanted to learn and gathered around him seasoned business managers who could help him. The technicians and brilliant dreamers that shaped the early firms, as well as the larger industry during its formative stages, now must develop into farsighted business strategists and managers or yield to others. Where they were once fathers of change with their new technologies and enterprises, they must now be able to plan for and manage larger change forces that lie beyond their control. Companies that rely primarily on marketing savvy must increasingly integrate R&D, operations, and culture to ensure the success of more ambitious strategies.

To stay ahead of the change cycle, companies will need to avoid some of the problems and mistakes seen in more mature industries. Worker dissent should not be suppressed but accepted as an opportunity to learn from the culture and effect a turnaround before the company experiences workforce alienation and the fundamental or total change that accompanies it. Wang, DEC, UNYSIS, and IBM ignored its consequences. Will the Microsofts and Intels of the industry be forced to endure the same hardships sometime in the future?

Lawrence J. Bolick

Lawrence Bolick is a vice president with the Cambridge Technology Partners of Cambridge, Massachusetts, where he directs the firm's network services group. Previously, he was a senior manager with CAP Gemini, Peat Marwick, and Coopers & Lybrand. He is one of the industry's leading authorities on networking technology and the integration of information and telecommunications systems. His clients have included Exxon, NYNEX, the Securities Industry Association, and AT&T.

Rouja Brzozowski

Rouja Brzozowski is president of Arbicon Consulting, a New York-based information technology training firm. Previously, she was with IBM and Chase Manhattan Bank, where she was responsible for the worldwide training and development of the bank's systems managers. Some of her recent clients have included Simon & Schuster, Mars Candy, Aetna Insurance, and Merck. Ms. Brzozowski is the author of the *I/S Skills Prototype Database,* which defines key skills and new roles for IT professionals.

9

Telecommunications: A Decade After the Big Bang

JEROME H. WANT

Partner, Organization Strategies, Inc.

No industry better represents a radically changed competitive environment than the telecommunications sector. With the breakup of Ma Bell a decade ago, we saw the overnight creation of:

- Eight new *Fortune* 50 companies,

- A two-tiered telecommunications industry with three primary long-distance carriers and the Baby Bells (now called regional Bell Holding Companies, or RHCs),

- Customer confusion with respect to how to procure and keep service at both levels, and

- Inflexible local rates coupled with cheaper long-distance rates from AT&T, MCI, and Sprint (the Big Three).

Unlike change in other industries, change in telecommunications immediately affected every American, and it will not stop— though many wish it would.

Many consumers still don't understand the structure of the industry (see Figure 9.1) and why local service has not improved. Basically, the industry can be traced back to the lack of competition in the predivestiture era of monopoly. Wherever one traveled in the United States, there was essentially one telephone company (AT&T) that served everyone (universal service) and was ultimately accountable to the public utility commissions (PUCs) in each state. AT&T's prime responsibility was to provide each customer with reliable service (dial tone), regardless of the cost. In remote areas like the Rocky Mountains, it was quite expensive to lay lines to isolated homes and villages. As a regulated company, AT&T could meet the challenge and needed to go to the PUC only when it needed a rate increase. As consumers, we were spoiled by the combination of high service levels, protection against the rapid rate increases by our state PUC, and one-stop shopping for all our telephone needs—local and long-distance.

If there was a downturn in the local economy, the service and costs were largely unaffected because the nationwide Bell system had deep pockets. Ma Bell did everything for us. In fact, some may remember that customers never even had to purchase a phone: the phone company just installed one, and the customer rented it for pennies a day. If it malfunctioned, the phone company replaced it at no cost. The only choices were color and whether the phone would be a Princess or a standard. People moving to another town or state just called the local phone company office, which established service at the new address. Within this monopolistic climate, the phone company exhibited certain operating characteristics:

- Subsidized universal service at an acceptable price,

- Slow time-to-market for products (thirty-six months),

- High-cost and high-quality manufacturing (in-house),

Figure 9.1
Structure of the Telecommunications Industry

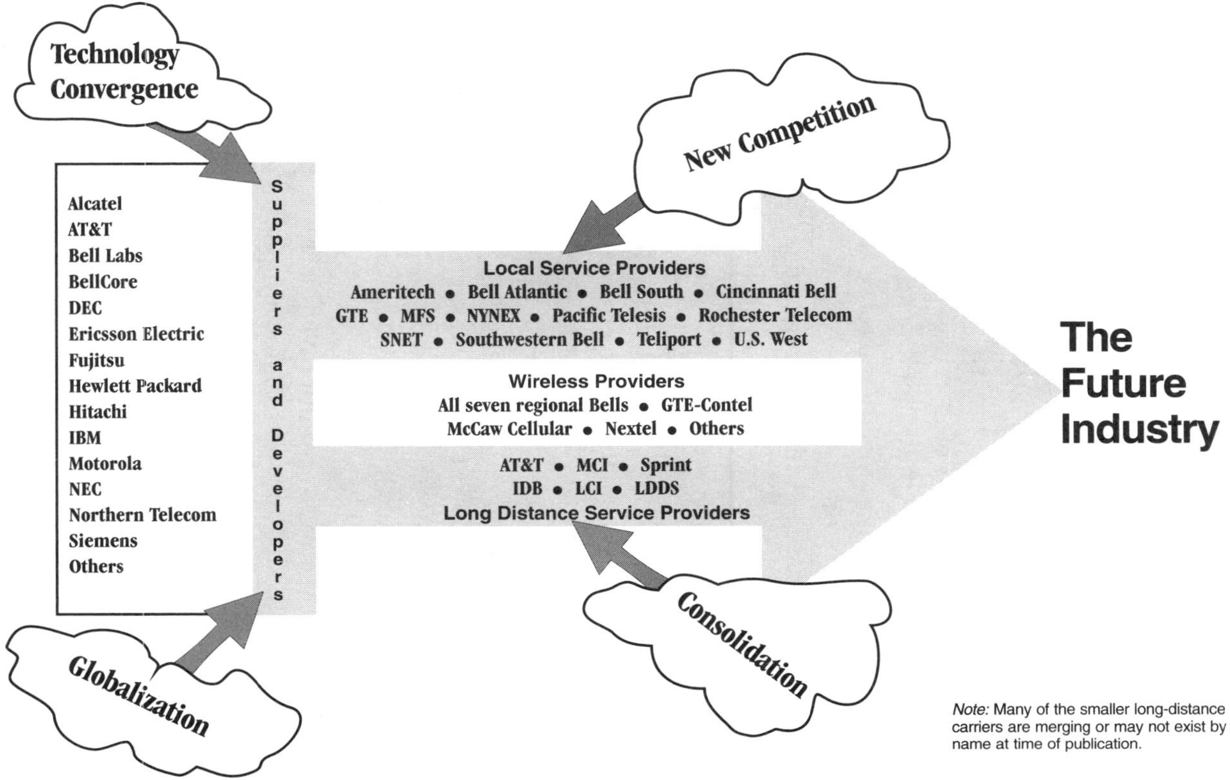

The Future Industry

New Competition

Consolidation

Technology Convergence

Globalization

Suppliers and Developers

Alcatel
AT&T
Bell Labs
BellCore
DEC
Ericsson Electric
Fujitsu
Hewlett Packard
Hitachi
IBM
Motorola
NEC
Northern Telecom
Siemens
Others

Local Service Providers
Ameritech • Bell Atlantic • Bell South • Cincinnati Bell
GTE • MFS • NYNEX • Pacific Telesis • Rochester Telecom
SNET • Southwestern Bell • Teliport • U.S. West

Wireless Providers
All seven regional Bells • GTE-Contel
McCaw Cellular • Nextel • Others

Long Distance Service Providers
AT&T • MCI • Sprint
IDB • LCI • LDDS

Note: Many of the smaller long-distance carriers are merging or may not exist by name at time of publication.

- Bureaucratic and ceremonial corporate culture nationwide,

- Cautious, conservative leadership, and

- Slow, incremental change both from within AT&T and from the marketplace in general.

Essentially, there was no need—or incentive—to speed products to market or to customize services because there was no competition. New technologies were slow to materialize and were slowly integrated into the telephone infrastructure. The culture of the phone company was geared to serve and satisfy the state PUCs. As a result, the phone company became a layered, bureaucratic organization charged with checking and rechecking its utility standards and procedures. To some degree, the seven regional Bell holding companies (RHCs) remain that way today since their core businesses—local service—continue to be monopolies to varying degrees. The growth potential for the regional holding companies has shifted to nonregulated services, such as cellular, information systems cable, PBX, and key systems.

Nevertheless, there were some benefits to the previous era of monopoly. Those ten-pound phones were so well engineered that they were virtually indestructible. It used to be said that you could drop one off the World Trade Center and then directly install it and it would work perfectly. Bell Labs was in the forefront of the best engineering in the world: they had the time, the best-qualified engineers, and a steady flow of revenues to support their projects (many of which had nothing to do with phone service). The Labs were a hot-bed of innovation that benefitted primarily the military and scientific sectors.

THE BIG BANG

From the moment that the divestiture took effect in the early 1980s, the entire industry was plunged into radical change. Many called divestiture the Big Bang. Within AT&T, in preparation for divestiture, a war began between the emerging regional Bells and AT&T over *future market roles* and the reallocation of people. The internal war over resources was not the only war going on at that time. The trade press predicted the "battle of the titans" between IBM and AT&T, a battle that never materialized because the convergence of computing with communications took far longer than was anticipated. If we gauge this change against the Business Change Cycle, it becomes clear that every player in the industry was struggling at the total change level. As America's second-largest corporation was broken apart, ten new organizations— AT&T, the seven regional Bells, Cincinnati Bell, and Southern New England Telephone—were created, not unlike an exploding supernova. It was the biggest business divestiture in history. Globalization and deregulation portend that change will continue to be rapid and radical in the telecommunications industry for the foreseeable future.

The Baby Bells

Within the seven new regional Bells, new assumptions, values, and missions had to be developed along with new strategies. The regional Bell companies were clearly starting over as new corporations. New management had to lead the change. Leadership and culture were especially hard issues for the regional companies because they traditionally received their marching orders from AT&T in New York and New Jersey for almost everything. The Baby Bells emerged from divestiture as new members of the *Fortune* 50, but with continuing responsibility to satisfy the PUCs along with tremendous overhead. They were limited to one product—local phone service—depriving them of the (then) more lucrative long-distance market. Nevertheless, market erosion was slower and smaller compared to AT&T: the Baby Bells lost less than 1 percent of market share over the decade and grew their cellular and enhanced telephone business (such as voice mail) impressively.

Despite their vast territories, the combination of stagnant

demographics and economic downturns undermined certain phone companies. Combined with fixed and stable populations, in some cases there was slower business growth. The effects of an economic downturn on a regional telephone company were more severely felt since they could no longer be spread over a nation-wide business. When the oil economy went into a prolonged decline in the mid-1980s, for example, Southwestern Bell suffered an erosion of revenue and profits as businesses closed and people moved away from Texas and Oklahoma. Southwestern Bell could not raid Illinois or New York for customers. Today, the regional Bells have begun to petition to courts to compete in states outside their region—which will increase competition if approved by the courts and may even produce lower rates.

Giant AT&T was also finding it difficult in the early period of divestiture. Initially, AT&T had to learn how to compete just to survive. It had to refine its mission (not just strategy) and was positioned at the fundamental or even total change level on the Business Change Cycle. Since divestiture, it has lost nearly 40 percent of its market share in certain segments of its long-distance business and has downsized by over 100,000 employees. MCI grew up as a tough, nonregulated street fighter. Its legendary founder, Bill McGowan, reinvented the industry with his push for a two-tiered industry with nonregulated long-distance service. The result was an entirely new climate of competitiveness for which MCI was already prepared. MCI had little to lose and a great deal to gain—usually at AT&T's expense. Today, MCI is a highly successful and aggressive company of nearly $13 billion in revenue, and Sprint is close behind. David has proven to Goliath and the world that he had more than a sling shot in his arsenal.

Within this radically changed environment, business conditions have changed from those of the monopolistic, predivestiture era. The following postdivestiture operating conditions now apply:

• Globalization of markets,

• Industry consolidation,

- Customized products and services,

- Faster time-to-market of new products (six to nine months),

- Lower cost of manufacturing (frequently outsourced),

- Convergence of technologies (such as computer technology with phone networks),

- Large-scale, proactive change, and

- Marketing and market-driven cultures.

Some of these forces of change, which had a profound effect on the major players' strategies and cultures, are revisited later in the chapter.

New Strategies and New Cultures

Culture and strategy are becoming major points of differentiation in the battle between the Big Three. Using my earlier definition of culture (shared beliefs about a company's ability to compete and how employees act on those beliefs), differences are more apparent among the Big Three than between the RHCs. Clearly, MCI has an advantage in that it has been an aggressive marketing company from the very start. It never has had to struggle to throw off the bureaucratic culture of the past. In addition, MCI has successfully resisted becoming bureaucratic as it has grown into a corporate giant. According to John Zimmerman, MCI's senior vice president for human resources, bureaucracy at MCI is equated with predictability of structure and process and the lack of timeliness (interview, February 13, 1993). Managers have always been close to the customer, and their customer service function has been a training ground for further advancement. This culture has served MCI well in projecting its strategy in the marketplace.

Unlike AT&T, MCI has shown little desire to diversify too far from its core business. Its acquisitions, mergers, and partnerships have all focused on strengthening and expanding its core long-distance business. Its commitment to build its own nationwide local network will also enhance its strategy while reducing its dependence on the RHCs (almost 47 percent of every dollar of revenue is paid back to the local phone companies for use of their local networks). In addition, MCI has been a superb marketing organization. It has gone to market first with such products as Friends and Family, 1-800-COLLECT, and pricing plans in the business segment. With British Telecom, it is now forming a worldwide business—Concert—to serve business on a global scale.

AT&T has had to play catchup at times, but with the lion's share of the market it historically believed that being a fast follower was acceptable. After all, the dominant vendor was never known for speed but, rather, quality at a premium price. As its culture has evolved, many vestiges of the old AT&T culture are beginning to disappear. Its original culture could be characterized as ceremonial, incremental, protective (protecting its base), and *very* bureaucratic. Its diversification into other technologies (information systems and computers) and the need to fight for market share is forcing AT&T to develop a more innovative and marketing-oriented culture. While AT&T always had to play catchup with MCI in product development and marketing, its new products (such as the AT&T Universal Card) have been well received by the marketplace.

AT&T's strategy to extend its core long-distance business includes information technology, networked applications such as video, and multimedia and information systems consulting. In the past, it was questioned for its far-ranging acquisitions, such as NCR. Now, with the projected growth in multimedia applications, those moves appear to be smart and farsighted (*appear* because the general track record of acquisition success has been poor and the former NCR has a long way to go to become a successful business unit within AT&T). In addition, it has recognized the future importance of wireless communications and is purchasing McCaw Cellular. For now, that gives AT&T the high ground in the cellular war.

In the past, lack of intense competition for the RHCs retarded any sense of urgency to change their cultures, but that is having to change with increased competition and business diversification. The RHCs have managed some stellar successes in cellular and enhanced services, such as automatic number identification (of the calling party) and public voice mail. Within their traditional business, they have learned that downsizing and cost reduction are not enough and that reengineering their processes will pay few dividends if they do not have the right people in place to assume the new responsibilities and tasks. Union-provided customer service, as measured by calls resolved on the first try, continues to be a problem for the telcos, based on data obtained from one of the Big Six and an independent consulting firm. Moreover, competing overseas will be different from competing in the United States, and moving into other industries here at home will require a less bureaucratic orientation in the marketplace. If they get strong competition from MCI's Metro division on the local network front (the original divestiture order from Judge Greene did not exclude MCI from that market), the RHCs could be faced with losing significant market share, as did AT&T in long-distance. In addition to long-distance providers such as MCI, smaller companies such as MFS (Metropolitan Fiber Systems) and Teleport, as well as the cable TV providers, will be competitors of the regional Bells.

NEW CHANGE FORCES

A decade after the Big Bang, the speed and complexity of change have increased. Despite its tremendous impact and implementation nightmares, divestiture was fairly simple and straightforward and had predictable consequences. Even those companies that have firmly positioned themselves in the marketplace will find the next decade of change to be challenging. Five major change forces are seen to be leading the next wave of change in the telecommunications industry:

- Globalization of markets,

- Convergence of technologies,

- Consolidation of the telecommunication industry, and

- Nontraditional competitors,

- Expansion into other industries such as media and entertainment.

Globalization of Markets

For decades, U.S. industries have complained that they have encountered closed doors when they tried to enter overseas markets but that foreign companies have been allowed to penetrate the U.S. market to become permanent and successful competitors. Telecommunications, however, is one American industry without peer anywhere in the world. Overseas markets are potentially a major new source of real revenue growth (along with wireless here at home). Moreover, foreign markets give telcos the opportunity to test drive new products and technologies before introducing them to the more demanding U.S. market.

U.S. companies are now being asked to develop networks for foreign countries. When they compete with European or Asian competitors, they frequently win, as Southwestern Bell did in Mexico and AT&T in Saudi Arabia (and Motorola won a contract for a wireless system in China). Bell South has wireless networks in more than a dozen overseas countries in Asia, Europe, and South America. In addition, MCI sold a noncontrolling share of its business to British Telecom in a shrewd move that gave it the cash to build and expand its own domestic network, while at the same time gaining access to the more open British telecommunications market through British Telecom's sales channel. Sprint did the same selling a portion of its stock to the French and German state phone companies (which must be approved by the Federal Communications Commission since markets in those countries have remained closed to outsiders).

Convergence of Technologies

The convergence of technologies may be the single most dominant change force driving the industry. Wireline and wireless networking, voice and data networking, and computers and communications all represent markets and technologies that are converging. Satellite technology now makes it possible to connect people and sites, almost instantaneously, anywhere in the world. Motorola's Iridium network holds the promise of connecting people anywhere in the world through satellite-linked cellular phone sets without being fixed to a physical site or network. Basic wireless communication (cellular and paging) has become a major portion of the industry, encompassing billions of dollars in revenue. AT&T's planned acquisition of McCaw Cellular (the nation's largest wireless network) and MCI and Motorola's recently purchased stakes in budding NEXTEL portend similar alliances in the future.

Of course, convergence has taken on new meaning recently as phone companies have moved to purchase cable television companies and even movie production studies (US West purchased 20 percent of Time Warner). The biggest and most noteworthy move in this area was Bell Atlantic's failed attempt to purchase Tele-Communications, Inc. (TCI). Despite court approval, the two companies were not successful in their negotiations (more about that later in this chapter).

Another noteworthy effort to merge two different companies around their compatible technologies was the failed effort by Sprint and EDS to merge. This was a potentially good idea that would have provided EDS with a telecommunication highway for its information systems, while giving Sprint access to a large EDS customer base.

Despite these initial false starts, the rapid advancement in developing and bringing new technologies to market will continue to be a driving force for merging companies across industry lines. Before long, the telecommunications companies will be the universal conduit for all information. Commercial networks are also developing that, like the research Internet, will promote business-to-business communications between customers, suppliers, and employees and further promote cross-industry communications and alliances.

Consolidation of the Telecommunication Industry

As noted above, technology convergence will become an ever-growing force behind consolidation of companies across and within industries. The failed EDS–Sprint merger will surely happen between two other parties. Sprint's merger with TCI, Cox, and Comcast may be a better business move in the long term. Of course, EDS is famous for having a more entrepreneurial "can-do" culture, created in the image of its founder—H. Ross Perot. The same issue apparently contributed to the failed Bell Atlantic–TCI merger. Like other Bell companies, Bell Atlantic is conservative. None of those characteristics could be attributed to Denver-based TCI, which was built around its driven entrepreneurial founder, Robert Magness. The public reason given for terminating both alliances was "business issues that didn't coincide" (that is, financial reasons), but it is safe to say that cultural differences played a major role as well. These oil-and-water cultural cases beg the question about how successful MCI and British Telecom ultimately will be, given their different cultures.

Consolidation also will occur in the second-tier long-distance business. The Big Three will always be with us, but there will be a major consolidation of the myriad of smaller long-distance companies under them—companies like WilTel, LCI, IDB, and LDDS. A fourth major long-distance company has emerged from the second tier through the merger of WilTel and LDDS. Companies also may be purchased by one of the Big Three or other types of companies, such as foreign public telephone companies.

Nontraditional Competitors

The recent personal communications services wireless-spectrum auction to dozens of smaller entrepreneurial companies promises that the next decade will spawn an entirely new industry built around selling individualized, customized services. These MCIs of the future will put added pressure on the established telcos of today. Furthermore, alternate access providers, such as Metropolitan Fiber Systems, will continue to enter the local market as competition accelerates.

THE INDUSTRY OF THE FUTURE

Since new and changing technologies will continue to emerge against a backdrop of deregulation and globalization, rapid and dramatic change in the telecommunications industry is expected to continue indefinitely. The telecommunications industry was founded on a breakthrough technology, and its sights will always be set on how the latest technology will help it expand the business or make it less expensive to run. In addition, some of the best R&D in the world comes from such companies as BNR (Bell Canada) Bell Labs, Northern Telecom, and Motorola, as well as a number of smaller up-and-coming companies like NEXTEL.

Characteristics of Telcos of the Twenty-First Century

With this in mind, the industry in the twenty-first century will see more radical change than in the past and will exhibit some of the following characteristics:

- Wireline communications will slowly decline in importance in favor of wireless personal communications, making the Dick Tracy watch a reality and demanding rapid time-to-market requirements typical of watches today.

- The volume of data transmission will exceed voice transmission.

- Business ventures among the regional Bells will be commonplace. (NYNEX and Bell Atlantic are now creating a joint wireless network to serve the entire Northeast, from Virginia to Maine.)

- The seven regional Bells will expand overseas to become premier builders and developers of phone networks. They will also hold significant equity in overseas phone companies, as did the oil companies in the 1950s and 1960s. The RHCs will also become premier regional long-distance carriers and ultimately will be strong players of interactive media.

- AT&T and MCI eventually will control roughly equal shares of the domestic long-distance market. Both will become major international players. Sprint, through alliances, will also grow significantly and could become a major player if it partners with the RHCs in the long-distance market.

- AT&T will take the high ground in converting its network to a value-added network and will extend its core business to multimedia networking and transition networking. As a result, interenterprise application networking will be commonplace for connecting businesses to consumers and suppliers.

- AT&T, MCI, and Sprint will become major providers of local network services.

- Many small local phone companies will go out of business or be purchased by the RHCs or large independents, such as GTE.

- Customer service will be instantaneous, and networks will never break, causing business customers to give up on the management of their networks to the phone companies.

- Employees in the industry will be challenged to become more innovative and entrepreneurial as a way to achieve security. Specialists with rare technical skills and managers with well-developed management and marketing capabilities will come to dominate the workforce.

- Businesses and consumers will experience more choice and better-priced performance at a faster rate because both customers and competitors will have become more sophisticated.

Ironically, interenterprise networking will create an instantaneous pricing exchange for goods and services much like financial trading today. In short, networking will make the telecommunications market more efficient.

Lessons Learned: Applying the Business Change Cycle

To succeed in the next century, the telcos will have to do more than restructure, downsize, and reengineer. Once an organization's processes have been redesigned and structure has been realigned, people must be trained for the new challenges facing them. People need support and a direction for change—or, as I described in Chapter 5, a culture. *Reengineering of processes without changing or enhancing people will lead to failure, especially if external markets dramatically change.* I would much prefer to have an organization staffed with effective people and bad processes than ineffective people and good processes because effective people will do on-the-job reengineering of the bad processes.

For that reason, the telco cultures will have to do more than change incrementally over time, especially if they are allowed to compete with each other. They must develop radical new strategies to change their cultures in dramatic, timely ways so that their culture matches the changing conditions in the marketplace. When plotted on the Business Change Cycle, the local telcos would now be within the directional phase of change (see Figure 9.2). New strategies have to be developed and operationalized with improved cultures and empowered midlevel management. Right now, much of the focus is on reengineering to cut operational costs and improve processes. That's good—but not good enough.

To accomplish this, the telcos will have to engage in a combination of massive retraining and refocusing efforts for their workforces. In the last decade, the telcos have spent prodigious amounts of money in training, awareness building, and recruitment of outsiders. This trend must combine and be augmented with high-risk compensation programs to truly drive culture

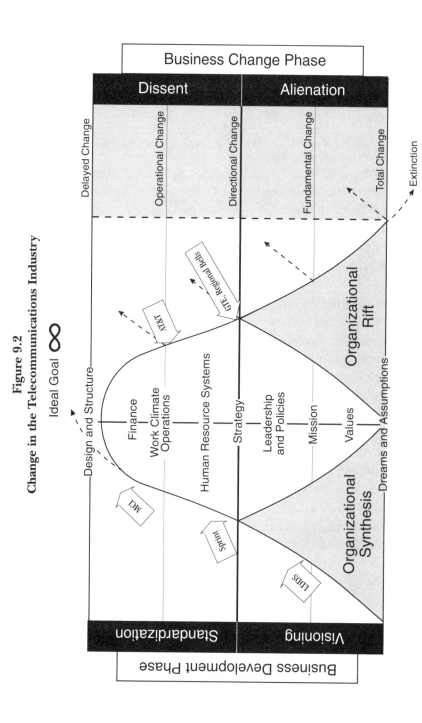

Figure 9.2
Change in the Telecommunications Industry

change. Furthermore, labor–management partnerships must be strengthened as they were in the manufacturing industry in the 1980s.

In addition, the telcos will have to replace or supplement much of the traditional telco workforce with people from other, more competitive industries. In some cases, the telcos have made mistakes by staffing leadership positions with people who have regulated backgrounds to run unregulated businesses and vice versa. In these situations, both have tended to fail. In the future, as markets deregulate, more and more emphasis must be placed on recruiting executive talent from the nonregulated sector.

MCI and Sprint are clearly on the developmental side of the Business Change Cycle. While they seem to be huge, even bureaucratic companies, they are also ventures born of the new age of competitive long-distance communications. MCI and Sprint have successfully developed their visions and are now in the standardization phase where they are standardizing their operations to better support strategy. AT&T is functioning on the change side of the curve, at the operational and directional levels, to deal with more effective strategy and improved operations. The Baby Bells are clearly functioning at the directional level—building strategies and cultures to support their repositioning in the marketplace.

The industry will continue to be dominated by radically changing conditions, and if there are no future big bangs, there certainly will be a lot of little explosions.

LESSONS LEARNED IN A RADICALLY CHANGING MARKET

What can be learned with respect to the management of market turbulence? Several lesson come to mind:

- Market convergence takes longer than expected. For example, the use of computers with communications and wireline and wireless networks took a decade to develop and converge.

The culture change associated with market shifts, such as convergence or deregulation, takes even longer due to deep-seated resistance to change.

- In highly competitive environments, one should stick to one's knitting to be successful (MCI—long-distance, RHCs—cellular and enhanced-services success). IBM's failed foray into the industry should serve as a reminder to remain focused.

- Fit the people to the task. Do not staff regulated positions with people from unregulated backgrounds and vice versa, unless you can provide prolonged training, culture change, and support initiatives. Not only does fitting the person to the task increase the profitability of success because of a skills and a culture match, but success promotes the further indirect benefit of fostering mutual respect of both cultures' values—which further increases the future probability of success.

- When markets are turbulent and changing, reengineering processes cannot make up for ineffective people or for a failed strategy. This is counterintuitive to traditional process thinking, which teaches, "Never blame the person, blame the process." This adage applies to stable market environments, not turbulent ones such as telecommunications. Hence, management must pay even more attention to the quality of the people rather than the processes because good people will perform on-the-job process redesign.

- Massive and frequently reinforced training and communications programs are required at organizations that are being forced by the market to diversify. The training has to concentrate on bread-and-butter competitive survival skills, such as project management, account management, and new product development.

- High-risk and high-reward compensation plans and union-management partnerships hold great promise for enhancing cultural change in the future telecommunications industry. These plans and partnerships, combined with systematic culture change strategies, will help companies prepare for even greater change in the future.

• Learning to manage change will be as important to success as managing people, technology, products, and markets.

Finally, strategy and culture alignment are a journey and not a destination, so avoid complacency.

Jerome H. Want

Jerome Want is a senior partner with Organization Strategies, Inc., a Madison, NJ change strategy consulting firm. Mr. Want has consulted to many of today's telecommunications companies and was a leading resource to the industry on the issues of culture change and executive development in the period just after the divestiture. Some of his clients in the industry have included: Southwestern Bell, Contel, US West, Northwest Telecommunications, AT&T and NYNEX. He also served as the internal director of Organization Design and Change Strategy for the Motorola wireless communications business. Mr. Want earned his doctorate from the University of Maryland, where he was a Maryland fellow. He is the author of a number of published articles on change and is the principal author of this book.

CHAPTER

10

American Health Care: Creating Order Out of Chaos

ROGER A. JONES
Executive Vice President, MEDCO Containment

Health care is an emotional, complex, and frequently disturbing industry. How often have we heard, "I'm happy as long as I have my health"? Whether or not we have our health, health care and this industry are not far from our minds. Health care encompasses the great promise and hope for new cures for illnesses like cancer as well as care for pregnant women who have never visited a physician prior to delivery. The cost of care and access for all, the fear of AIDS, and the ethical questions raised from genetic research all converge in the public's perception of this industry. As politicians position and battle over the structure and extent of government involvement in the future of health care, the perception of this industry by the average citizen becomes pivotal in the national debate. The current discussion on national health care will forever change the future of the industry.

Treating the sick and the infirmed is as ancient as humankind. The father of medicine, Hippocrates, lived and taught over 2,400 years ago, yet it has only been 125 years since surgeons learned the importance of washing their hands before surgery. Much has changed in the past hundred years in health care—and much in the past twenty-five years—yet health care, as an industry, is already experiencing such radical change that entire companies are being transformed—or they will not survive. The changes in the health-care industry are being fueled by the demand for care from a growing and aging population, by technology and research that produce miraculous results, by uncontrollable increases in costs, by unending finger-pointing within the industry, and by a government that seeks to regulate the entire industry to ensure that health care is available for all Americans.

AN INDUSTRY IN CRISIS

Health care is an industry in crisis. The fundamentals and the structure of the delivery, consumption, and financing of medical services are being redefined, requiring companies to change to capitalize on the unknown. This industry will change. The rewards from this vast opportunity will go to companies that realize that not only is the industry changing, but the company itself must change in order to compete in this new order.

The Business Change Cycle provides a means for understanding and responding to radically changed business conditions. It also provides us with an excellent framework for capitalizing on change where the winners and losers will include both current household institutes, as well as new entities to the industry. To accomplish this, we briefly trace the progression of health care in America, starting with its roots in post-Revolutionary days and moving to its current standards and practices.

An Overview

The first hospital in the United States was the Pennsylvania Hospital, built in 1790 in Philadelphia with the assistance of Benjamin Franklin. A mere 150 years ago, medical technology consisted of little more than manual tools like the scalpel, pliers, and the hammer. Today, multimillion-dollar magnetic resonance imaging (MRI) machines transmit computerized images to other computers for further diagnosis. There are wonder drugs, and microscopic surgery is performed under high-powered optical equipment employing space-age technology. Health care is big business. Expenditures for health care in the United States are approaching trillions of dollars a year, and millions of people are employed in thousands of different businesses in hundreds of separate industry segments.

In the same country where patients recover from heart and lung transplants in a matter of months and tiny premature babies are cared for in high tech neonatal nurseries, millions of people are without the most basic care, and others are turned away from overcrowded facilities. Over 38 million Americans are without health insurance. Doctors are cautious to treat due to fears of malpractice allegations. We all are frightened of viruses like AIDS, whose medical costs may exceed $50 billion by the decade's end, absorbing about 5 percent of the total Medicaid budget. The total annual cost of personal health care (care directly involved with the treatment of patients) is approaching three quarters of a trillion dollars—over 12 percent of the GNP (the largest proportion of the GNP for any industrialized nation) and rising every year.

In 1993, the nation's total personal health-care bill was over $700 billion, with the average per capita expense over $3,000. The wonders of technology and the cures it represents add to the crisis as demand, expectation, and costs continue to increase. Too frequently, we have redundant technology within the same treatment area, adding to the inefficient and excessive cost of treatment. Richard D. Lamm, the former three-term governor of Colorado says, "Too many technologies are beneficial only at the margin. They too often prolong dying without prolonging life." An aging population will add demands for more care, miracle cures, more services, and more expense.

Health care is changing, and *the businesses engaged in health care will have to change significantly if they are to remain competitive and effective.* In looking at Jerry Want's Business Change Model, it's clear that total change is being experienced at all levels of the industry:

- Established assumptions and values do not meet the demand for care or financing.

- There is no current agreement on basic objectives, vision, or business strategies that will carry the industry into the next century. On the other hand, the opportunity to forge a winning strategy is up for grabs.

- Leaders within the industry frequently lack a grasp of the magnitude of impending change or the ability to forge a strategy that will chart a winning course. Running a business 10 percent more efficiently than it ran in the past will not lead to success.

- Industry leaders are too frequently spending time, talent, and resources on strategies based on the old paradigm and are not preparing for new opportunities.

- Professionals and users of the health-care system are becoming alienated as care becomes a commodity of differentiated quality and reliability.

Daniel Callihan, in his book *What Kind of Life: The Limits of Medical Progress* (Simon and Schuster, 1990, p. 185), goes well beyond the need for corporate change when he says, "The health care system will and must change.... Most reformers have wanted to work within the present set of national values about health, hoping that by devising some ingenious fresh mix of them, a new system could be born.... We will have to change not just the mix and balance of these values, but the values themselves." Perhaps it is self-evident, but if society at large reorders its basic values as it deals with health care, the businesses that service that society will surely experience significant change.

A Fragmented Industry

The health-care industry is much more than just hospitals and doctors. The obvious players in the health-care industry are physicians, nurses, hospitals, medical-equipment and hospital-supply companies, insurance and managed-care companies, and pharmaceutical and research laboratories. But the industry also includes clinics of all sorts, medical group practices, data-analysis companies, consulting firms, utilization review organizations, and legal and financial professionals dedicated to health-care issues. The list goes on and on, including giant firms like Becton Dickenson and Johnson & Johnson, as well as small entrepreneurial firms like Invacare Corporation, which makes wheelchairs, Meta Health Technologies, which provides information-management systems to hospitals, and Medical Data North, which helps physician offices manage their patients' records. Clearly, the businesses in health care are fragmented and diverse. Vertical integration of the delivery segments of the industry (medical, nursing, hospitals, insurance, and managed care) is being attempted by some of the largest institutions (like Humana and Aetna) and smaller hospitals (like the Columbus Medical Center). To some degree, they have been successful in cutting costs and improving efficiency.

The industry is global: research and manufacturing of products and technology are exported or imported to every country on the planet. Joint ventures with foreign companies are becoming commonplace. Giant companies like Merck and DuPont have formed joint ventures, just as have smaller companies like Medtronics and ALZA in the medical and pharmaceutical fields. The most successful mergers have been between foreign and U.S. pharmaceutical companies, as seen in the Astra-Merck venture between Astra Pharmaceutical (Sweden) and Merck, and the Beecham (U.K.) consolidation with SmithKline. Consolidation in pharmaceuticals has continued, as Bristol Meyers purchased Squibb, and Merck purchased MEDCO Containment. As technology becomes more sophisticated and services more expensive with the ever increasing demand, it is expected that the federal, state, and local governments will increasingly regulate the health-care industry.

Health care as an industry is a complex maze of interlocking, dependent businesses and institutions. For example, medical-supply companies are involved with research and development and manufacturing of the product, which is distributed by others, prescribed by independent physicians, administered by specialists, funded by individuals, employers, or the government, reimbursed by third parties, monitored by independent review companies, and regulated by the government. There is nothing formal or even historical about the way these businesses related. They simply evolved into the current industrial complex we know today, and this lack of logical structure can easily change as new alliances, consolidation, and entrepreneurial determination shape a new order (see Figure 10.1).

Figure 10.1
Gridlock in the Health-Care Industry

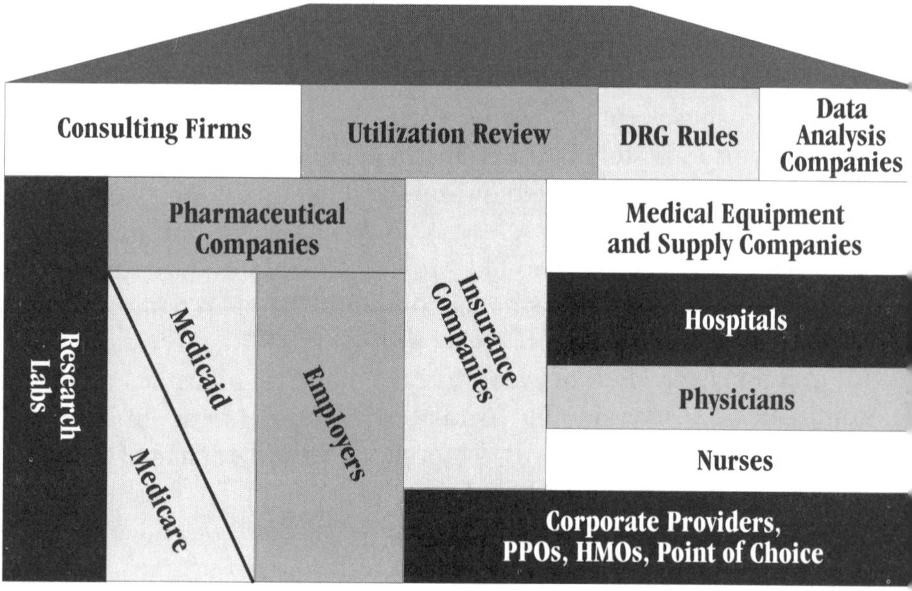

Uwe Reinhardt, the Princeton economist and expert on health care, has said, "At its best, the American health system is unmatched anywhere in the world. At its worst, no other industrialized nation would ever want to match it" (Callihan, *What Kind of Life*, p. 72). Callihan is more emphatic saying, "It is not actually a system at all, but a collection of programs and disparate institutions, neither coherently conceived nor coherently operated. Efforts to achieve any significant efficiency reforms by the most commonly employed—and commonly venerated—methods are inevitably bound to fail. Those methods, a combination of incentives and disincentives, carrots and sticks, make use of false perceptions and faulty premises. They want to insert into good behavior a fundamentally deranged system, one whose problems mount with each passing year" (*What Kind of Life*) Both Reinhardt and Callihan are talking about a health-care delivery system and not the health-care industry as a greater entity; however, there is considerable agreement that the health-care system is out of control and is bound to come under even stronger regulatory controls. As the health-care system changes, so will the entire industry that supports and services the system. Increasingly, society is having to deal with the moral, economic, and social issues of health care as all become integrated into one complex system: *the flash point is access and cost.*

Health care often makes headlines with dramatic stories of miraculous breakthroughs in research or in medical achievement or for some miserable failing of practice or administration. The pressure—to provide needed care for all, at costs society is willing to bear, while producing outstanding physicians and researchers, improving technology, and fulfilling America's insatiable appetite for more advances—is coming to a bursting point.

CHANGES IN DELIVERY, REIMBURSEMENT, AND REGULATION

Changes and refinements in the delivery, reimbursement systems, and regulatory environment have occurred nearly as fast as they've occurred in research and technology. In 1847, doctors joined together to form the American Medical Association, dedicated to raising the standards and performance of physicians. In 1910, the first group health insurance contract was issued to Montgomery Ward & Company, covering their employees and families. By 1930, the first health maintenance organization (HMO) was formed, Blue Cross was created, the Social Security Act was passed, private insurers had begun to provide surgical coverage, and the first Blue Shield plan was offered. In the 1930s, more government regulation was passed, and government-supported organizations grew, including the National Institutes of Health. In the 1940s and 1950s, insurance coverage, both publicly funded and privately offered, flourished. The Hill–Burton Act, passed in 1946, supported and encouraged massive hospital construction all over the country. The 1960s introduced Medicare and Medicaid. In the 1970s, the HMO Act assisted in the establishment and expansion of HMOs, and the Employee Retirement Income Security Act (ERISA) encouraged the growth of self-insurance of employee benefits. *However, the problem of reimbursement and coverage is simply that we have fewer available resources to cover ever-increasing costs.*

The Role of the Physician: So Long Marcus Welby

The role of the physician has changed since the days when house calls were expected of your family physician. Thirty years ago doctors brought their black bag to the home to diagnose illness, care for the sick, and offer medical advice and personal comfort. The doctor was part of the family memory bank, and loyalties were binding in both directions. There were few specialists and fewer clinics. Over time, the family has changed, and so have the role and practice of the physician. Clinics and medical group practices and panels of providers have now replaced house calls. Increasingly, the individual's choice of doctors is being directed and limited by managed-care "preferred provider" panels. More and more conditions are being treated by specialists who have little time to deal with the whole person. Referrals from one physician to another are commonplace as practitioner and patient both strive to seek elusive cures. We all can reminisce about those good old days when physicians were an important fixture in the family's life history and patients had a special rapport with their family doctor, but those days are history.

Physicians today heatedly discuss the administrative burden of a seemingly endless stream of paper as they endure the process of precertification, followed up with concurrent review, only to be further questioned on postutilization review by firms that are hired by employers or local governments. The physician can be bombarded by a myriad of medical-necessity review organizations, each one different, each one demanding immediate response. Daily, qualified, productive physicians are leaving the practice of medicine because of these restrictions on their judgment or intrusion on their time. Yet the businesses controlling the practice of medicine are flourishing as purchasers and payers of health care insist on the need to monitor, control, and gather data on medical and surgical patterns, practices, and outcomes—and they, too, add to the costs of health care. This reflects a bureaucratization of the larger industry, as well as a struggle for power or control. Ultimately, the patient all too frequently feels the impact of less effective care and more cost.

THE INDUSTRY OF THE FUTURE

In the near future, health care, in all its complexity and interdependencies, will change significantly from what we recognize today. Despite much discussion and conjecture about the type and form of that change, it is not feasible to predict how this industry will change in the future. All that is certain is that total and radical change within the industry is forcing companies to change to stay competitive and that the pace and magnitude of the change will force companies to adopt significantly different approaches to organization, management, and information. *The entire health-care industry and each of its components will have to develop strategies for turning themselves around on Jerry Want's Business Change Cycle.* The best we can do is evaluate the market and social forces that will generate change, examine current business structures and partnerships with legislators, position businesses for change as a condition of existence, and capitalize on the emerging change by going beyond survival to produce and add value. The focus on any health reform bill from Congress will be on cost and coverage. This means that insurance companies will be the first sector to be affected, but ripples will be felt throughout the entire industry.

Change—both directional change (the strategy of delivering health-care services) and fundamental change (the mission of the system)—will come to this industry sooner than later. If the entire industry is experiencing total change, then the specific businesses within the industry will have to adapt to the change in their environment or they will soon fail. At this point, we can make the following assumptions about possible future changes in health care:

- The population is *aging*, and the potential for living longer is increasing whether individuals are generally healthy or ill. Currently, 12 percent of the population is sixty-five years or older, and in thirty years that population will exceed 20 percent of the population. (Callihan, *What Kind of Life*, p. 185).

- *Research* will continue to produce miraculous results, forcing society to make hard choices about resources, ethics, and expense.

- As *technology* produces more expensive equipment, existing technology will become less expensive and more accessible.

The site of many services will change to the home or local clinic, while larger institutions specialize in equipment and its supporting staff. Technology will continue to offer more solutions to health problems, resulting in increased demand, higher costs, and improved individual medical results.

- The *volume of information* is exploding. "It took from the time of Christ to the mid-eighteenth century for knowledge to double. It doubled again 150 years later, and then again in 50 years. Today, it doubles every 4 to 5 years. More new information has been produced in the last 30 years than in the previous 5,000" (Callihan, *What Kind of Life*, p. 69). The near future will see a transformation of information into usable knowledge by a variety of disciplines and businesses within the industry.

- *Accessing information* and making it understandable will fundamentally change the way medicine is delivered and administered. Physicians will have ready access to sophisticated data on practice patterns, protocols, outcome statistics, and patient information. The overwhelming amount of paper processing—with pre-, concurrent-, and postutilization review, claim processing, statistical reporting, and medical records—will be done with computers linked together to share information. The potential from the consolidation of meaningful information within the delivery system will provide great opportunity for new businesses that are adept at sophisticated data gathering, evaluation, and dissemination.

- Without government intervention, a *widening health gap* between those who have access to health care and those that do not will continue to grow. Costs will continue to rise as the population grows and ages, new cures are found, new technology is more available, and illnesses such as AIDS consume more resources.

- We will have some form of *national health policy and national health insurance,* at the very least, for the uninsured. The political debate now focuses on access to the delivery system, the degree and level of care, and how society will pay the bill. The debate is highly politicized, but reform will come.

• *Employers* will become more directly and actively involved with the broad issues of employee well-being.

• The current excess of physicians will reverse itself, and the *number of practicing physicians* will decrease in absolute numbers. Of those remaining, the number entering a specialty will increase (unless restricted by the government, as proposed).

• The *site of care* will change as less efficient hospitals are consolidated or forced to go out of business, while specialty centers like Pittsburgh Hospital for transplants and Massachusetts General Hospital for burns become more effective and competitive. Home care and long-term care will increase significantly, as will segments that provide equipment, technology, and service to this emerging segment.

CORPORATE CHANGE IN THE
HEALTH-CARE INDUSTRY

There is a growing consensus that businesses currently in the health-care industry will undergo at least directional change as their environment changes around them. Most will experience fundamental change as their missions and justification for existence are challenged. Some segments and companies in the health-care industry (such as pharmaceutical and high tech companies) have historically been externally focused and adaptable as new technology, discovery, and products forced change to occur, while other health-care industry segments (insurance companies, managed-care companies, and hospitals) changed more slowly. In the coming decade, these service-based companies will change more rapidly as they adapt to the blurring of industry roles and the changes offered by technology, competition, and government intervention. The health-care services business involves hundreds of billions of dollars, is technology sensitive, impacts a broad base of consumers, will manage huge volumes of information, and continues to be highly regulated. We can engage in a lively debate over how much, what form, and where the changes will occur in the services segment of the health-care industry, but there is little disagreement that change—at least directional change—is coming.

For simplicity, we can divide the health-care industry into two large segments. The technology- and research-based companies (such as pharmaceutical, hospital supply, and medical-equipment companies) make up one segment, and the service- and transaction-based companies (such as hospitals, utilization review organizations, HMOs, insurance companies, and managed-care companies) make up the other segment. Physicians as individuals or as they practice in small groups are not discussed in this chapter, which is devoted to the corporate business structure within the health-care industry. Physician group practices will play a significant role in the future, affecting how the rest of the industry competes and adapts to change. Nevertheless, we may be seeing the end of the physician-entrepreneur role. Doctors will be employees or will be affiliated with larger corporate managed-care organizations.

TECHNOLOGY- AND RESEARCH-BASED COMPANIES

The technology- and research-based companies survive by capitalizing on their ability to leapfrog the competition by introducing new products, marketing, and innovation. Exploring possibilities, identifying emerging demand, and investing in research or strategic partnerships keep these companies involved with the management of change. Johnson & Johnson evaluated its marketplace, strengths, and weaknesses and pursued a joint venture with Bristol Meyers to sell proprietary drugs in those markets in which Johnson & Johnson had a particularly strong marketing presence. Successful managers in these companies tend to see themselves as managing change rather than managing an established process or function.

Although these successful technology- and research-based companies deal with a changing marketplace daily, they are must keep up with the rate and form of change. People are quick to formalize and standardize their lives, thought, and behavior, and managers constantly attempt to fine-tune their overworked formula for dealing with change. Managing by formula, however, no matter how successful in the past, will not help companies that are determined to stay competitive in a rapidly changing marketplace. Companies also can suffer from the mesmerizing effects of focusing on the competition's latest product or innovation which blinds them to fundamental changes in the industry. High tech companies risk much in the decade of the 1990s if they lose a broad perspective. It makes good short-term sense for large drug companies to create joint ventures or form partnerships to take advantage of the innovation provided by their smaller partners. Merck and Astra is one such example. But this formula cannot replace the basic need for large companies to invest in R&D, stay competitive in the long run, and reinvent their corporate cultures so that they can cope with change.

Want's model for business change explains the nature of change as it affects all organizations, and it applies especially to those in the health-care sector (see Figure 10.2). Every company exists by balancing internal and external forces that are changing independently of one another. *In health care, the external changes will be so significant in the coming decades that nearly every company in the industry will feel the impact, often at both directional and fundamental change levels.* Managing this degree of change is difficult and filled with risks of its own. Those risks will be less if industry leaders carefully evaluate the potential changes emerging in this industry and find ways to cooperate with their counterparts in the service and transaction sector.

Figure 10.2
Change in the American Health-Care Industry

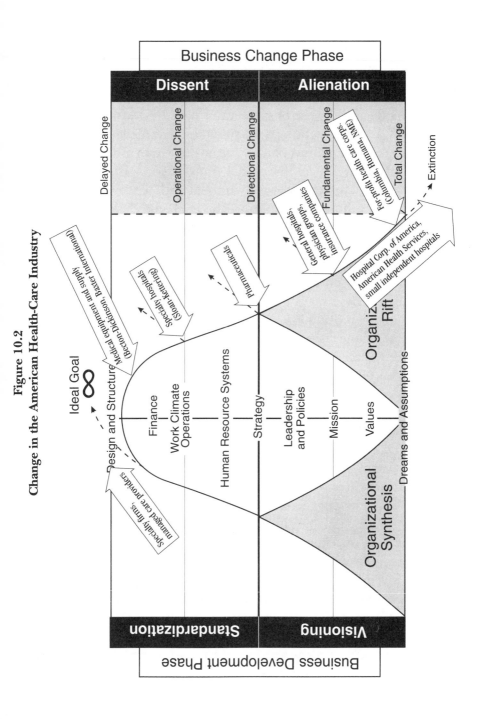

Service- and Transaction-Based Companies

The service- and transaction-based companies, like hospitals and managed-care companies, face a far more serious challenge in the coming decade. These organizations have slowly developed large process- and transaction-based systems to handle large volumes of individual personal events and reams of paper on a postservice incurral basis. In Want's model, they have *overstandardized* the business, making it excessively bureaucratic and inflexible. The pressure for these companies to change comes from upheaval in the health-care industry. Companies that have been successful and well managed in the past will face the need to change again as the demands from consumers, competitors, and government require more than the processing of paper or people.

Many of these service and transaction companies pride themselves on promoting long-term employees and expecting them to lead in the same fashion as their predecessors. They have spent time and energy on employee issues and internal staff developmental programs and feel quite satisfied with this historical approach to employee seniority. The key question, however, is whether these employees and their managers can manage change: *Can they transform their outlook and skills to deal with the reality that change—and not tasks or functions or process—is to be managed?* In order to achieve this transformation in any real time, the CEO must be willing to look at the very fabric of the company—its culture and the abilities of the staff. Let's not put the cart before the horse. Since history's first marketplace, managers have been preaching the need to adapt to, or capitalize on, change. The idea that the only constant in business is change is not novel. All too often, however, senior management looks inwardly to identify areas that must change when in fact the most profound change is coming in the marketplace.

Hospitals

Because many health-care executives do not see the potential depth of the changes we are facing in this industry, they propose superficial remedies to more complex problems. Future health-care legislation will be the panacea (not the whipping boy). Too frequently, hospital administrators and their consultants promote improving staff productivity and physician relations as the solution to dealing with the competitive changes occurring in their sector. These hospitals are considering actions like inviting doctors to join their board of directors, expanding hospital amenities for physicians, reassessing medical staff privileges, enhancing community image, and promoting a collegial organization culture. All this may be worthwhile but will not result in long-term success unless management grasps the trends in the broader industry and understands the impact of these trends and changes on the hospital as a "people system."

Several hospitals used to service the same geographical area, with a resulting duplication of service, excess capacity, and waste of resources. The industry no longer supports this kind of redundancy, and competitive (or regulatory) forces will reward the better-positioned provider. James Cooks says, "The hospital industry is overbuilt and overequipped, and it is overbuilt and overequipped primarily for the benefit of the physician, who are its true clients. Physicians are very much interested in high technology equipment, and the hospitals, in order to compete for the physicians and patients, equip themselves with a lot of high technology equipment" (*Forbes*, April 30, 1990). Cook's comments are directed at hospitals and physicians, but a red flag should also be directed at the high tech manufacturers. Richard Lamm further observes, "One of our main excesses is that we have too many redundant, duplicative, superfluous technologies in too many locations. *America is simply not rich enough to afford the current level of duplication of medical technologies.*"

MANAGED-CARE AND INSURANCE COMPANIES

The huge insurance, managed-care, and utilization review companies have succeeded at managing transactions—from processing claims to enrolling HMO members to processing utilization information. They are very good at these tasks, and computers will continue to replace the human in the middle of transactions. The value will come from their ability to provide information from a variety of sources on a real-time basis through highly trained specialists at the critical point in the decision path. One has to wonder at the huge investment these companies are making to process paper.

Throughout the service- and transaction-based segment of the health-care industry, companies are coming to grips with the definition of *service* for the coming decade. As more transactions are made by computer, people's expectation of service will change from "Did they get the paperwork correct?" to "Did I receive the best information and advice?" The very definition and concept of service will change, and so will these companies. In the present climate, the insurance companies are being seen as the villains. Their refusal to serve all, their interference with physician prerogatives, and their failure to comply with contractual commitments to the patient have opened the door for criticism from all participants. The insurance sector will be subjected to the greatest change in the first wave of health-care reform.

AN INDUSTRY IN CHANGE: LESSONS LEARNED FROM THE BUSINESS CHANGE CYCLE

Corporate Vision and Mission in Changing Companies

According to the Business Change Cycle, any company that is going through fundamental or total change needs to carefully reexamine its corporate vision and mission. Given their own vision for the industry, companies must forge successful missions and reassess the required values in order to compete successfully in the marketplace. Merck reevaluated its vision of its traditional role as the leader in pharmaceutical research and production and concluded that as a major player in managed health care, it needed to directly affect consumers through benefit programs that cover employees and retirees. Merck's purchase of MEDCO Containment, the country's largest prescription-benefit manager administering drug programs for the country's largest employers, set a new standard of integration within the health-care industry. This visionary step linked research, manufacturing, and distribution to the consumers in a way that will improve the quality of health care while controlling cost for plan sponsors.

Corporate Leadership and Staffing for Change

A broad knowledge of the industry, an insightful vision of the future, and a clear sense of corporate mission are essential prerequisites for leaders to direct the corporation into the future. Fundamental change begins first with executive leadership as noted in the Business Change Cycle. It is not good enough to be well-disciplined and capable managers: top executives must consistently and visibly display strong leadership abilities. Leaders stand out, personify the vision, and make believers of workers, investors, and customers. A military friend turned CEO is fond of stating, "A leader takes the hill; a manager keeps the hill."

A newly formed company or one that is growing from its infancy can have a dynamic leader that is the change agent and rallying post. Well-established companies that are undergoing directional or fundamental change, however, must have many leaders empowered at all levels to point the way and attract people to the cause. Those lacking this leadership can expect to slide down the Business Change Cycle to total change and possible extinction. Empowering management with the leadership mandate is difficult for many CEOs. People who have proven leadership skills realize how rare those skills are. The visionary leader will be reluctant to give loyal managers leadership responsibility when they have not proven their ability or willingness to lead. Leaders can rock the boat: they tend to focus more on end results rather than internal process, can be independent, and sometimes express frustration at the slow pace of change.

Managers, especially incumbent managers, have learned the way things have been done historically within the defined corporate structure. They are good at getting people to work within the accepted process, and they frequently are proud of their team-building or consensus-achieving skills. These skills are needed and rewarded in stable companies where direction is clear and workers understand their roles and can rely on the rules of behavior.

Fundamental change will not occur if leaders and management teams continue to use the same approaches, skills, and attitudes that they've always used. Innovation and flexibility are badly needed in the industry. *It must attract quality leaders who can capitalize on change while productively retaining and motivating key existing management.* This workable combination recognizes and values the existing management's performance within the guidelines and rules established by prior management. It offers a tradition, stability, and continuity that will be essential as the new company emerges. The dynamics of the industry will reward companies that bring talent in from the outside, that see new possibilities, and that can manage change. This new approach does not signal an abandonment of nurturing existing talent or a lessening commitment to employee development. Filling key positions with the best talent in the marketplace will bring new ideas, new emphasis, and healthy challenge to the existing order.

Too often a board of directors will bring in a CEO from the outside with a mandate for change but without the resolve, direction, or courage to expect other staff changes. At best, the new CEO can reshuffle the deck but will face an invisible wall of entrenched resistance from the existing staff. Facilitating directional or fundamental change by finding outside leaders is not a popular theme today. We must prepare for a changing industry that requires visionary leadership capable of managing change.

Business Strategy and "the Facts"

All too frequently businesses that are in need of fundamental change begin the process by reexamining their strategies. This approach is attacking the problem in the middle rather than at its source. Business strategies must be based on facts about the industry, the competition, the markets, and the position of the company as it exists today. Success requires that information be factual, complete, and current. This requirement may appear to be self-evident, but unless key people are, in fact, well informed about the industry and are recognized within the industry as being informed about current competitive and market issues, it is very probable that the facts are limited or questionable. CEOs managing change will want to challenge the information historically accepted by their organizations. When faced with the frequently heard, "That's the way we've always done it," they need to discover the real source of the knowledge base.

Large service- and transaction-based bureaucracies that successfully evolved over time are generally not skilled or equipped to evaluate underlying trends in the industry or market and formulate workable proposals to capitalize on directional or fundamental change. This reality adds to the volatility of the industry as nimble, more market-sensitive players may catch the Goliaths asleep. Huge hospitals are losing revenue to local surgicenters and home-care companies. Insurance companies will be shocked when technology permits an upstart computer company, or perhaps a giant like American Express, to handle the transaction aspects of claim payment along with much of the utilization review through parallel computer systems.

The Workforce of the Future

The health-care industry has shown steady growth in the numbers of professionals it has employed. This will necessarily change—especially in the general hospital sector, as beds are reduced. This will hit hard the effort that is needed to change attitudes, behaviors, and commitments—the industry's culture. Attempting to transform people who have never managed change (or may have resisted it) into managers who can effectively capitalize on the constant nature of change may require more time than the marketplace and the competitive forces will allow. Good leaders are hard to find, but they make the difference between success and failure. As the industry realizes the value of bringing key people in from the outside with broad business skills, all companies will risk losing good people to the competition. In addition, traditional boundaries and conflicts between medical and administrative staffs will have to be eliminated. The competitive advantage will go to companies that retain and attract the best talent. To do that, they must foster cultures that promote risk-taking innovation, empowerment, and a strong mutual commitment between management and staff. The industry, as large as it is, can accommodate several companies in each segment with this advantage. In this scenario the strong will get stronger, and the weak will be absorbed. The strongest competitors will be those that dedicate themselves to hiring top practitioners of change, while developing and challenging their skills in an environment that rewards results.

Roger A. Jones

Roger Jones is executive vice president for MEDCO Cost Containment Services Company of New Jersey. MEDCO is the nation's leading manager of prescription drug programs for corporations, government, and union organizations. Previously, Mr. Jones was eastern region president for Equicor, a nationwide provider of managed care services and funding to the health care industry. He earned his bachelor of science degree in business administration from Bucknell University.

11

The Pharmaceutical Industry: What's Driving the Change?

ROBERT N. WILSON
Vice Chairman, Johnson & Johnson

SARAH E. HENRY
Special Consultant, Organization Strategies, Inc.

The entire health-care industry reflects a unique dynamic where the mere anticipation of change is itself becoming a major force for change within individual companies. All participants are scrambling to position themselves for profitability in the dimly seen, but much heralded, world of health-care reform. The public clamor for cost containment, political promises of expanded coverage, and growing clout of health-care purchasing cooperatives have created an industry beset by a siege mentality. Pharmaceutical manufacturers have been particularly vulnerable to these pressures.

FROM ALCHEMY TO BIOTECHNOLOGY

The pharmaceutical industry had its roots in folklore and the cottage-based compounding of herbs, seeds, oils, and fats into curative potions and remedies. Nineteenth-century advances in transportation and distribution made it possible, for the first time, to produce patent medicines in bulk for later sale to a mass market. Over time, the hucksterism of the carnival barker gave way to a scientific and research-dependent industry. It was grounded in chemistry and progressively applied molecular biology, biochemistry, physical chemistry, computer modeling, and other sophisticated disciplines to the development of medicine. Unlike many comparable consumer products, drugs must indisputably demonstrate their safety and efficacy, or they will not be permitted to be marketed. Further, if products don't work as well as competing products or other modalities work, physicians won't prescribe them, and the public won't use them.

Consequently, new products and new technologies have been a constant spur to change within the industry. Every drug runs the risk of being eclipsed by a cheaper or more effective substitute. However, as long as a particular drug enjoys patent protection, price has traditionally been a matter of secondary importance. But today, even this ground rule is changing. Cost containment has become a matter of national and global concern. Although the shape of health-care reform in the United States remains uncertain, new strategies and new configurations are emerging as an entire industry realigns itself to cope with an unpredictable future.

STRUCTURE OF THE INDUSTRY

The pharmaceutical industry can be divided into two major groupings: research-based pharmaceutical developers and generic manufacturers. In addition, the research-based pharmaceutical companies collaborate with a wide variety of biotechnology companies, academic research institutes, and special technology companies in the development of new medicines and improved delivery systems for existing ones (Figure 11.1). The mission of the generic pharmaceutical companies is to produce and distribute low-priced copies of pioneer pharmaceutical products. These

Figure 11.1
Structure of the Biopharmaceutical Industry

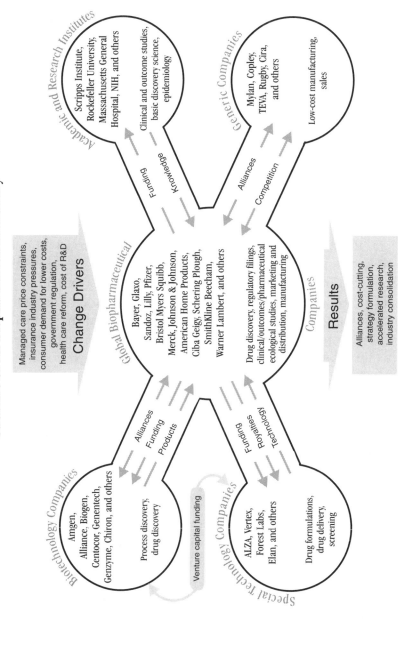

ucts. These generic copies are typically reformulations of older drugs that have lost their market protection due to patent expiration. Most important, these companies do not develop or invent drugs, nor do they conduct research designed to expand or improve the safe and effective use of their products.

By contrast, the mission of the research-based pharmaceutical sector is to conduct the research and development programs necessary to transform basic science into cost-effective medical treatments. These research programs also aim at improving the quality of life enjoyed by patients while determining the appropriate dosages required for various treatments. These enterprises are usually large, global businesses that support internal and academic biomedical research programs. They manufacture and distribute their products on a worldwide basis.

Although the generic drug producers are of considerable economic importance in the United States and are significant in national health-care policy, the research-based companies invent 90 percent of all new pharmaceutical products. The ability to create innovative drugs, manufacture them with near-zero tolerances for potency and safety, and then communicate their benefits to medical professionals is the key to competitive success. This requires a unique and complex mix of skills within each successful company.

The pattern of market concentration for pharmaceuticals is very different than it is most other high technology manufacturers. No single company accounts for more than 5 percent of the worldwide market. This diffusion also characterizes the U.S. market, where the largest company, Merck, holds a 6 percent share and it takes the top twenty companies to account for about half the U.S. market. Individual companies do, however, hold larger shares of specific therapeutic categories such as ulcer treatments, high blood pressure, cancer therapies, or antibiotics. A company strong in one category often tends to reveal weaknesses in other product areas. This absence of market dominance has fostered a diverse and productive research climate, permitted the simultaneous pursuit of different scientific visions, and has led to a wider array of new medicines for the public.

Paradoxically, even though no one company holds a large market share, the industry is characterized by a relatively large number of financially capable and highly profitable businesses. These companies undertake large, high-risk research and costly development programs. They conduct clinical investigations in major teaching hospitals worldwide where appropriate treatment protocols are developed for their products. And, finally, they market their new drugs through educational programs aimed at medical professionals.

CHANGE FORCES IMPACTING THE PHARMACEUTICAL INDUSTRY

For most industries, the source of change usually comes from a single source or maybe even two: in banking it's deregulation, in telecommunications it's the effects of divestiture, and in information technology, it's emerging new technologies. The pharmaceutical industry is beset by half a dozen change forces and all at the same time.

The High Cost of Product Development

The industry is also characterized by long lead times for product development. The full implications of these lengthy lead times is a critical factor in understanding risk and reward in the industry. Regulatory oversight and the need to demonstrate both safety and efficacy consume substantial time and money. Between seven and ten years and approximately $350 million are required to bring a new drug to market. This interval is calculated from the point when a new compound is actually discovered. There have often been years of work invested before a new compound is actually developed. Usually, the new compound or molecule is patented immediately since the investment in its discovery must be protected against others who are pursuing similar research. As a result, a major portion of a new product's seventeen-year patent life often has elapsed long before the product reaches the market.

This relatively short product life, when measured against the research investment required, significantly raises risk. In 1993, United States–based research pharmaceuticals spent $11 billion on research and development. The typical pharmaceutical company invests nearly 15 percent of sales in research as compared to other research-intensive industries, which invest 6 percent of sales in research. And for every one compound that eventually receives a federal license, 5,000 others are "dry holes." Consequently, no more than one drug in three ever recovers the full research investment dedicated to its discovery, evaluation, and manufacture.

The pharmaceutical industry began globalizing in the first quarter of the twentieth century. Global competition occurs among U.S. companies like Merck, Pfizer, Bristol-Myers Squibb, Eli Lilly, American Home Products, and Johnson & Johnson, as well as among competitors like Sandoz, Roche, and Ciba-Geigy of Switzerland, Bayer and Hoechst of Germany, Glaxo and Burroughs Wellcome of England, and the new British-American hybrid, SmithKline Beecham. Alliances among these companies have been and continue to be very important in understanding the industry. Cooperation has run the gamut from simple cross-licensing agreements to highly complex joint ventures in research, marketing, and manufacture—all to optimize the cost of product development.

Cost Containment: The Regulator Without a Face

As health-care costs have consumed an ever-larger proportion of gross national product, service providers have jockeyed to demonstrate that their costs are under control while implying that the real problem lies elsewhere. The research-based pharmaceutical companies, together with insurers, have made easy targets. The result has been to rapidly expand the use of generic copies of pioneer drugs in lieu of new or emerging technologies. This has made it even more difficult for the inventor of a pioneer drug to recover the investment made in research and the facilities needed to isolate, produce, and distribute that particular discovery.

This pressure is particularly severe in the United States, where employer and governmental demands for cost containment are driving an ever-larger percentage of the health-care system into a managed-care setting. Large, well-organized health-care systems are now representing the consumer, which increases the pressure for cost containment. The speed with which patients are being moved from supervision by personally selected physicians to groups that manage an individual's care for a fee is astonishing. During the six years from 1987 to 1993, managed-care organizations increased their share of the market from 17 percent to over 50 percent. Excellent care is available through these managed-care providers, but some restriction in choice is exercised to contain costs.

Because of the purchasing power of managed-care organizations and their ability to control the number and specific names of drugs authorized for use with their patients, they can now demand sizable discounts from manufacturers. Other group purchasers, including national health plans and even some treatment review organizations, are similarly pressing pharmaceutical companies for discounts based on volume and the placement of specific drugs on their reimbursement lists. As a result, the proportion of industry sales made to individual consumers based on their own preferences and physician recommendation is in sharp decline. Clearly, the number of pharmaceutical detail representatives will decrease over the next decade.

In most cases, only a few products are authorized for reimbursement in each treatment class, with generics preferred. Delisting of a pioneer or patented drug can have a devastating impact on company earnings. Not surprisingly, price competition has sharply increased throughout the industry. This has created an effect similar to the deregulation of the airline and trucking industries, creating pressure for consolidation and partnerships.

Worldwide Government Regulation

Although proposed government commercial regulation of the industry is new to the United States, the worldwide pharmaceutical industry has long been subjected to regulation by most governments in both the developed and the undeveloped world. In Europe and Japan, pharmaceuticals are further subjected to commercial regulation by state-run or state-mandated health-care programs, strict price controls, and approved lists of drugs for reimbursement. Until recently, only the United States and Germany had unregulated markets where market conditions alone were the determiners of price, and now Germany has begun to regulate and control the price of drugs.

In state-run health-care systems, a drug must be on the list of approved drugs for reimbursement or it essentially does not exist in the marketplace. State-mandated controls in France have led to good science and research support for the pharmaceutical industry but a negligible presence in discovery. This is significant to an industry that is truly global. American companies have drawn 40 to 60 percent of their business outside the United States. European companies have similar market profiles. So the impending health-care measures in America will have a tremendous impact on the global industry.

Biotechnology: The Expansion of Risk

The pharmaceutical industry is uniquely dependent on the end products of applied science. This reliance on technology involves a never-ending search for better and more effective products and techniques and an ever-growing commitment of funds. In fact, research expense has been doubling in terms of real dollars every five years for the past two decades—just $0.6 billion in 1970 but approaching $11 billion in 1992. The new, so-called biotechnologies, involving the production of biological and organic agents, are more expensive than ever.

Development and production costs are also escalating with the introduction of these synthetically manufactured organic agents. Separate production facilities are often required for certain product classes in order to avoid the risk of cross-contamination. The pharmaceutical industry is required to replicate products every day, which will predictably and reliably deliver pharmacologically active substances measured at the thousandths of a gram level. At the same time, basic research has produced an explosion of knowledge relative to biological processes that can be applied to drug discovery and development.

In the successful discovery of a new medicine, research costs represent only about 20 percent of final development expense. The research phase, however, is the least determinate in terms of time required to a successful conclusion. Development (accounting for 80 percent of expense) is a many-faceted activity that encompasses clinical testing, the development of large-scale manufacturing processes, product-stability testing, quality-assurance procedures, and the management of the regulatory licensing and approval process. Because of the critical mass required for global development, the large pharmaceutical companies will continue to be well positioned to be key players in bringing new medicines to the world market.

All major companies have extensive development capabilities. Therefore, the dominant strategy for gaining access to cutting-edge biotechnologies has been consolidation between companies, an expanded effort to form alliances with emerging companies, and maintenance of high levels of support for university-based basic research. These alliances take many forms: equity investment, joint ventures, partnerships, progressive investment commitments based on development of a concept, and permutations of these arrangements. The research field is now too wide and too active for any one company to effectively explore all possibilities in-house. The small discovery companies are chronically in need of capital and usually do not possess the size or sophistication to manage the development process themselves. A productive symbiosis is the natural outcome for research and development firms.

The continued financial strength and viability of the global pharmaceutical industry is of vital importance to biotechnology companies. Biotechnology appears to offer the most promising route to improved treatment protocols for reversing, halting, or even curing the most difficult metabolic diseases. Gene therapy is perhaps the most difficult and sophisticated of the new molecular approaches to treatment, yet it promises the most profound and physiologic intervention for disease states, particularly for those that are genetically based. These latter diseases are typically devastating to a person's quality of life and frequently end in early and painful death for those afflicted. Further, with today's technology, treatment and care for these patients is often expensive, both in terms of cost of treatment and loss of productivity for the society. Gene therapy may well turn out to be the only successful approach to conditions such as Huntington's chorea, sickle cell anemia, Cooley's anemia, hemophilia, Tay-Sachs, Down syndrome, and familial hypercholesteremia, each of which affects many thousands to literally millions, depending on the disease. Further, genetic links are important—even if not entirely identified—components of schizophrenia, alcoholism, many cancers, cardiovascular disease, and possibly multiple sclerosis and cystic fibrosis. The way is long and extremely expensive to find answers in this science, and while the limited successes to date with the bubble baby syndrome are tantalizing, they are mere beginnings. However, the cost-benefit tradeoff clearly favors the commitment of effort, resources, and the long timeline that these research and development programs require.

The downside to this emerging technology is that the reliable production of these agents demands for entire buildings a level of contaminant-free environment that was, until just a few years ago, difficult to achieve within a single research flask. These facilities are highly specialized and demand an extraordinary investment in specialized vessels, instrumentation, filters, and clean rooms. A key consideration is that these are actually biological products that require special handling and refrigeration. Yet drug development of any kind requires large-scale investment and long-term commitment because of the high cost and shortened product life that flows from the long years of a drug's patent life that are spent in study and regulatory review.

This investment requires global access to markets in order to maximize the chances of recovering an adequate return on capital. Therefore, companies are coming to terms with the fundamental decision about whether to seek their future as broad-line, balanced competitors or to pursue a niche strategy. Niche players, however, will still need access to global outlets for their specialized products. In either case, both the market and emerging technologies are contributing to increasing globalization in this already global industry.

Industry Consolidation

Industry consolidation is not just a source of change in the pharmaceutical industry: it is also a product of the numerous change forces that are simultaneously impacting the industry. Continued consolidation of the worldwide pharmaceutical industry may be inevitable with increasing regulation abroad and the prospect of some form of government regulation in the United States. Through alliances and international mergers like those between SmithKline and Beecham and between Astra and Merck, European companies are better able to market their products in the United States market while U.S. drug makers are better positioned to enter European markets through their European partners and subsidiaries.

Nevertheless, worldwide cost containment—not regulation—is the *major* contributor to industry consolidation. The skyrocketing cost of drug discovery and development is now beyond the reach of many small and midsize companies like Carter-Wallace (which abandoned drug research in late 1993), and it is testing the resources of many larger manufacturers.

Horizontal consolidation on the company and division levels and joint ventures between large companies exist largely for the purpose of creating greater scales of economy in R&D and in marketing. Several have included Roche/Genentech/Syntex,

Ciba-Geigy/Chiron, SmithKline/Beecham, Merck/DuPont, Marion/Merrell/Dow, American Home Products/American Cyanamid, Sanofi/Sterling, and the biggest in the U.S. sector—Bristol-Myers/Squibb. The Bristol-Myers/Squibb merger has been not just the largest but possibly the most complementary designed consolidation: it created a more competitive pharmaceutical company by providing a presence in most therapeutic categories. Squibb was strong in R&D in creating cardiovascular drugs and diagnostic agents and producing a wide array of ethical drugs while adhering to long-term strategies. They were a patient and process-oriented company. Bristol-Myers was also doing research, primarily in the cancer treatment field, psychotropics, and antibiotics, but they were stronger in over-the-counter consumer products. Bristol-Myers was also very bottom-line oriented, and the pressure to produce was more visible in Bristol-Myers than in Squibb. As one unified company, BMS is a more formidable competitor in the marketplace because of its significant presence in a number of therapeutic categories.

Vertical consolidation has the effect of extending a company's reach into sectors where it historically has had little strength. Merck's acquisition of MEDCO—a pharmacy-benefit manager (PBM)—is a classic example that surprised the industry but that may pay dividends in time.

In the minds of many people, Merck has been the premier research-based pharmaceutical company in the industry. It has been unmatched in its ability to discover new medicines and apply them with novel forms of action on the patient. This has allowed it to demand premium prices for its products. So why would it purchase a pharmaceutical cost-containment company for $6 billion? MEDCO doesn't just distribute drugs at discount prices through mail order, it also manages the lists and costs of drugs for health insurance plans and managed-care institutions. This will allow Merck to place its drugs on MEDCO-managed lists more frequently than it normally would, and it also allows Merck to earn MEDCO's PBM fees, which are a new revenue channel for Merck.

Another example of vertical integration again involves Merck in a joint venture with Johnson & Johnson. Merck has no real ability to market products to the consumer—specifically, prescription drugs that the FDA *may* approve for over-the-counter or non-prescription use. These product conversions help both Merck and Johnson & Johnson to participate in the cost-containment trend toward more self-medication by the patient. J&J gains access to additional products from Merck's vaunted product pipeline and Merck benefits from J&J's superior consumer-marketing clout. These are all examples of how the industry is coming together through mergers, alliances, and joint ventures to better cope with change forces that are beyond the control of individual companies.

WHAT DOES THE FUTURE HOLD?

Few other industries have experienced the radical change that has rocked the pharmaceutical industry in recent years. Externally, health-care reform, cost containment, and the advent of market Darwinism has battered stock prices and profit margins. Internally, biotechnology advances, service and product diversification, and industry consolidation have created an entirely new set of demands on managers. Hostile takeovers are being seen for the first time as companies attempt to position themselves horizontally or as vertically integrated health-care providers. Agreements between pharmaceuticals and pharmacy benefit management administrators (PBMs) are streamlining distribution while providing patient-therapy-effectiveness data. All is in flux.

Industry analysts are predicting further restructuring, which will result in a handful of powerhouses supported by many niche players. This is all occurring in an environment with the threat of heavy, some would say oppressive, governmental regulation. Few adversarial regulatory schemes are required to support increased levels of collaboration and the development of new drugs and treatment methods. Industry restructuring will also blur traditional organizational boundaries as former competitors find it advantageous to share information and methods. Simultaneously, the globalization of the market will demand cross-cultural sensitivity and marketing know-how. The internal structure of pharmaceutical companies will also change. Chains of command will have to be shortened so that spans of control are extended from a current industry standard of 2.7 to 3.2 reports to one supervisor to a projected 5.7 reports to one supervisor.

Customer Changes

Perhaps the most unprecedented change for pharmaceuticals is the still-evolving character of their customer base—not the ultimate medical needs of patients but the person who is actually purchasing drugs on behalf of the patient. Traditionally, the independent physician-practitioner was regarded as the customer, and large salesforces serviced the needs of individual physicians. Although the physician remains a significant market, PBMs, HMOs, hospitals, pharmacies, and insurance companies now dominate the marketplace. These changes have created powerful pressures for the selection of the most cost-effective therapies. At times, pharmaceutical companies are finding themselves treated as vendors rather than as professional collaborators.

Pharmaceuticals are also being asked to assume many of the costs of operations formerly shouldered by retailers. Huge accounts like WalMart can and do demand individual store demographics and planograms. Some pharmaceutical companies are partnering with large accounts, such as Wal-Mart, to their mutual advantage. These large, savvy customers recognize their power and wield it with little brand allegiance. This emerging marketplace carries implications not only for strategy but for structure, business processes, technology, marketing, sales, manufacturing, R&D, distribution channels, and the workforce. In short, all that constitutes total organization change.

All of this is transpiring at a time when tight financial markets and eroding profit margins create resource constraints unfamiliar to the industry. Therefore, timely and accurate innovation will be the hallmark of competitive survival. Appropriate speed of thought and action will prove critical if this transition is to be navigated successfully.

Workforce Changes

Ambiguity and uncertainty are among the few certainties facing the industry workforce—organizational dissent over the Business Change Cycle. Despite this, performance standards have not been merely raised but have leapfrogged past all previous expectations. Fewer people are being asked to do much, much more. As strategies, value chains, and business processes change, work itself—how and where it is performed and the skills needed for highly effective production—has dramatically changed. Companies require extremely flexible, diversified, and high-achieving workforces that can be quickly deployed to carry out business strategies. The desire and adaptability to constantly and quickly learn will be required of all employees, regardless of their assignment or job level.

In other words, all employees will be expected to evidence competencies traditionally demanded of senior management. All employees must have widely based and continually updated knowledge and understanding of the industry, as a whole, as well as their own company—its finances, processes, organization, and products. They must become customer and market centered while adopting a service-oriented work ethic. And, finally, they must be able to work effectively in high-performance teams, alliances, and partnerships forged with customers, vendors, suppliers, and, occasionally, even competitors. Negotiation, influencing, coalition, and network-building skills will prove invaluable. Interestingly, many of the global pharmaceutical companies have been evolving these approaches over a number of years.

The emerging pharmaceutical marketplace is one that will require the juggling of multiple, often conflicting, demands. Communication skills will have to be finely honed, including cross-cultural understanding. Most of all, employees must be able to think systematically—identifying and analyzing complex relationships, patterns, and trends. They must possess high personal autonomy, together with the motivation, discipline, and self-esteem required to be self-directed decision makers. Most important, employees must have a high tolerance for ambiguity, and they must embrace change, not resist it.

Leadership Changes

Industry executives will be expected to focus more on results while better understanding the implications of change on the company's ability to compete. SmithKline Beckman was a good example of a company that relied too long on older, well-established products. Its R&D lost its focus and drive for keeping the pipeline stocked with new products, forcing the company to relinquish its independence to Britain's Beecham.

Schering Plough is an excellent midsize company that would seem to be a candidate for acquisition in the current environment. Nevertheless, its well-regarded CEO, Robert Luciano, has signaled the company's intention to maintain its independence by increasing Schering Plough's focus on becoming more results oriented in its labs while linking them more closely with its marketing capabilities.

Merck took the unusual step of going outside the industry to find its new CEO, Raymond Gilmartin, the successful CEO of medical-instruments-producer Becton Dickinson. He faces a formidable challenge integrating the R&D culture of Merck with the mail-order and distribution mentality of MEDCO.

As time and industry changes progress, the profile of pharmaceutical managers and executives will also have to change to reflect a broader grasp of business and societal issues. They must begin to think as change managers who never rely on static or friendly market conditions.

DIRECTIONAL CHANGE FOR
THE PHARMACEUTICAL INDUSTRY

The entire pharmaceutical industry is being confronted by directional change, according to Want's Business Change Cycle. Change is coming from the marketplace with a dizzying array of pressures and new competitive rules for the road. As a result, strategies will have to change for every company, and any that do not adapt will fail. Given that the industry is so uniformly burdened by these change forces (and that it is in the early phases of change), it is appropriate to place most of the major pharmaceutical companies on the change side of the Business Change Cycle and at the directional-change level (see Figure 11.2). In two to three years, there will be increased differentiation between the companies as some succeed with their change strategies while others fall behind on the change cycle.

Changing company structures, intercompany alliances, and mergers will not be enough to make a company successful. It will have to examine closely how well its executives plan and lead and how well prepared its culture is for being responsive to an increasingly unpredictable and hostile marketplace. In an industry where the typical company is segmented, there will have to be a move toward seamless organizations. R&D will have to work more closely with marketing as distribution channels and product buyers change. Human resources will have to do more to prepare, evaluate, and promote talent so that the larger enterprise retains its competitive edge. Most important, each company will have to maintain a strong vision for both its workforce and for the marketplace.

Figure 11.2
Change in the Biopharmaceutical Industry

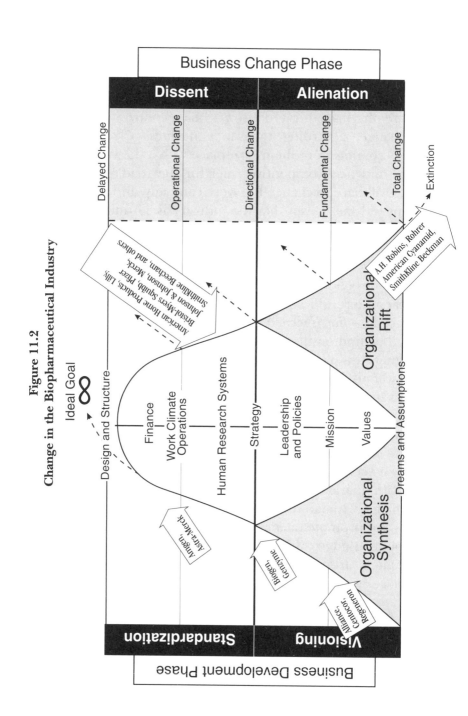

Robert N. Wilson

Robert N. Wilson is vice chairman of the board of directors of Johnson & Johnson, the diversified health-care company. Mr. Wilson also serves as the vice chairman of the executive committee. Mr. Wilson is responsible for Johnson & Johnson's Corporate Office of Science and Technology, as well as the company's Worldwide Environmental Policies and Programs Task Force.

Previously, he was with the Ortho Pharmaceutical Corporation, a subsidiary of Johnson & Johnson. In 1977, he became the president of Johnson & Johnson's Dental Products Company, and in 1979, he was appointed president of Ortho Pharmaceutical.

Mr. Wilson is a member of a number of organizations and societies, including the board of directors of the Pharmaceutical Research and Manufacturers of American (PhRMA), the board of directors of the Scientific Advisory Board of the Center for Advanced Biotechnology and Medicine, and the Executive Committee of the Pharmaceutical Partners for Better Health Care. He earned his bachelor's degree from Georgetown College of Kentucky.

Sarah E. Henry

Sarah Henry is a special consultant for Organization Strategies, Inc., a Madison, NJ change-strategy consulting firm. Dr. Henry is a leading authority on workforce dynamics and human resource strategy. Previously, she was director of organization development for Warner-Lambert and director of human resource planning and development for Sterling/Winthrop Pharmaceuticals.

Dr. Henry has also held senior consulting positions with Towers Perrin and the Renaissance Strategy Group, serving clients in the areas of organization design, culture development, work-process engineering, and leadership development. Some of Dr. Henry's clients have included Chrysler-Mitsubishi Diamond Start Motors, Detroit Edison, Ameritech, AT&T, and Kraft Foods.

Dr. Henry has been a member of the Metropolitan New York Association for Applied Psychology, the Human Resource Planning Society, and the Society for Industrial/Organizational Psychology. She earned her bachelor's and master's degrees from the University of Kansas, and she holds a doctorate in industrial and organization psychology from Stevens Institute of Technology.

Change on Wall Street: The Decline and Fall of a Giant

J. JENNINGS PARTIN
The Diameter Group

People who are curious about Wall Street are reminded of it nearly every day as the Dow Jones Industrial averages are quoted on news broadcasts throughout the world. While most may not understand the inner workings of the financial center of the world, they have formed an impression of life in the financial marketplace through films like *Wall Street, Working Girl,* and *Bonfire of the Vanities,* which have popularized and reinforced Wall Street stereotypes. Hollywood has taken certain license with the character traits of those who work in the banking and brokerage industry, but real-life examples of Wall Street personalities are accurately described in books such as *The Predators' Ball* (a story about the junk bond empire at Drexel Burnham Lambert) and *Liars Poker* (an inside look at bond trading at Salomon Brothers). Whether portrayed on the screen or observed in real life, Wall Street values are both complex and paradoxical—but they are no different than values found in many other large organizations.

The management challenge of overseeing such a complex fabric of people and styles is immense. Traditional solutions don't fit, but there are no precedents for professional management practices. Instead, a star system and practices have evolved (tailored to fit the situation) that, in a high-transaction environment, don't lend themselves to change or innovation. And although the institutions built on these practices grew over decades, they have fallen in a fraction of that time, as was the case of E. F. Hutton in 1987–1988 and Drexel Burnham Lambert in 1988–1989. More recently, incidents led to the resignations of the chairman and the president of Salomon Brothers in August 1991.

In 1993 and 1994, we saw the indictment of Merrill Lynch, Kidder Peabody, and Prudential Securities for fraudulent trading and selling practices. Some of these irregularities may be understandable (if not acceptable) in that entirely new products and opportunities for investing (such as derivatives) have opened up that are not well understood by senior management, the public, or even regulators. The increased utilization of computer technology also has made it easier to cross the boundaries of best professional practice.

This chapter describes is how one Wall Street institution— E. F. Hutton—grew and died an ignoble death. It reconstructs the themes that led to the development of the firm's distinctive personality, which later became the source of its vulnerability and demise. The firm's failure will be interpreted using Jerry Want's Business Change Cycle as a diagnostic device for understanding the critical issues that existed but went largely unnoticed.

The firm sensed some of the changes that needed to occur as described in the change phase of the Business Change Cycle. However, internal dissent among senior managers, personal agendas, and missed windows of opportunity led the firm to do too little, too late. *The speed with which the company moved through the operational, directional, and fundamental change stages was much too rapid for the leadership to sense and respond to.* In a matter of months— beginning with Shearson's initial probe in the fall of 1986 and accelerating through the summer of 1987 until the fall of 1987— the company's rocket-like fall could not be stopped.

CHANGE FORCES ON THE STREET

Change in the investment banking and brokerage industry has been overwhelming. Most of us watch with fascination as the latest scandal forces a key resignation, as in the case of John Gutfreund, or the failure of an entire firm, as with Drexel Burnham Lambert. Most Americans may feel that these events have no effect on them personally, but Wall Street affects us all, as these firms have become the driving force behind most corporate mergers, the financing of business expansion, and the investment of trillions of dollars of pension fund monies.

Growth and size have been the major driving forces behind the industry for the past thirty years, recently followed by increased monitoring and regulation of the industry. Until Donaldson Lufkin & Jenrette went public in the early 1970s, all firms were private partnerships. Eventually, all but a few of the firms went public to protect themselves from suits and to identify additional capital for expansion. *Nevertheless, the culture of the privately held partnerships that worked out of sight of the public and of regulators has been slow to change.* Some individual traders and high-level officers continue to engage in questionable practices that yield drastic consequences for themselves and their firms, especially as the opportunities for enriching oneself have increased with the dramatic increase in revenues that are handled by these firms.

The dramatic growth and change that have occurred in the industry are demonstrated by the following:

- In 1970, the market saw a record high trading day of 50 million shares; today, a trading day of 300 million shares is not unusual.

- In 1968, Merrill Lynch had a total value of $250 million; by 1990, it had a market share value of around $3 billion, making it the largest American investment firm (at the same time, Nomura Securities was valued at over $46 billion).

- Seven of today's top ten firms were not even in the top ten in 1968, and at that time, a company like Morgan Stanley had only 250 employees (including clerical staff).

Much of this growth was fueled by the passage of ERISA in 1974, ensuring the vesting and portability of pension funds. In 1975, fixed commissions for brokers were abolished, forcing the failure of many companies that could no longer compete. As pensions flowed into the brokerage houses, pension managers demanded lower fees for high-volume transactions. The operations of firms also were affected as they could no longer manage the volume of transactions that flooded their offices. Merrill Lynch was the first to recognize this need and led the industry in backroom computerization and automation.

Another landmark event came in 1977 with the creation of high-yield (junk) bonds. This fueled the leveraged buyouts of companies, which invited mergers and acquisitions. Some of these ventures were highly beneficial, creating such companies as MCI and Compaq. In addition, other countries—Germany, Japan, and a number of Middle Eastern countries—were now able to grow their own economies without the help of the United States. This also fueled the growth of securities markets in London, Tokyo, and Hong Kong, forcing U.S. securities firms to open operations overseas.

The growth of technology, trading volume, and overseas markets and economies forced U.S. firms to specialize:

LEADING RETAIL BROKERS:

Merrill Lynch
Dean Witter
Paine Webber
Smith Barney Shearson
Kidder Peabody (no longer in existence)
Prudential Securities

LEADING MERGERS AND ACQUISITIONS AND CORPORATE
UNDERWRITERS:

Morgan Stanley
Lazard
Drexel Burnham (no longer in existence)
Goldman Sachs
Merrill Lynch
Salomon Bros.
Lehman Bros.

LEADING BOND TRADERS:

Bear Stearns
Salomon Brothers

The biggest bomb to hit Wall Street recently was the crash of October 1987. Careers were ruined, thousands of jobs were lost, and entire firms were liquidated or taken over by firms outside Wall Street or by larger survivors on the Street. The irony of the October 1987 crash was that since most Wall Street firms were no longer private partnerships (they were publicly traded companies), their stock value crashed along with most other companies, making them vulnerable to takeover.

THE HUTTON LEGACY

Mention the name of E. F. Hutton prior to 1985 and most people would smile, lean forward, tilt their heads with a hand cupped over one ear, and pretend to listen intently. "When E. F. Hutton speaks, people listen" was one of the most successful advertising campaigns of all time. Not only did it reap huge benefits for the firm, but it also won several awards for its advertising excellence. But this public awareness was simply an external recognition of what people in the firm for decades had experienced for years. Like other long-lived firms (Hutton was founded in 1904), a lore was handed down from one employee to another, which helped create and maintain a distinctive culture.

Perhaps the earliest legend is about Bet-a-Million Gates, a high-rolling, flamboyant financier. In 1905, Gates was visiting the West Coast and went to Hutton's San Francisco office to execute a trade. According to the story, he promised the office manager that he would give Hutton all his business if the firm could execute the trade in fifteen minutes. By using its private Western Union line, it did the trade in less than three minutes, which began a long relationship between Gates and Hutton.

Another early story about company heroes involved the great San Francisco earthquake. When Edward F. Hutton persuaded the president of Western Union to provide the firm with a private line to San Francisco, it was a major coup because private lines were available only to Denver at the time and no other California brokerage firm had one. The line proved to be a distinct trading advantage on April 18, 1906, when the earthquake struck San Francisco at 5:13 A.M. According to the legend, Richard Mulcahy, manager of the San Francisco office, recovered his books and chartered a fishing boat to Oakland. At Oakland's Western Union office, he persuaded the office manager to open Hutton's private line and then sold off his client's interests in companies with San Francisco operations before anyone in New York knew about the quake.

A CULTURE BASED ON FEW RULES

Employees who came to work for Hutton in the early 1980s soon found themselves in a company that could be characterized as paternalistic, permissive, generous, forgiving, proud, and, generally speaking, a great place to work. The headquarters was then located in the Battery Park area of Manhattan in the heart of New York's financial district, easily accessible to most employees. Compensation levels were at or above the market for most jobs, with the possible exception of back-office operations (below average) and brokers (above average). The firm offered benefits comparable to other Wall Street firms but less generous than major companies in other industries. The emphasis was on cash income—slightly below average salaries with high incentive compensations or bonuses. For several years prior to 1985, everyone in the company got an annual bonus ranging from hundreds to millions of dollars.

There were few rules, and those that did exist usually could be ignored, if employees didn't openly flaunt their rule breaking. Forgiveness was often easier to get than permission, especially in uncertain or overlapping areas of responsibility. Aggressive employees were able to do nearly anything they wanted to do, provided they didn't arouse the wrath of the power elite, the heavy hitters who brought fee and commission income to the firm. On May 2, 1985, all of this changed—forever.

THE HUTTON FIASCO

The bubble that finally burst on May 2, 1985, had been a long time in coming. The decline and decay of Hutton was, for the most part, obscured from rank-and-file members of the firm. They continued to live in the aura of the Hutton traditions and were proud of their association with the company. The roots of the fall were a labyrinth of complex dealings that went unnoticed for months and, in some cases, years before they were ever known by the general population.

The Guilty Plea

May 2, 1985, marked the beginning of what was to become a public viewing of the events that led to the firm's eventual collapse. Every major news service carried the announcement that E. F. Hutton had plead guilty to 2,000 counts of wire fraud for check kiting. In simple terms, the company admitted to moving funds between accounts in different banks in such a way as to take advantage of the float and earn interest on money that was not on deposit in the proper accounts. While many individuals and companies have done this from time to time, Hutton was accused of developing a "money mobilization system" to do this on a grand scale. While no customer accounts were involved, the sums were large. One small bank in Pennsylvania was systemically overdrawn by $900,000 per day for the last few months of 1981. Similar occurrences were found in other banks in Pennsylvania and New York during the 1981–1982 time frame. Although the practice had long since ceased, a grand jury returned an indictment leading to the guilty plea, which marked the first public sign that things were askew in E. F. Hutton.

While the check kiting scheme was the most widely known white-collar crime of its time, two other episodes in the Hutton story are indicative of what was happening to the firm. Internally they were referred to as FAMCO and the Aubin case. They illustrate that the company leadership was out of touch with the company's culture, which later contributed to its demise.

FAMCO

In December 1983, Hutton entered into an agreement to buy mortgages from First American Mortgage Company (FAMCO), which operated mostly in Maryland. These mortgages were unusual in that they carried very high usury rates (as high as 18 percent at the time) and up-front points of as much as 30 percent of the value of the loan. Then, as now, the only people interested in such terms are desperate. As a result, many borrowers were paying extremely high interest rates (in some cases 100 percent or more of the principle). Since Hutton was making extremely high margins on this business, it apparently never occurred to anyone that things were amiss when FAMCO failed to submit agreed-to reports of its operations. As it later turned out, FAMCO was using the cash flow from new loans to pay off overdue payments on bad loans (a Ponzi scheme). Because the requirements for reporting results were not enforced, Hutton never knew the desperate condition of the mortgage company and continued to buy FAMCO mortgages at the rate of $10 million per month. Even after Hutton discovered that the company was in default of the terms of its agreement, FAMCO was given a letter that these terms would be waived. Finally, in November 1984, a Hutton accountant visited a branch office in Arkansas and discovered that E. F. Hutton would need to foreclose on millions of dollars of bad loans. One company lawyer was then assigned full time to this case in order to minimize further losses and exposure—but more than money was lost by this incident.

The Aubin Case

The Aubin case in another example of misguided trust and lack of oversight. Long before the present national savings and loan debacle became widely known, Hutton had its own S&L crisis. From 1980 to 1984, a customer named Aubin and a Hutton broker in Houston together managed to get Hutton to do some unusual things. The customer and his associates opened as many as thirty-nine margin accounts at one time. A margin account is similar to a revolving credit account in which a customer is able to borrow short-term funds from the firm to buy securities on credit, provided that the full amount of the transactions is paid within a specific time period (such as five days from the date of the transaction). The Aubin group required settlement of their personal trades the day after their trades were made, while taking as much time as allowable to pay any monies due to Hutton. Aubin had insufficient funds in his accounts, but by writing checks on accounts he had just settled, Aubin was able to use Hutton's own money to finance his future trades. By the time Hutton discovered what was happening, Aubin owed Hutton more than $40 million. To pay off his debts, Aubin proposed to settle his account using the assets of two S&Ls owned by a friend. The S&Ls' financials indicated that they were worth more than $100 million. With these assets, Aubin was allowed an even higher line of credit. His trading appetite increased and over the next few months, he drew down another $40 million in equity until his losses left him with a $10 million deficit in his accounts. In March 1986, the Federal Home Loan Bank Board placed the two S&Ls into conservatorship because of numerous illegalities. Hutton was left holding the bag for $48 million, which was over $2 million more than the company earned in 1985.

And so, the latter days of E. F. Hutton were marred by revelations of impropriety that were evidence of an inner decay of growing proportions. Indiscretions and poor judgment were not new: customer complaints are routine in the securities industry. Management oversight required that branch managers ensure that customer trades were consistent with stated investment objectives and were within acceptable degrees of prudent levels of financial risk. The major difference in these cases is the magnitude of the money made or lost.

Failed Values

On reflection, one could make the case that these cases were aberrations in an otherwise ethical work environment. After all, these cases involved only a few dozen of over 30,000 employees. The headquarters and local field offices continued to participate in worthy projects. For example, many offices allowed community fundraisers to use their funds to solicit for worthy causes. This was, after all, the same company that ran soup kitchens during the Depression. *But over the years, there were manifest changes in the values, leadership, management styles, management systems, compensation, rewards, and vision of the company.* These were the roots that provided so little sustenance during the final days.

THE ROOTS OF THE FALL:
FAILED VALUES AND FAILED LEADERSHIP

It may be said that values are the key elements that combine to form a distinctive corporate culture. Every company has a culture that serves as the glue that holds together sometimes disparate elements to form the fabric of the company. At Hutton, traditional values—always putting the client first, ensuring that the client understood his or her investment objectives and how the prospective transactions met those needs—were becoming secondary. Brokers were not measured in terms of customer satisfaction. They were rated in terms of sales volume and production credits—the stepping stones to financial success and career advancement in the latter-day Hutton, as well as the grounds for its final failure. On the Business Change Cycle, failed values and mission represent the need for total change (see Figure 4.5 on page 83).

Packaged Products and Promotions

In the early days of the firm, when the securities business was less complicated, the level of trust between client and broker was sacrosanct. The company, for the most part, sold only stocks and bonds, which were fairly easily understood securities. During the 1970s and 1980s, however, new investment vehicles emerged that were much more complicated, making it easier to shave explanations to get a buy. The new language included CMOs, CATs, upper floaters, not to mention annuities and other packaged products. In the last days of Hutton, there were branch offices that rarely sold stocks and bonds staffed by brokers who sold *only* packaged products (such as life insurance and annuities). The commissions on company products were higher than other companies' products, and sales campaigns were designed to push certain products. Not unexpectedly, quotas soon replaced customer needs and investment strategy as the prime motivators of broker behavior.

Ethical Indifference and Apathy

After the guilty plea in May 1985, the firm hired Judge Griffin Bell (attorney general in the Carter administration) to conduct an internal investigation to determine what remedial actions should be taken. Judge Bell recommended Hutton retain the Ethics Resource Center, a not-for-profit firm headquartered in Washington that he had worked with in the past. The Ethics Resource Center worked with a committee of representatives appointed from each major unit of the company. The committee worked for several months in the fall and spring of 1985–1986 to draft a credo or statement of values and beliefs that would be the guide to future ethical behavior. This is a difficult assignment for any organization, but especially so for a group that was under siege by the press, the federal government, and its own employees. After several meetings and ethics statement revisions, the consensus was that the result was unimpressive and far from what was needed to make a bold statement and chart a new course. A final committee report was issued but never widely publicized. A program called "Red Light, Green Light," consisting of case studies and the credo, was offered twice to two groups of field employees but later was dropped for lack of interest. The agenda remained: make money.

Hired Guns

Beginning in the spring of 1986 and over the next year, there was a deliberate attempt to jump start the company's lagging performance by recruiting some hired guns. The firm's president had concluded that Hutton executives who had grown up in the company didn't have the talent, insight, or commitment to shake things up and reach for higher levels of performance. Within a period of twelve months, the firm hired a new chief financial officer, general counsel, head of trading, head of marketing, head of corporate finance, and head of management information systems. They came from Deloitte Haskins and Sells, Debevoise and Plimpton, Citicorp, American Express, Merrill Lynch, and Salomon Brothers. Each brought his or her own lieutenants to fill key positions. Since these were senior positions, the top of the hierarchy was soon populated by new people in nearly every function, many of whom had little, if any, experience in the brokerage business but were seasoned professionals in their own areas—largely outside of Wall Street.

The results were disastrous. Most of the new breed had employment contracts that guaranteed their compensation for two or three years and protected them from any downside risks, including a change of control. Moreover, they came convinced that Hutton was sick and that they had the medicine that would cure the illness. *This wasn't a situation that encouraged consensus building, teamwork, mutual goal setting, and agreement on what needed to be done.* As the values and beliefs of each unit became polarized, no statesmen emerged who were capable of bridging the differences. Balkanization of the firm had set in.

Leadership

Power quickly shifted to the new elite. Over a twelve- to eighteen-month period, one group emerged in the corporate headquarters that wanted to run the firm according to its rules and another group emerged in the field that attempted to disassociate itself from the people and events that it believed had brought such shame on the company and its employees.

As a result of this concentrated infusion of new people, new forces were unleashed in the company:

- People with employment contracts often acted in their own interests, based on the incentives included in their agreements.

- New functions (such as marketing and management-information systems were established, which either were substantially different in approach or had a different reporting relationship, or both.

- Factions became evident and manifested themselves in terms of when they assumed their duties, to whom they owed their allegiance, and whether they were from Hutton or from the outside.

The effect was to transform a traditional, old-line Wall Street firm into an entanglement of counterproductive and conflicting goals and management styles. Subcultures developed that occasionally arose in opposition to one another and were ultimately harmful to the firm. The result was a continuing struggle to reach an inner harmony that never lasted. Depending on one's position and tenure in the firm, the attitude was either "These guys are ruining the firm" or "These people are acting as though nothing happened. Can't they see the handwriting on the wall?" Neither position provided much room for accommodation of the other. The runaway train to failure was accelerating.

MANAGEMENT SYSTEMS

The introduction of new values, systems, and people significantly affected the firm, but the condition of the management infrastructure made the situation even more critical. The structure for communicating changes was tenuous. Although the company was in a high transaction environment (i.e. millions of transactions each day), important communication was still done verbally. Essential information traveled according to the "networks" that existed. The new people and functions created "disconnects" which resulted in huge gaps in the information individuals had about what was going on. The grapevines flourished.

Except for controls that were mandated by the regulatory agencies (and there were many), the company itself had few rules. As the headquarters staff grew and took in people from outside the company, the need for systemization increased, but the appetite for written rules didn't. Operating procedures were one thing; management practices were another. The remedy was to develop guidelines and apply them consistently without formally publishing them. The new general counsel favored this verbal approach because he felt that if a policy couldn't be enforced, then the lack of a written policy would benefit the company's defense should litigation result. In effect, practices emerged that were sanctioned by the new leadership but became evident by the organization at large only as individuals personally became involved with them.

Another example of the failure of management systems was in the business-planning system. The company had existed since 1904 but had no unified, bottoms-up business planning system until at least 1986. Attempts had been made to introduce a corporate planning system from the branch level up and within each function as early as 1982, but there was no simple way to integrate plans, share goals, or affix accountability for results. In actual practice, the budgeting system allowed the finance and accounting departments to forecast accruals for year-end bonuses. The business plan itself was known only to a few and of no practical use in running the business on a day-to-day basis.

Compensation and Rewards

In a business that exists to make money, it's not surprising that a high value is placed on wealth—becoming wealthy and staying wealthy. This goal permeated the firm, but it could be achieved only by those in a position to take advantage of opportunities. The groups that were most affected by the reward system were the brokers, corporate finance people, and company officers. Brokers often came from working-class backgrounds, while corporate finance people typically came from the better graduate schools. They all came to the business to build their own wealth and put out great individual effort to achieve it. Successful brokers were typically in their offices between 7 and 8 A.M. (Eastern time) and didn't leave until the market closed and often worked into the evening. When corporate finance people were working on a deal, they often worked twenty-hour days for weeks until the deal was done. Little wonder that few retire from the industry and many burn out after only a few years in the industry. A relatively short tenure is widely accepted. Hence, an extreme emphasis is placed on doing the deal *now*—"take the money and run."

The compensation systems were set up to capitalize on this philosophy. Brokers were paid commissions, and investment bankers were paid fees. Corporate officers were paid bonuses, if they weren't "producers." Over the years, Hutton developed a reputation for "packaged products" that carried "production credits" far greater than commissions paid on stock and bond transactions.

This eventually led to a system of discordant but interlocking love–hate relationships that were maintained by a common desire to make money. The compensation system acknowledged this by disproportionately emphasizing cash and incentives. Further rewards were available to the inner circle in the form of stock options and stock grants, which were initially offered to senior vice presidents and above and later to vice presidents. Since there were hundreds of vice presidents, inclusion in the program was less of a distinction than the amount of the award received. Those that were recruited from outside the company often came in with stock guarantees equal to or greater than their total annual compensation for two or three years.

Such emphasis on the accumulation of wealth led to a single-minded approach to scorekeeping. The performance appraisal system that did exist was used mostly in the branch offices and with lower-level exempt employees. The real measure of performance was in the form of salary increases and year-end bonuses. For many employees, bonuses often exceeded their salary by several times their base pay. This was the scorecard that really mattered— and that has come to plague virtually all of Wall Street.

One of the best-known examples of this was Hutton's "annual taffy pull," in which every department head made recommendations to his or her boss for promotions, salary adjustments, stock options and grants, and year-end bonus amounts. Ultimately, the head of the division or managing director had to convince the chairman to accept his recommendations. It was widely understood that this was not an objective decision but rather a subjective one based on the biases of the chairman and whether or not he liked the department head or person in question. Hutton had created a star system and was loathe to change it, even to save the company. Since the firm had no generally acceptable cost-accounting system, no one argued that people were being paid according to their contributions to the firm and its profitability, but simply that their skills were needed on the team for the team to succeed.

VISION

The company had undergone such major change and been under such minute scrutiny internally and externally that no broad consensus could be found on how to manage change. To the contrary, factions mobilized their forces to achieve their objectives at the expense of others. In the period following the guilty pleas, a powerful group from the broker-dealer organization (the director's advisory council, composed of million-dollar producers) on at least two occasions called for the resignation of the chairman. After the chairman retired, similar plays were made to unseat the president. The field organization advocated withdrawing from investment banking. Investment bankers wanted to be a separate organization. Eventually, both groups were somewhat appeased when the firm was divided into an Individual Investors Groups and a Capital Markets Group (along lines similar to what Shearson did in 1990 with Lehman Brothers). Clearly, this is an example of a company that has lost its vision, direction, and identity. The result was a badly fragmented company.

The 1986 annual report announced a new departure for the firm: "We will not be a financial supermarket." The message went on to say how Hutton intended to stay close to its customers and do what it knew best. These turned out to be hollow words because nothing of any consequence changed. The powers that ruled the divisions were intractable. For example, during a 1987 freeze on all hiring except revenue producers, over 100 people were hired in corporate headquarters.

STRATEGIES TO SAVE THE COMPANY

By the spring and summer of 1987, several internal groups were aware that the firm was in trouble and, in characteristic fashion, began to address the problem independently. Each group tried to impose its vision of the firm and its future, its own analysis, and its own remedy on the others. Their approaches were radically different: systematically reduce overhead, refocus and resize the firm, and sell the firm. The latter group initially wanted to sell the company to a group that would allow the company to remain intact as a stand-alone entity.

Cost Reduction

The systematic overhead-reduction approach was favored and advocated by the corporate controller's department. Borrowing from McKinsey and Company, Project NOVA (National Overhead Value Analysis) was born. Each department was to closely examine every program and position to assess its fit with the espoused mission of the organization. Teams of people were trained to conduct audits of other departments (not their own) and submit recommendations to the NOVA committee, which was responsible for approving the savings that the department would then implement. The NOVA target was $100 million, but the teams could recommend cuts totalling only $40 million; these cuts were never implemented. The final meeting of the NOVA committee was canceled some six months later (and never rescheduled), when the firm was about to lose its credit rating and faced a severe cash shortage.

Downsize and Refocus

The second approach to saving the company originated in the marketing and strategic development unit. Its plan to take an objective look at the financial-services market, identify competitors in each segment the company was now in, evaluate competitive strengths and weaknesses, determine which niches the firm could compete in, and resize or refocus the firm accordingly. Using a small group of outside consultants, this group developed a change strategy that included the following: eliminate up to 1,000 positions immediately, reduce the regional retail network to half its regions, eventually close half of the offices (200), and reconfigure the capital markets group to perform only those functions the retail network required. This was radical surgery. The president received the consultants' report and recommended that it be shared with certain members of the finance department for their concurrence with the financial assumptions. Those meetings were held, but in the meantime, the third group had acted—and the downsizing group's recommendations were never acted on.

Sell the Company

The third group's plan was to sell the company. The head of the corporate finance department, who also represented the company a year earlier as an outside investment advisor, joined the company with a lucrative employment agreement and an opinion that the company needed a substantial infusion of outside capital to survive. The stock market engaged in a minor free fall on Monday, October 19, 1987, that saw Hutton's stock plummet from 30⅛ to 16¾ and started the move to auction the company to the highest bidder. Of course, many factors contributed to the decision to sell the company, but this view was held by several influential people, including former officers, who were also in a position to profit personally if a sale could be arranged.

The first two strategies—reducing overhead and downsizing— were tactical, incremental actions that had little effect on the real issues confronting the firm—*failed leadership and culture.* Ego con-flicts, value differences, permissible behavior, coalitions borne of a common need to make money, and self-serving agendas all influenced the ultimate state of the once-proud company. Based on Want's hierarchy of corporate culture, Hutton had become balkanized, chaotic, and predatory—sure signs of failure. When it finally happened, the end came swiftly, but the tell-tale signs of the impending disaster were apparent for months prior to the fall.

A MODEL FOR DISASTER: TOTAL CHANGE

Hutton's spectacular failure is a case study of what not to do when faced with total change (see Figure 12.1). It also shows that the more serious the change conditions, the more difficult it is to save the company from itself. Even if the change strategies of cost reduction and downsizing had been appropriate, no one in the company was committed to their success. In fact, resolving opera-tional and directional change issues cannot resolve other more imbedded change problems found at the fundamental and total change levels. The first real signs of trouble came with external directional change through deregulation of brokerage commis-sions and the intrusion of other financial-service institutions into the securities trading arena. This forced Hutton and other Wall Street firms to begin controlling costs. Hutton even tried building a discount firm with the larger firms, but it failed. Hutton's failure to deal with directional change precipitated its continuing slide toward total change and extinction. In the final analysis, the company was sold at a bargain basement price—$29¾ per share—to a firm (Shearson Lehman Brothers) that was reported to have offered over $50 per share only one year earlier. The reduced operating costs that Hutton had considered were achieved under the new owners within six months of the acquisition. Most of the people with employment agreements executed their rights regard-

Figure 12.1
Change in the American Securities Industry: Wall Street

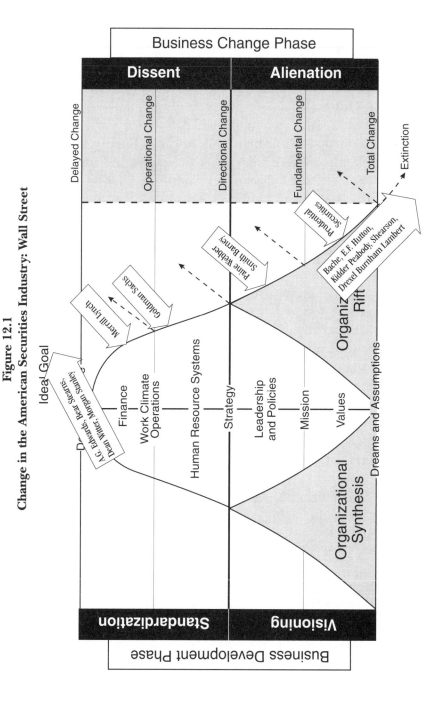

ing a change of ownership and received one or more years of compensation. Other large producers were able to move to competitors' firms, often bringing entire groups or offices with them and receiving substantial signing bonuses in the process. Of the original Hutton management committee, only two members were retained by the new owner. After two years, the Hutton name was dropped from the Shearson Lehman Hutton name and the company returned to its preacquisition identity. Since then, Shearson and Lehman were both divested by their parent company, American Express. Shearson has more recently merged into Smith-Barney, another brokerage firm, and Lehman Brothers has spun off as an independent investment banking firm.

As soon as Hutton's historical mission and values were no longer at work in the firm, it was time to deal with them. But to accomplish a renewal, strong leadership was needed that was empowered to make sweeping changes. The leadership never came forward, and Shearson Lehman had no desire to try to rein in and manage the chaotic culture at Hutton. It was having enough trouble with its own.

THOUGHTS ON WHAT MIGHT HAVE BEEN

Today, E. F. Hutton is a fading memory. Looking back on what happened to the firm, one might come to the following conclusions:

- The free marketplace did what it was supposed to do, since the company wasn't competing well enough to survive as an independent company.

- The improprieties and the self-serving decisions of a few were able to adversely influence the lives of thousands of people who had no voice in determining their fate.

- Organizations and leaders that don't adapt to changing conditions are destined to fail.

- The misdeeds of the past led to the development of a corrupt company that didn't deserve to survive.

No matter which of these positions, or some combination thereof, one might take, substantial financial, career, and psychological losses occurred needlessly or to a greater extent than was necessary. The firm could have taken several steps that would have made a difference in the outcome, including the following:

- Develop a cost-accounting system that more accurately determined profitability, purge the company of unprofitable products, and reduce operating costs (operational change);

- Revise its banking practices and remove all people who had contributed to the problem from their positions (fundamental change);

- Develop a vision of the company that positioned the company in markets where it could compete effectively, and restructure the organization accordingly (directional change).

- Develop a code of business practices, that every person in the company understood and personally endorsed (fundamental change);

- Modify its reward system to compensate people equitably who contributed to the success of the entire company and not just the success of their own personal or group interests (directional change); and

- Concentrate on building a new consensus among company leadership, and refrain from hiring or promoting anyone who wasn't committed to helping the total company succeed (fundamental change).

While these post-mortem insights have the benefit of 20–20 hindsight, they are, nonetheless, fairly well-documented and understood principles of organization change. The fatal flaw here was that no one in a senior leadership capacity in the company was able to identify or recommend any corrective actions until it was too late. The cost issues were known, but their seriousness was not acknowledged until "the wolves were at the door." The moral and ethical issues were known by people who were in a position to do something about them early on, but no one had the courage to speak out or felt that they warranted any attention. The reward system that fostered these behaviors was never seriously questioned. Cost containment received more attention than the behaviors rewarded by the compensation system. Leadership was seriously flawed from very early times. The leaders that emerged at E. F. Hutton during the 1970s and 1980s were, in many ways, a product of the time and not significantly different than those found in other firms on the Street. They failed the company, the shareholders, and the thousands of employees whose lives were permanently affected. The leaders didn't have a vision for the entire firm. Their vision was a narrow, win-or-lose view that had no room for accommodation or compromise for the greater good. It was this stubborn insistence on the rightness of parochial thinking, self-dealing, and self-promotion that brought to an end one of Wall Street's great legends.

Some have laid blame for this colossal failure on two people— the former chairman and the former president of E. F. Hutton. While both men had serious leadership flaws, however, they were not the instrumental cause of the demise of the firm. The dysfunctional policies and practices that evolved over a single decade disconnected an entire firm from the precepts that had allowed it to flourish for eight decades. E. F. Hutton became another ordinary Wall Street firm because:

- Its leaders were insensitive to the danger signals that were manifest in the excessive cost escalation and ethical lapses of the late 1970s and early 1980s;

- Emphasis on near-term revenues led to a proliferation of products that were promoted regardless of their profitability or strategic significance; and

- Once it was recognized that the firm was in danger of failure (total change), the company leaders naively assumed that new outside capital (a White Knight) would save them, which was preferable to self-administered strategies for managing total change.

In the final analysis, Hutton leaders either couldn't see the blight that had permeated the firm or were too feeble to make the hard decisions required to mount a comeback. And so, the artless leadership of a few did something the firm's fiercest competitors couldn't: it brought down a Wall Street giant without firing a shot. It was an inside job. In plotting other industry players on Want's Business Change Cycle, it would seem that few have learned from the painful lesson at Hutton.

J. Jennings Partin

J. Jennings Partin is the founder and principal of the Diameter Group, a consulting firm specializing in the management of organizational and cultural change. Mr. Partin has spent over twenty years as an internal change agent serving such companies as Zenith Electronics Corporation, RCA Corporation, and IU International Corporation. His most recent corporate position was senior vice president for human resources and strategic development for E. F. Hutton Group, Inc. Mr. Partin has a doctorate in behavioral sciences from Indiana University.

PART III

Conclusion

13

Managing Radical Change to the Horizon

Change—an uninvited guest who is always at his or her best when welcomed.

—June Graham and
James Spencer

I am convinced that the greatest barrier to managing business change is an overreliance on outdated practices that have long lost their usefulness. Corporate leaders evidence an inordinate attachment to their outdated processes, practices, and strategies, even when they no longer fit the current competitive landscape. Managers frequently seem not "concerned with determining what decision is best, but [rather] what is acceptable" (Ackoff, *The Democratic Society*, Oxford University Press, 1994). Consequently, companies fail to make the most of emerging opportunities in the marketplace. Entire companies and not just their strategies, are failing.

Countless project teams and task forces have been assembled to ponder the dynamics of knowledge transfer, information exchange, reengineered processes, team building, total quality management, and other quick fixes. These are all worthy concepts, and I utilize them on occasion with my own clients. Nevertheless, real *measurable* change can be achieved only through altered beliefs and behaviors—by letting go of comfortable and familiar practices, no matter how successful they once may have been. If aging policies and methods survive periodic and careful scrutiny, then they may remain viable in a climate of change. The radical change the business world is now experiencing demands that we resist inordinate attachments to what we do or how we do it.

THE THREAT OF CHANGE
A Case Study that Demonstrates
Personal Commitment to Top-Down Change

Several years ago, I was called in by the CEO-owner of a manufacturing and distribution company to determine why previous interventions had done little to stimulate the company's growth. A badly needed, state-of-the-art assembly line had been installed, the company's structure had been assessed and modified, new cost-monitoring procedures had been implemented, and a formal performance management system installed. Nonetheless, after years of steady growth, the company was dead in the water, and the owner was considering selling the business rather than "maintenance manage" a static business.

In interviews with senior and middle managers, I determined that virtually no one was actually cooperating internally with the interventions. When they tried, communications soon became hostile. Conflict dominated every officers' meeting, while one-on-one discussions were burdened with hidden agendas and negative, self-defeating motives. Turf battles originated at the top and insinuated their way into day-to-day operations on the production line. Deadlines for existing clients were being missed, quality was deteriorating, and the company was turning away new clients for fear it couldn't meet their expectations. At the same time, a major new competitor was coming onto the scene backed by heavy foreign investment and a new technology. The problems I found were clearly not ones of efficiency that could be resolved with the usual nostrums like cost monitoring or restructuring.

When I shared my findings with the CEO, I suggested he sell the business (indeed, he was *not* a maintenance manager). Alternatively, I suggested that he needed to undertake a wholly new direction, characterized by profound change, that would require him to put a lot of himself on the line. This change effort would necessarily be centered on altering the behaviors, beliefs, and commitments of his executive team—starting with a long look in the mirror. Many CEOs would have found a reason to pass on such a proposal. In this case, the CEO fully embraced my recommendation.

It proved a difficult transition for members of the executive team since they had to confront their own inadequacies, as much as one other. Managers began to understand the nature of their individual management styles and how these were fundamentally incompatible with the needs of the business, not to mention the expectations of the marketplace. More important, they began to identify their unique emotional needs and personal issues. Only then were they able to appreciate how these forces played themselves out through specific workplace behaviors. No one was more successful in making a personal transformation than the CEO, and other officers quickly discovered he was a tough act to follow. Before they could successfully deal with the issues facing the company, they had to deal with their own issues and behaviors. The leadership change process continued with the "professionalization" of the officer group, as well as middle management.

Within three years, the company doubled its gross revenues and greatly expanded its customer base. On-time delivery also improved dramatically. Officers and managers were

(continued)

working with each other and, consequently, had become more effective decision makers. This success grew out of the personal change effort undertaken by the CEO and his officers before they attempted to drive it down into the organization. Today (seven years later), the company has quintupled in size since its decision to implement a change process. It's not only an industry leader in terms of volume but is now viewed by its customers as a leader in innovation, quality, and reliability. New accounts are migrating to the business from larger and more sophisticated competitors, testing the organization's ability to meet even higher levels of customer demand. The management team is now faced with directing a significantly expanded company where a tendency to fix things may distract them from the continuing need to steer the right course for the organization in a radically changed business environment. Still, the compass remains pointed at the center of the company—the CEO and his managers.

This is not an atypical example of the way in which individual behavioral change can lead to organizational change. It does not imply, however, that an entire company can change through the efforts of senior management alone (as noted in Chapter 5, the senior officer group at Chase Manhattan Bank embraced a similar process). What was unusual in this case study was the CEO's readiness to embrace a difficult process that involved considerable personal risk taking. Similarly, a painful change in behavior, values, and belief systems has been initiated at the Denny's restaurant chain, where highly publicized and self-defeating discrimination toward African American customers nearly ruined the entire company. It is always less painful when a change effort is launched proactively, rather than being forced on a business as the result of a crisis unpleasantly communicated by the marketplace.

NECESSARY COMMITMENT
FOR MANAGING RADICAL CHANGE

Few of us can honestly say we enjoy change or look forward to changed conditions: perhaps we may enjoy someone else's change or the rare occasion when the outcome is obvious, but not real, unpredictable change. The unknowable consequences of change are frightening. For that reason, those who claim they are committed to change are to be feared, if not avoided. *What do they know that the rest of us don't know?*

Faith in the Process

Successful change managers understand that the change process—not artificial "crystal balling" or futile attempts to control change conditions that are well beyond the reach and grasp of any company—is the key to successfully anticipating, understanding, and managing change. Openness, thoughtful planning, and proactive management of various change challenges will increase the likelihood of success, while ensuring a good fit between the business and the changed environment.

Eliminating Bias

In order to increase the chances of achieving the best possible outcome, it is critical to eliminate all bias from the change-management process. The most honored business icons and sacred cows should be examined and questioned, while hidden agendas must be brought to the surface. Previously suppressed ideas should be reexamined, and the squeaky wheels deserve a second hearing—not more oil. Those who claim to know exactly what the end product of change should look like need to be taken with a grain of salt. Their hypotheses, however high in the organization they were formulated, should be forced to pass a reality test throughout the business and in the marketplace. *Change management is not about an end product—but an unending process.*

Change Is About Development and Not Just Growth

Too often we try to quantify the goals of change: "How much can we grow the company's return on investment in the next three years?" "By reengineering our operational core, we can cut three layers from the organization, saving X dollars." "We can immediately improve company culture by cutting 35 percent of our workforce." When appropriate processes for quantifying or measuring change exist, use them. Nonetheless, change is about *quality:* the quality of decision making, leadership, employee commitment, service to the customer, cooperation, innovation, fairness, openness, and, ultimately, performance. These quality benchmarks should never be appraised as separate, unrelated measures but as interdependent and interactive components required for a *whole* system or business organization.

Holistic Change Management

Change intrinsically involves the entire organization—not just one function or division or one or two layers of management. It definitely isn't about just the stockholders. Failure to include everyone in a change process will alienate those who have been excluded and eventually doom the process to failure. Russell Ackoff identifies the key actors as *stakeholders* (*The Democratic Corporation*, Oxford University Press, 1994). The company is a reflection of many interests and contributions that go far beyond investors: employees, who contribute their ideas and careers; suppliers, who provide the necessary management resources (this includes consultants, accountants, and lawyers, who collectively share their intellectual capital); customers, who constitute the lifeblood of the business; and the public, which counts on the company as a source of employment, tax revenue, needed products or services, and wealth creation. These stakeholders constitute the company's ecosystem or suprasystem.

Courageous Leadership and Empowerment

Change leaders understand that courageous, farsighted leadership is required to produce successful change. There are good reasons that businesses are rarely hotbeds of innovation and change. The CEO must answer to directors, and those directors are responsible for protecting the investment of the company's shareholders. Most corporate directors are CEOs of other companies. Middle managers are discouraged from initiating change. Too many suggestions from a manager are often viewed as making waves rather than doing what one was hired to do. Nothing short of courageous, farsighted, even visionary leadership is required at the top, accompanied by the genuine workforce empowerment and broad consensus building in support of change throughout the organization. Only after a company's *official* leaders demonstrate their commitment to change will change leaders begin to emerge down the line. Once top-to-bottom commitment is evident, the entire organization can embrace a change agenda. Otherwise, rank-and-file employees will be hesitant and fearful of the consequences of undertaking behavioral change on their own.

Innovation and a Futures Orientation

Despite the seemingly endless array of ingenious and innovative products that have been produced for the marketplace, the processes and thinking governing the management of corporations has been anything but creative. Imaginative thinking and a focus on the future is required—especially when a sea change in thinking and behavior is required. Few companies seem able to look ahead without nervously glancing backward to gain their bearings. In part, this is due to their obsession with past results, which were used to control decisions about people, ideas, and processes. Companies are often incapable of allowing anyone inside to lead—unless, of course, they are authorized. Unauthorized leaders—natural leaders—in combination with innovative thinking and behaviors are almost always threatening to the corporate status quo. John Kenneth Galbraith refers to this phenomenon as the corporate pursuit of the "culture of contentment" (*The Culture of Contentment,* Houghton Mifflin, 1992).

RECURRING PATTERNS AND PRACTICES

As Part II's examination of change in seven industries suggests, certain recurring patterns seem to emerge regardless of the industry.

The Shock of Change

CEOs and senior managers repeatedly misjudged the rate and scope of change in their industries. Business leaders in the airline industry underestimated the impact of deregulation on cost structures and, just as critically, the cost of competition with smaller, startup niche companies like Southwest Air. Despite having several years to prepare for the breakup of AT&T, most industry executives were slow in developing their strategies and preparing their cultures and management capabilities for the new marketplace. They relied far too heavily and too long on the courts for permission to grow and expand, believing their territorial hegemony could carry them through. The health-care and pharmaceutical industries nervously braced themselves for health-care reform designed in Washington, while reform was quietly cropping up at the grassroots level across the country. Technological changes in the information-management industry quickly rendered obsolete main-line products at companies like Wang, IBM, and DEC—forcing thousands of layoffs that reached all the way to the executive suite. On Wall Street, officers of major firms like Kidder Peabody and Prudential Securities ignored the misdeeds (and their consequences) that had previously occurred within the industry and then looked the other way as a wave of fraudulent practices brought down their companies. In manufacturing, American auto manufacturers and steel producers took more than a decade to regain their competitive edge after the shock of Japanese competition. Only now are they learning how to compete in a truly global environment.

Incremental Responses to Change

When change washed over each of these industries, the initial response was to downsize, usually followed by more downsizing, called reengineering. It seems that only when a company is confronted by extinction does it begin the truly manage itself and the changed conditions around it. Some companies went so far as to oust their CEOs: Stemple at GM, Akers at IBM, Lego at Westinghouse, Lippincott at Scott Paper, and Winters at Prudential. Nevertheless, their successors appear to be doing the same familiar things. Change management is a proactive and far-reaching endeavor. It's difficult, if not impossible, to try to play catchup with change.

Overreliance on the Magic Bullet

Too often technology has been relied on to redress fundamental problems within companies. Expectations for information technology have been unrealistically high, fostering as many problems as solutions. Research labs have been pushed to produce breakthrough products at a rate faster than the scientific method can match. Advanced communications systems have replaced workers like secretaries and customer-service professionals, who also solved problems and coordinated processes for their bosses and customers. In many cases, mechanization of the production process may have reached its capacity to replace skilled workers. Companies must begin changing their management capabilities, strategies, decision-making practices, cultures, and attitudes to enthusiastically embrace change. The magic bullet doesn't really exist.

Excluding People from the Change Process

Personally, my greatest concern about change and its impact on the business world is the tendency for executives to eliminate people from the change equation. Business leaders prefer to hold the change-management process hostage to an elite group of officers, planners, and directors. This diminishes the creativity and innovation that are always so badly needed when a company finds itself challenged by radical change. Even worse, too many companies think the change process is hindered by the involvement of employees. They apparently believe that only through radical downsizing can their organization subsequently launch a radical new course toward change. In fact, change is *inherently* about people. Business organizations should be among our most dynamic social systems. The workplace has become the embodiment of worker fulfillment and commitment, but that will not continue unless companies return the commitment. We cannot hope to be successful in implementing business change initiatives without factoring in the impacts and economic advantages of change for the social systems that corporations comprise. If businesses continue to throw workers overboard whenever their companies are challenged, the social fabric of the workforce and larger society may be irrevocably ripped apart and businesses will feel the impact.

THE FORK IN THE ROAD

Contrary to conventional wisdom in the business community, change is not synonymous with crisis or revolution. Companies can plan for, anticipate, adapt to, and manage—even if they cannot control—change. The choice does exist. Change need not always be unfriendly or threatening, and when it is, this threat often can be attributed to the company's lack of preparedness and internal resistance to the realities of the marketplace. No industry or company can avoid change, regardless of the resources at its command. Increasing numbers of companies are beginning to recognize that they can and should be part of change. But too many companies still resist change or convince themselves they can tiptoe their way through the minefields of change, all the while relying on incremental, outdated strategies that do little more than segment and weaken the organization.

Change—radical change—is synonymous with competitiveness. Companies that genuinely wish to succeed and lead and not simply survive are making change strategies the focal point of their business strategies. Those that wish to lead and thrive are making change their goal, which substantially enhances their opportunity to overcome and benefit from a *radicalized* marketplace. Companies that cling to old practices and strategies—companies that merely wish to survive—are destined to become the bottom feeders of their industries.

As corporations have grown in size and power, expanding their reach to markets around the globe, they have increasingly acted as though they were free from the pressures of market forces. Companies continue to dump inferior products into the marketplace with little regard for consumer needs and for the down-line consequences to the business. Customer service is often perceived as a necessary evil or, at best, a cost center—not as an additional opportunity for building customer loyalty. Growing waste and its associated costs are blamed on the workforce, rather than on poor management. Archaic human resource practices and autocratic, military-style hierarchies are slow to be recognized for the obsolescence and the hindrance they now represent to a company's competitiveness.

As change inevitably intrudes itself into the consciousness of society—in politics, personal life, and the prose of corporate annual reports and consulting firm brochures—one might be led to believe that the "Age of Aquarius" was just around the corner. Instead, I fear that too many mediocre and incremental practices of the past have merely been reformulated to masquerade as real change. As Eli Ginzberg and George Vojta warn, "If leaders of existing corporations continue to demonstrate that they are unable or unwilling to change, a virile democracy [and competitive marketplace] will find new approaches to accomplish its objectives" (*Beyond Human Scale*, Basic Books, 1985).

However, if foresighted business leaders join with flexible workforces, then companies can evolve to meet the challenge of radical change that will continue to confront their industries long into the future.

INDEX